Property Values and Race

PUBLICATIONS OF THE
COMMISSION ON RACE AND HOUSING

Where Shall We Live? Report of the Commission on Race and Housing

Residence and Race: Final and Comprehensive Report to the Commission on Race and Housing by DAVIS MC ENTIRE

The Demand for Housing in Racially Mixed Areas: A Study of the Nature of Neighborhood Change by CHESTER RAPKIN AND WILLIAM G. GRIGSBY

Privately Developed Interracial Housing: An Analysis of Experience by EUNICE AND GEORGE GRIER

Property Values and Race: Studies in Seven Cities by LUIGI LAURENTI

Studies in Housing and Minority Groups edited by NATHAN GLAZER AND DAVIS MC ENTIRE

Property Values and Race

Studies in Seven Cities

BY LUIGI LAURENTI

SPECIAL RESEARCH REPORT
TO THE COMMISSION ON RACE
AND HOUSING

UNIVERSITY OF CALIFORNIA PRESS

BERKELEY AND LOS ANGELES 1961

Prepared under the direction of
DAVIS McENTIRE, *Research Director*
Commission on Race and Housing

UNIVERSITY OF CALIFORNIA PRESS
BERKELEY AND LOS ANGELES
CALIFORNIA

CAMBRIDGE UNIVERSITY PRESS
LONDON, ENGLAND

Foreword

Property Values and Race by Luigi Laurenti reports the findings of one phase of a broad study of housing problems involving minority racial and ethnic groups, conducted for the Commission on Race and Housing under the direction of Davis McEntire.

Where the members of minority racial and ethnic groups should live—whether in segregated communities or dispersed through the general housing supply—is a social problem of large and growing importance in American cities. To inquire into this problem was the purpose of the Commission on Race and Housing, formed in 1955. The Commission is an independent, private citizens' group, not a part of any other organization. Its work was made possible by a grant of $305,000 from the Fund for the Republic. The Fund's participation was limited to financial assistance, and it is not in any way otherwise responsible for the studies carried out for the Commission or for its conclusions.

The following persons have served on the Commission in their individual capacities and not as representing any organization or group:

GORDON W. ALLPORT
  Professor of Psychology, Harvard University, Cambridge, Massachusetts.
ELLIOTT V. BELL
  Chairman of the Executive Committee and Director, McGraw-Hill Publishing Company; Editor and Publisher, *Business Week*, New York.

LAIRD BELL
Attorney: Bell, Boyd, Marshall and Lloyd, Chicago.

REVEREND JOHN J. CAVANAUGH, C.S.C.
Director, University of Notre Dame Foundation, Notre Dame, Indiana.

HENRY DREYFUSS
Industrial Designer, South Pasadena, California, and New York.

PETER GRIMM
Chairman of the Board and Director, William A. White and Sons, New York.

COL. CAMPBELL C. JOHNSON
Assistant to the Director, Selective Service System, Washington, D.C.

CHARLES S. JOHNSON
President, Fisk University, Nashville, Tennessee. Deceased.

CHARLES KELLER, JR.
President, Keller Construction Corporation, New Orleans, Louisiana.

CLARK KERR
President, University of California, Berkeley.

PHILIP M. KLUTZNICK
Chairman of the Board, American Community Builders, Inc., Park Forest, Illinois.

HENRY R. LUCE
Editor-in-Chief, *Time, Life, Fortune, Architectural Forum, House and Home,* and *Sports Illustrated,* New York.

STANLEY MARCUS
President, Neiman-Marcus, Dallas, Texas.

HAROLD C. McCLELLAN
President, Old Colony Paint and Chemical Company, Los Angeles. Resigned following appointment as Assistant Secretary of Commerce in 1955.

WARD MELVILLE
President, Melville Shoe Corporation, New York.

FRANCIS T. P. PLIMPTON
Attorney: Debevoise, Plimpton and McLean, New York.

R. STEWART RAUCH, JR.
President, The Philadelphia Saving Fund Society, Philadelphia.

ROBERT R. TAYLOR
   Secretary and Executive Director, Illinois Federal Savings and
   Loan Association, Chicago. Deceased.
JOHN H. WHEELER
   President, Mechanics and Farmers Bank, Durham, North Caro-
   lina.
EARL B. SCHWULST, CHAIRMAN
   President and Chairman of the Board, The Bowery Savings
   Bank, New York.

   Professor Robert K. Merton of Columbia University, Professor
Stuart W. Cook of New York University, and Dr. Robert C.
Weaver, formerly State Rent Administrator of New York, served
as research advisors to the Commission.

   The central focus of research undertaken for the Commission
was on the problem of inequality of housing opportunity connected with racial or ethnic distinctions, with emphasis on the
situation of Negroes, Puerto Ricans, Mexican-Americans, and
Orientals. The research was national in scope and endeavored to
comprehend all major ramifications of a very complex problem
—its causes, impacts and consequences, and directions of change.
Some thirty special studies and research memoranda were prepared for the consideration of the Commission by the Research
Director, his assistants, and coöperating social scientists in a
dozen universities.

   The Commission has previously published its own conclusions
and recommendations in *Where Shall We Live?* (University of
California Press, 1958). A comprehensive report of the findings
of the entire study, by the Research Director, is in press. In addition, several of the particular inquiries which are of wide interest
have been or will be published; the others are available in the
library of the University of California at Berkeley.

   In authorizing publication of research reports, including the
present study by Dr. Laurenti, the Commission on Race and
Housing believes that the research was conscientiously and com-
petently carried out, in accordance with high scientific standards. However, the Commission assumes no responsibility for the
accuracy of specific data in the various reports, nor does it neces-

sarily endorse all of the interpretations and conclusions drawn by the authors. Persons desiring to know the position of the Commission are referred to its own report.

EARL B. SCHWULST, Chairman
Commission on Race and Housing

New York City

Preface

Among the theories and beliefs supporting the exclusion of non-whites from white-occupied residence areas probably none is more frequently encountered than the idea that the presence of nonwhites depreciates property values. The wide currency of this belief and its frequent invocation in support of racial exclusion justifies a serious effort to test its validity in fact.

As described in other reports to the Commission on Race and Housing, there exists in American cities generally a marked and obvious association between nonwhite residence patterns and areas of blight and decay. From this observed association, many have assumed a causal connection, asserting that the former is the "cause" of the latter. To the critical mind an alternative hypothesis readily suggests itself, namely, that the incidence of blight may be due to nonracial causes, with the nonwhites merely being obliged, through poverty or social pressures, to live in the blighted areas.

As Dr. Laurenti's report points out, the second hypothesis has been gaining ground at the expense of the first one. The belief that nonwhite entry into an area causes property values to fall is neither so firmly nor so widely held as it once was. However, there is little solid factual evidence for either hypothesis. The lack of evidence results from the difficulty of disentangling the factor of change in racial occupancy from other possible influences upon property values, in order to measure the effect of that factor by itself.

It is the particular merit of Dr. Laurenti's study that he has been able to do this on a limited scale. His study utilizes a type of scientific experimental method. A number of areas character-ized by varying degrees of nonwhite entry are selected for study. Each area is paired with another area in the same general vicinity of the same city, comparable in significant respects with the study area but without a history of nonwhite entry. The trends in sales prices of homes in the two areas are then compared, beginning from a date prior to the entry of nonwhites into the "test" area. In this way, providing that "test" and "control" areas are really subject to the same value influences apart from racial change, it is possible to isolate the factor of nonwhite entry and detect its effects. The evidence obtained through this research procedure represents an original and substantial contribution to knowledge of race and property values.

In addition to his original studies, Dr. Laurenti reviews the pertinent writings of real estate and appraisal experts and the findings of other studies. The present report may, therefore, lay claim to being a comprehensive treatment of evidence available at the present time.

DAVIS MCENTIRE, Research Director
Commission on Race and Housing

Author's Acknowledgments

What might now be termed a pilot study for this investigation was carried out for the Real Estate Research Program of the Bureau of Business and Economic Research, University of California at Berkeley, during 1951. Dr. Paul Wendt, Director of the Real Estate Research Program and Professor of Finance in the School of Business Administration, directed the work. His constructive guidance fundamentally influenced the initial study, as well as that which followed, and much that has been done could not have been done without his generous assistance. The planning and execution of the initial study also owed a great deal to the advice of Catherine Bauer Wurster, Lecturer in the Department of City and Regional Planning, and Martin B. Loeb of the Department of Social Welfare. Other individuals and agencies, too numerous to list here,[1] helped to gather and shape the materials which culminated in a report published in July, 1952, under the title: "Effects of Nonwhite Purchases on Market Prices of Residences."[2]

Further research on the subject continued on an individual basis during 1952 and 1953, leading to the publication of a second article in 1954: "Real Estate Price Behavior in Neighborhoods Entered by Nonwhites."[3] Again, Dr. Wendt's guidance and editorship were invaluable.

In 1955 the Commission on Race and Housing, operating under

[1] See Appendix B.
[2] *The Appraisal Journal*, XX, no. 3 (July, 1952), 314–329.
[3] *Bay Area Real Estate Report*, Fourth Quarter, 1954, pp. 61–65.

a grant from the Fund for the Republic, undertook a major investigation of the housing problems of minority groups in the United States, under the direction of Professor Davis McEntire of the Department of Social Welfare, University of California, Berkeley. The broad scope of the Commission's inquiry naturally included the question of how real estate values are affected by the presence of nonwhites. The work already done on the problem, as described above, was considered by the Commission's Research Director to constitute an adequate base from which to launch a broader study. At his invitation, work was begun in August, 1955, to widen the geographical coverage of the earlier research and bring the statistics up to date.

The major difficulty of this study has been the collection of sufficient and accurate market data. This difficulty could never have been overcome without the coöperation of the real estate profession in the areas studied, on both an individual and institutional basis. For the California areas the bulk of the data was gathered from the files of the following agencies whose coöperation is gratefully acknowledged: the Multiple Listing Service of San Francisco, O. T. Peterson, Executive Secretary, and Seifert Eberts, Office Manager; the Multiple Listing Division of the Oakland Real Estate Board, Loren Mowrey, Executive Secretary; and the Southern Alameda County Real Estate Board, Margaret Fowler, Executive Secretary. For the Philadelphia areas studied, extensive statistics were compiled from the Philadelphia Real Estate Directory, Inc.

The following persons supplied very helpful background information about economic and population changes in the neighborhoods studied: Herbert Hotchner, formerly Administrative Assistant, Redevelopment Agency of the City and County of San Francisco; Edward Howden, formerly Executive Director, Council for Civic Unity, San Francisco; James Lash, formerly Director, Redevelopment Agency of the City and County of San Francisco; Seaton Manning, Executive Director, Urban League, San Francisco; John McDermott, formerly a staff member, Commission on Human Relations, Philadelphia; and Robert Pitts, formerly Racial Relations Officer, Federal Housing Administration, San Francisco. Other assistance is listed in Appendix B.

The revision of a preliminary report, completed in June, 1956, was greatly facilitated—and the report contents were significantly strengthened—as a result of suggestions and comments received from those who took the trouble to review it. I should like to give special thanks to Robert H. Armstrong, Armstrong Associates, New York; Catherine Bauer Wurster, Lecturer, Department of City and Regional Planning, University of California; Laird Bell, Commission on Race and Housing; Dr. Ernest M. Fisher, Professor of Urban Land Economics, Columbia University; Dr. Robert C. Weaver, formerly Administrator, Temporary State Housing Rent Commission, New York; Dr. Paul F. Wendt, Professor of Finance, University of California, Berkeley.

This study would not have been possible without the strong support provided by the Research Director and the staff of the Commission on Race and Housing. Dr. McEntire's methodological and editorial supervision helped greatly in the analysis and shaping of the material, and his steady encouragement made the long task endurable. Katherine Eardley prepared the charts; June Harvey managed the editorial details through several revisions of the manuscript and prepared the index. Other members of the staff who assisted in the study were Milton Nason, Mary Allison, Betty Lou Kirtley, Montgomery Woodruff, Betty Aycrigg, Lois Ness, Jessie Omura, and Eleanor Randolph.

To all these, and to everyone else who helped, my deepest thanks.

Luigi Laurenti

Contents

Tables

Figures

Maps

PART ONE

*Approach and
General Findings*

I

The Problem

In the time it takes to read this report perhaps a thousand homes will be sold in America. They will differ widely in size, shape, location, age, and price, but each will be solving, for some span of a family's life, the problem of shelter.

The thousand families buying these homes will all have entered the housing market in their local communities, seeking to buy the best house they can afford. It can be estimated that at least fifty-six of the thousand buyer families will be nonwhite,[1] and of these, all but two or three will be Negro. In seeking a home, these fifty-six buyers will, like white customers, have to stay within personal budget limitations. Unlike whites, however, they will meet additional restrictions. They will find their search for a home held inside certain geographical bounds because (1) the community may, for a complex of reasons, resist their moving into certain neighborhoods; (2) individual white property owners, in deference to community attitudes, or for reasons of their own, may refuse to sell to them; (3) real estate brokers and agents, motivated by a combination of community pressures, real estate codes of ethics, instructions of sellers, and personal feelings, may

---

[1] In 1950, nonwhites accounted for 10.5 percent of the total population and owned 5.6 percent of all owner-occupied units. In 1940 they owned 5.1 percent. There is every evidence that nonwhite homeownership is still increasing, absolutely and relatively. Negroes own over nine out of every ten nonwhite owner-occupied homes. *United States Census of Housing: 1950*, Vol. I, *General Characteristics*, chap. 1, "U. S. Summary."

The term "nonwhite," as generally used throughout this report, refers to the three racial or national-origin groups which figure most prominently in the changing population patterns of the neighborhoods observed: Negroes, Chinese, and Japanese. Negro families account for 95 to 100 percent of the total nonwhite population in the areas studied, so that "nonwhite" and "Negro" may—for all practical purposes—be considered interchangeable in the over-all context of the report. Wherever reference is made to Census figures, however, it must be remembered that the Census definition of "nonwhite" is broader than this, taking in all non-Caucasian groups.

direct them into limited areas "approved" for nonwhite residence; and (4) real estate loans may be unavailable—or available only on terms less favorable than those for white borrowers. That Negro and other nonwhite customers do not have access to all the houses for sale in their local community is a widely recognized and accepted fact of life.

Both social and economic arguments are used to justify the restricting of nonwhites to separate residence areas. Charles Abrams groups these arguments under three fears: fear of losing social status, fear of losing established neighborhood associations, and fear of losing investment.[2] Robert Weaver, in *The Negro Ghetto*, reports that the following reasons have been given as justification for opposing Negro (and presumably other nonwhite) neighbors:

[1.] fear on the part of many white people that the presence of any colored persons in the neighborhood will cause serious depreciation of existing property values;

[2.] reluctance of some whites to share public and community facilities with Negroes;

[3.] fear of losing social caste by living in a neighborhood with Negroes;

[4.] opposition of owners of property occupied by colored people to expansion in the supply of such housing;

[5.] apprehension lest change in racial composition of a community will upset existing political balance;

[6.] vested interests in maintaining existing homogeneity of nationality-religious neighborhoods;

[7.] resentment against alleged efforts of Federal officials to superimpose social changes upon a local community; and

[8.] entrenched racial prejudice.[3]

Whites who object to nonwhite neighbors may be broadly classified under two headings: those who object for a variety of social or personal reasons, and those who are concerned only about the economic loss they may suffer.

Those in the first group insist that whites and nonwhites must not live in the same neighborhood—at least not as equals (non-

---

[2] Charles Abrams, "Race Bias in Housing," statement sponsored jointly by the American Civil Liberties Union, National Association for the Advancement of Colored People, and American Council on Race Relations (July, 1947), pp. 24–28.

[3] Robert C. Weaver, *The Negro Ghetto* (New York: Harcourt, Brace and Company, 1948), p. 214.

white domestic servants have usually been accepted without
question as residents in the white neighborhoods they serve, in
the South as well as the North).[4] The entry of nonwhites, this
group maintains, injures the social status of the neighborhood,
with serious consequences for the white residents and their associates. Not only is neighborhood social status damaged, but since
many white families move out of the neighborhood, established
association patterns are disrupted.

Those in the second group, who might be willing to accept nonwhite neighbors on social grounds, may yet feel they must defend
the all-white neighborhood pattern in order to protect their real
estate investment. The threat to property values is also relied
upon but not usually openly cited—as an additional reason by
many who oppose nonwhite neighbors on grounds of "social un-
desirability."

No other reason, in fact, is more frequently and strongly urged
in support of racially separate residence patterns than that nonwhites depress property values. This is a widespread belief and
one of crucial importance because it governs or at least rational-
izes many practices of real estate brokers, builders, and financial
institutions—as well as the actions of homeowners.

Its origins cannot be determined exactly, but they go back at
least to 1910, when cities in several border and southern states
began enacting segregation ordinances. These cities were concerned about Negro families' moving into all-white blocks and
viewed such moves as threats to the necessary "social distance"
between the races.[5]

When these city, and later state, segregation laws were tested
in the courts (which pronounced them unconstitutional), their
defenders said they were needed to preserve the general welfare,
peace, and social good order of the community. It was argued
that a major cause of neighborhood friction was that the entry
of a Negro family into a white block cut down real estate values.

---

[4] Cf. Charles S. Johnson, *Patterns of Negro Segregation* (New York: Harper
and Brothers, 1943), pp. 8–12, and *Negro Housing*, Report of the Committee on
Negro Housing for the President's Conference on Home Building and Home
Ownership (Washington, D. C.: The Conference, 1932), pp. 35–45.
[5] San Francisco also "pioneered" race segregation ordinances, in 1890, with
one aimed at the Chinese. However, the property value argument does not seem
to have been used to justify the ordinance.

Counsel for the city of Louisville, Kentucky, for example, alleged that values dropped from 30 to 60 percent following Negro entry.[6]

Fear of the economic threat believed to be created by non-whites' moving into white neighborhoods was a significant factor in originating and spreading racial restrictive covenants in northern and border state cities during and after World War I. Property owners tried to keep the hundreds of thousands of Negroes and other nonwhites who were pouring into urban centers confined to already established racial areas by pledging not to sell or rent surrounding "white" property to them. Until the U. S. Supreme Court in 1948 declared such covenants judicially unenforceable, they were, for three decades, formidable barriers to nonwhites who sought housing outside the racial ghettos.

Along with these legal barriers existed several other restrictive measures—still quite effective today in creating and perpetuating segregation. These included agreements, practices, and codes of ethics among real estate boards and brokers; the development of exclusive neighborhoods; the neglect of the nonwhite market by private builders and sources of finance; and local political action to restrict nonwhites to certain areas.[7] Behind these, too, stood—and still stands—the white's fear of what nonwhites may do to his real estate investments.

The question of what happens to real estate values when non-whites come to live in a previously all-white neighborhood has taken on renewed importance in the years since World War II, for in this period, to a greater extent than ever before, the non-white need for better housing has coincided with an ability to purchase it. Many cities, especially in the North and West, have experienced such increases in nonwhite population that the areas formerly "set aside" for nonwhites have proved entirely inadequate to house them. These developments have led to the entry of nonwhites into scores and even hundreds of formerly all-white neighborhoods across the country.

There is no question but that many more white neighborhoods face the prospect of losing their uniracial character. Their residents, like others before them, will doubtless be more or less agitated over what the change will mean for the value of their

---

[6] *Buchanan* v. *Warley*, 245 U. S. 60 (1917).
[7] Weaver, *The Negro Ghetto*, p. 211.

properties. A factual study of the question should therefore be of wide interest to residential property owners.

Concrete data, such as the present study attempts to provide, should also be of interest to the professional worlds of real estate, housing finance, urban planning, and government, for all must cope, in one way or another, with the problem of where racial minority groups shall live in American cities.

PLAN OF THE BOOK

The material in this book has been organized to provide, first, a general report on the study and its findings and, second, a more detailed analysis.

Part One is the general report. It states the problem under study, reviews theories of race and property value, describes how the present study was conducted, and summarizes the findings. This Part will probably constitute, for most readers, sufficient information on the study and its conclusions.

Part Two is intended for readers interested in the details of price behavior in the various cities and neighborhoods studied. The data and analysis are presented area by area, with a summary for each city. Also included in Part Two are chapters on two subjects significantly related to the main problem: the financing of transactions in mixed versus all-white neighborhoods and the standards of property maintenance by nonwhite owners.

Some further details of research methodology and sources of data are presented in the Appendices.

II

Theories of Race and Property Value

Before presenting the factual evidence from the several studies which have been made concerning the effects of racial change on property values, it will be instructive to examine the positions taken on this subject by real estate and finance spokesmen, land economists, and others. Most of their conclusions are unaccompanied by supporting evidence, although such evidence may have been observed by the writers. However, several statements are based on actual field study, and these findings are discussed in later sections of this report.

In examining the statements that have appeared over the past forty years, an evolutionary shift in their scope and tone becomes apparent. Generally, the earlier ones are marked by much more sweeping and unqualified predictions. This is particularly true of statements in real estate textbooks and articles. These are examined first, followed by a survey of the price behavior predictions made by three other groups: real estate brokers, lenders, and builders; professional students of housing; and the Federal Housing Administration.

THE PROFESSIONAL REAL ESTATE LITERATURE

Professional writings have probably played a continuing role in shaping the beliefs that motivate brokers, builders, lenders, and appraisers. They reveal what theories have been and are accepted in the real estate field.

Thirty to forty years ago, the pronouncements of the real estate experts were uniformly gloomy concerning what would happen to prices if a nonwhite should move into a white neighborhood. The following are representative of the 1923–1933 period:

It is a matter of common observation that the purchase of property by certain racial types is very likely to diminish the value of other property in the section.[1]

With the increase in colored people coming to many Northern cities they have overrun their old districts and swept into adjoining ones or passed to other sections and formed new ones. This naturally has had a decidedly detrimental effect on land values for few white people, however inclined to be sympathetic with the problem of the colored race, care to live near them. Property values have been sadly depreciated by having a single colored family settle down on a street occupied exclusively by white residents.[2]

The mere threat . . . of an undesirable encroachment [differing race or nationality] must many times be recognized by a reduced unit value for the house.[3]

Neighborhoods populated by white persons have been invaded by colored families, and often aristocratic residential districts have suffered tremendous lessening of property values because of the appearance of a Negro resident.[4]

It is in the twilight zone, where members of different races live together, that racial mixtures tend to have a depressing effect upon land values—and therefore, upon rents.[5]

In the next group of statements, dating from 1932 to 1955, there appears a clear tendency to think about the problem more critically. The depressing influence of nonwhite entry is still asserted, but is qualified to various degrees by the recognition of other factors such as socioeconomic levels, physical condition of the neighborhood before entry, and price ranges of homes in the area:

Families in any particular class, who rise in economic status, move to a better district. If they have a degree of inferiority they damage that community, displace the occupying class, and lower values. . . . Most of the variations and differences between people are slight and

[1] Ernest M. Fisher, *Principles of Real Estate Practice* (New York: The Macmillan Company, 1923), p. 116. Cited in Charles Abrams, *Forbidden Neighbors* (New York: Harper and Brothers, 1955), p. 155.

[2] Stanley L. McMichael and Robert F. Bingham, *City Growth and Values* (Cleveland: The Stanley McMichael Publishing Organization, 1923), p. 181. Cited in Abrams, *Forbidden Neighbors*, p. 159.

[3] George A. Schneider, *California Real Estate Principles and Practices* (New York: Prentice-Hall, Inc., 1927), p. 315. Cited in Abrams, *Forbidden Neighbors*, p. 160.

[4] McMichael and Bingham, *City Growth and Values*, p. 370.

[5] Homer Hoyt, *The Structure and Growth of Residential Neighborhoods in American Cities* (Washington, D. C.: Federal Housing Administration, 1939), p. 62.

value declines are, therefore, gradual. But there is one difference in people, namely race, which can result in a very rapid decline.[6]

Certain racial and national groups, because of their lower economic status and their lower standards of living, pay less rent themselves and cause a greater physical deterioration of property than groups higher in the social and economic scale. . . . Land values in areas occupied by such classes are therefore inevitably low. Part of the attitude reflected in lower land values is due entirely to racial prejudice, which may have no reasonable basis. Nevertheless, if the entrance of a colored family into a white neighborhood causes a general exodus of the white people, such dislikes are reflected in property values.[7]

In the appraisal of homes, general data covering the city and surrounding territory must be considered. . . . Even more intensive must be the study of the immediate neighborhoods . . . ; characteristics and background of the residents of the neighborhood; presence or threat of intrusion of discordant racial groups; and other conditions having a bearing on the present and future desirability of the location.[8]

It [the effect of Negroes on property values] has a most important bearing on future developments in our housing program. Appraisers are interested in the problem from many angles. In addition, they desire the problem to be considered objectively from one specific point; i.e., does Negro occupancy have a tendency to blight only the area where it occurs, or does it blight the surrounding white area, with a corresponding decrease in valuation and loss of tenants . . . ? It cannot be denied that his presence in large groups has the effect of blight upon the surrounding property. The first blight which we must mention is the mental blight or the depreciation in psychological worth. Some Negroes may take better care of their property, they may be as law abiding, they may have an equal education, they may in fact be just as fine citizens as their white neighbors, but we all know countless neighborhoods and communities where the presence of one Negro family will cause many white families to move out. There is an immediate falling off in rentals of surrounding property and a corresponding depreciation in value, more Negro families move in and then the returns are greater and the color line blight moves to the next block. . . . In fairness, we must admit it is not always the Negro occupancy alone which causes blight; the contributing factor

---

[6] Frederick M. Babcock, *Valuation of Real Estate* (New York: McGraw-Hill Book Co., Inc., 1932), pp. 88 and 91.

[7] Homer Hoyt, *One Hundred Years of Land Values in Chicago* (Chicago: University of Chicago Press, 1933), p. 314. Cited in Abrams, *Forbidden Neighbors*, p. 160.

[8] David Neiswanger, M.A.I., "Appraising the Small Home," *The Appraisal Journal*, V, no. 2 (April, 1937), 124.

may be the age and condition of buildings in which these people are housed that causes the trouble.[9]

The third type of depreciation is economic obsolescence. This is a loss of value which comes from conditions outside of the property itself, such as: 1. an oversupply of houses in the area; 2. change in character of use in the neighborhood; 3. legislative enactment, such as zoning changes; 4. proximity to nuisance; 5. racial infiltration; 6. under- or overimprovement. . . . Economic depreciation can be measured by making a careful comparison of value between property in the subject neighborhood and in ideal neighborhoods.[10]

Racial encroachment has less effect on high-grade property than upper-medium, medium, or lower-medium grades. Perhaps the reason for this is that only the select representatives of the encroaching race come into high-grade property.[11]

During the 1940's, three new ideas were advanced by several appraisers and other real estate professionals. The first two were (1) that minority occupancy might only "threaten" values, and (2) that while nonwhites might cause market disruptions which would *temporarily* depress prices, eventual neighborhood stability would move prices up again. Some said prices would settle at a level below the old one; others maintained they might return to the previous level, or even higher:

From this we may generalize that, in the city that houses a large percentage of people of foreign birth, or their children, or that contains a substantial minority percentage of people of races other than white, residential real estate values in the older districts bordering those at present inhabited by the minority peoples will exist in a state of threatened status quo.[12]

Frequently the presence of inharmonious racial, national, or income groups in an adjoining area represents a threat to property values.[13]

That the entry of non-Caucasians into districts where distinctly

---

[9] Elsie Smith Parker, "Both Sides of the Color Line," *The Appraisal Journal*, XI, no. 3 (July, 1943), 232–234.

[10] A. M. McDonald, "Appraising Residential Property," *The Appraisal Journal*, XXI, no. 2 (April, 1953), 264.

[11] Thurston H. Ross, "Market Significance of Declining Neighborhoods," *The Appraisal Journal*, XXIII, no. 2 (April, 1955), 203–211. This article analyzes the market problems of declining neighborhoods in general, with only incidental reference to racial factors.

[12] Arthur A. May, *The Valuation of Residential Real Estate* (New York: Prentice-Hall, Inc., 1942), p. 75. Cited in Abrams, *Forbidden Neighbors*, p. 165.

[13] Arthur M. Weimer and Homer Hoyt, *Principles of Real Estate* (3rd ed.; New York: The Ronald Press, 1954), p. 373.

Caucasian residents live tends to depress real estate values is agreed to by practically all real estate subdividers and students of city life and growth. Infiltration at the outset may be slow, but once the trend is established, values start to drop, until properties can be purchased at discounts of from 50 to 75 per cent. . . . Later, when a district has been entirely taken over, values tend to re-establish themselves to meet the needs and demands of the new occupants.[14]

Should a shift to a buyers' market start in any neighborhood, prices of less attractive houses are the first and most detrimentally affected. This has been markedly true where the shift is from white to Negro population, and the first two or three houses are usually sold to Negroes at a few hundred dollars above the market. In a few months sales prices drop below prices for comparable houses on white-owned and occupied streets. After the change is past the halfway mark, prices stabilize at an average price of perhaps 10 per cent below prices of comparable houses in white neighborhoods. The loss of price, however, is much greater on a street of mansion-type houses or on a street of sub-standard housing. Rentals are about the same in like quarters, whether rented by whites or Negroes.[15]

In a recent edition of *McMichael's Appraising Manual*, a basic reference, the author modifies the pessimistic predictions about values in transition areas that appeared in earlier versions:

Whether rightly or wrongly, some families avoid or leave a neighborhood of mixed race or national origin. This reduces the market for homes in the area and consequently may at first affect values adversely. As the neighborhood takes on its new character, and assuming equal maintenance of all property, value trends may reverse.[16]

The third new opinion that developed during the 1940's is that nonwhite entry does not harm—and may even improve—values. In a 1942 ruling on a race restrictive covenant case in the U. S. Court of Appeals for the District of Columbia, Chief Justice Groner evidently felt that the technical real estate evidence was favorable to values, for he said:

---

[14] Stanley L. McMichael, *Real Estate Subdivisions* (New York: Prentice-Hall, Inc., 1949), pp. 204–205.

[15] George A. Phillips, "Racial Infiltration," *The Review of the Society of Residential Appraisers*, XVI, no. 2 (February, 1950), 8. Quoted with permission of the Society of Residential Appraisers, 7 South Dearborn Street, Chicago 3, Illinois.

[16] Stanley L. McMichael, *McMichael's Appraising Manual* (4th ed.; New York: Prentice-Hall, Inc., 1951), p. 169. For his earlier statements, see footnotes 2, 4, and 14.

The evidence satisfies us that the effect . . . [of a racial change in neighborhood occupancy] is to make the market value of property on Thirteenth Street . . . greater for colored occupancy than for white. There is also evidence to the effect that the local citizens association, upon learning that appellants' vendor contemplated selling to appellants or other Negroes, tried to procure a white purchaser, and that one of the appellees himself had purchased the house . . . from Home Owners Loan Corporation for $2,000 less than the corporation was offered by a colored bishop . . . the covenant would merely depreciate all the property in the block. . . .[17]

Perhaps the best known statement by a professional appraiser supporting the view that nonwhite occupancy may actually be beneficial to values appeared in 1945. In introducing George W. Beehler, Jr.'s article, the editor remarked that "his reasoning and factual support for it establish a new concept for appraising areas under transition of occupancy." In Beehler's own words:

. . . to show that values have increased, we can cite sections newly occupied by colored during the past two or three years that have increased in value from 60 to 100 per cent on the average. This is due, primarily, to the fact that values in these sections, occupied by white and subject to colored encroachment around the edges, have remained static, while the colored section surrounding has felt the usual increase in values due to the so-called housing shortage and the changing economic value of the dollar as represented by its purchasing power. Then, within a six-month period, when colored occupancy enters a new block it picks up as much as the surrounding sections already occupied by colored people in a much shorter period of time. From that point on the values continue to increase along with other areas.[18]

During the process of racial transition, properties move through three stages of price behavior, according to Beehler's analysis. These are (1) an initial period of stagnation followed by (2) continued stagnation or slight price declines, but eventually reaching (3) a period of rising prices:

[17] *Hundley and Hundley* v. *Gorewitz, Bogikes and Bogikes*, U. S. Court of Appeals for the District of Columbia, December 14, 1942, cited by Robert C. Weaver in *The Negro Ghetto* (New York: Harcourt, Brace and Company, 1948), p. 268, n.
[18] George W. Beehler, Jr., "Colored Occupancy Raises Values," *The Review of the Society of Residential Appraisers*, XI, no. 9 (September, 1945), 3–4. Quoted with permission of the Society of Residential Appraisers.

White owners ordinarily do not want to be the first to put in colored and the other white people will not buy in the block, so that the only market is that made by the speculator who is buying to hold for a substantially increased price. Then, when the block is first broken, panic sets in among the remaining white owners and sales signs suddenly appear on more than half of the properties. For a short period after that the white owners compete with one another on prices in their desire to vacate. During this period prices either are at the old static figure or in some cases slightly under. When the panic ceases and most of the properties exposed for sale have been sold at this static figure, then gradually prices increase until the block becomes predominantly colored and then the remaining white owners secure a substantially higher price than those who sold earlier.[19]

The new price level holds up firmly and continues to move in accordance with city-wide trends, although Beehler states that the increase in better, newly established nonwhite sections is slightly higher than in similar white areas. Beehler concludes that "Neighborhood values in areas newly occupied by colored people have sharply increased and *will continue to increase.*" He feels this statement will be "startling" to the one out of ten "real estate men [who are] still living fifteen or twenty years in the past when *all* colored occupancy had an adverse effect on real estate values."

Beehler's prediction is challenged by another appraiser, Oscar I. Stern, well known for his articles in the professional journals. He doubts that colored occupancy will increase values over a period of time in the Philadelphia neighborhoods discussed.[20] Stern agrees that pent-up Negro demand for homes resulted in premium prices, but defines the premium as "exploitation" rather than an addition to value. He concludes that values in transition neighborhoods may be *sustained,* in comparison with similar all-white neighborhoods, but will not stay relatively higher permanently. However, he ends with the firm view that "It is a fact, the axiom that colored infiltration collapses the market is no longer true."

In a later article Stern observed that "Neighborhood mutations

---

[19] *Ibid.* Quoted with permission of the Society of Residential Appraisers.
[20] Oscar I. Stern, "Long Range Effect of Colored Occupancy," *The Review of the Society of Residential Appraisers,* XII, no. 1 (January, 1946), 4–6. Quoted with permission of the Society of Residential Appraisers.

have been accelerated. The old notion of Negro infiltration adversely affecting values is now shopworn. We are striking blindly at a situation, ignorant of its causative background. We lack a realistic program to handle it." [21]

In a general analysis of the market significance of declining neighborhoods, the professional appraiser Thurston Ross holds that nonwhites, under certain conditions, may stabilize or possibly enhance values in such neighborhoods.

In poor and slum sections racial encroachment sometimes raises the economic standards of the neighborhood. There are instances where obsolescence has been arrested and a number of additional years of useful life given a neighborhood by racial encroachment, particularly when older people are displaced by younger groups of the encroaching race. Furthermore, a sufficient identity must be given the neighborhood so that the market is stimulated to encourage additional members of the encroaching race to come into the area, thus keeping the market active, rather than by being depressed by the loss of a favorable identity because of the encroachment of only a few members into the neighborhood.[22]

Reconsideration of long accepted generalizations about race and value is strongly urged by Belden Morgan, formerly deputy chief appraiser of the FHA office in Los Angeles. He writes:

Right now a change is taking place in appraisal thought with respect to the opinion held on the effect of the "infiltration" or "invasion" of minority groups on white neighborhoods. . . . To approach this problem without prejudice is difficult indeed. Over the years we have been brought up with deeply ingrained emotional feelings that we cannot shake off with ease simply by saying we will. Inevitably, some reservation of prejudice will be retained, and we probably will not be free of it for several generations. Most appraisal texts treat the problem from the viewpoint of 20 years ago when it was commonly believed by nearly all that the presence of Negroes or other minorities in a neighborhood was a serious value-destroying influence. . . . There are many locations where such generalizations are no longer true.[23]

[21] Oscar I. Stern, "The End of the Restrictive Covenant," *The Appraisal Journal,* XVI, no. 4 (October, 1948), 439.

[22] Ross, *The Appraisal Journal,* XXIII, no. 2, 205.

[23] Belden Morgan, "Values in Transition Areas: Some New Concepts," *The Review of the Society of Residential Appraisers,* XVIII, no. 3 (March, 1952), 5–9. Quoted with permission of the Society of Residential Appraisers.

It is significant that Morgan is one of the few real estate representatives writing in the field who encloses words like "infiltration" and "invasion" in quotation

These recent statements indicate a readiness on the part of professional real estate people to analyze actual developments as they occur. Evidently, "automatic" reduction of an appraisal because nonwhites are in the neighborhood is no longer considered to reflect real value conditions, at least by some appraisers and brokers.

It is possible that the older statements are not so much erroneous as out of date. The years since 1940 have witnessed great changes in social and economic conditions and in the status of nonwhite minorities—changes that have altered the character of racial occupancy in housing. Further changes must inevitably come, and they will in turn qualify present-day statements about race and value.

THE REAL ESTATE BROKER, LENDER, AND BUILDER

As one would expect, the beliefs held by those in the housing industry reflect the professional literature very closely. It is instructive to observe, nevertheless, how the broadly worded theories and generalizations in the literature have more specifically worded counterparts in the field of practice.[24]

The Broker.—Many brokers and salesmen belong to local real estate boards, which in turn make up the National Association of Real Estate Boards. The local boards, numbering over 1,100, control the bulk of real estate selling activity in most communities in the country. Members are known as "realtors" and are bound to operate their businesses in accordance with the NAREB code of ethics, as well as their own local codes. For a quarter of a century,

---

marks. Such punctuation suggests that the user does not wish to go along with the implication that nonwhite entry is literally an infiltration or invasion of a white neighborhood.

In this connection, the vocabulary frequently encountered in the literature describing nonwhite population movement around or into a white area is indicative of the tension and hostility felt by many whites. Words like "threat," "encroachment," "encirclement," "penetration," "intrusion," "infiltration," "invasion," "infestation," "inundation," and "infection" appear to be consciously or unconsciously chosen to draw a parallel between the manifestations of war and sickness on the one hand and the entry of nonwhites into white areas on the other.

[24] Beliefs and attitudes concerning race and property values held by members of the housing industry are, of course, related to more widely held racial attitudes. The general subject of racial attitudes in housing is treated in two special studies prepared for the Commission on Race and Housing: Claire Selltiz and Stuart W. Cook, "Studies in the Social Psychology of Race and Housing" (unpublished), and Helen E. Amerman, "Studies of Attitudes Toward Housing and Race" (unpublished).

up to its revision in 1950, Article 34 of the National Code stated: "A realtor should never be instrumental in introducing into a neighborhood a character of property or occupancy, *members of any race or nationality,* or any individual whose presence will clearly be detrimental to property values in the neighborhood." [25]

As revised, the article now stipulates: "A realtor should never be instrumental in introducing into a neighborhood a character of property or use which will clearly be detrimental to property values in that neighborhood." [26]

Despite this rewording, most realtors appear to understand the article in the same sense as before, and to continue to act accordingly. In addition, most local real estate boards have their own code of ethics forbidding members to introduce "detrimental" minorities into neighborhoods.[27] Any realtor who violates the code is subject to expulsion or suspension from the local board, a penalty that would have disastrous effects on his real estate business. Property owners in the neighborhoods where he handles real estate may take their business elsewhere, and he may lose valuable business contacts. Thus, even those who might be inclined to challenge the old generalizations about nonwhites and property values are given pause by the thought of the direct economic losses and group pressures that could follow.

Very few systematic inquiries into broker and lender attitudes and practices have been made. One recent study, however, is based on interviews with representatives of sixty-four real estate firms and ten mortgage lending institutions in San Francisco,[28] and presents evidence on the general opinions and business methods encountered in the real estate field.

An important aspect of broker behavior emerged in response to the question, "What direct or indirect information do you have regarding what happens when a nonwhite family first moves into

---

[25] National Association of Real Estate Boards, *Code of Ethics,* adopted June, 1924. Italics supplied.

[26] *Ibid.,* revised November 17, 1950.

[27] The comment made by one broker is typical: "Our Code doesn't mention race, but certain things are understood." Personal interview, San Francisco, October 5, 1955.

[28] Constance C. Jensen, John Lindberg, George L. Smith, "The Minority Group Housing Market in San Francisco, with Special Reference to Real Estate Broker and Mortgage Financing Practices" (unpublished Master's research project, School of Social Welfare, University of California, Berkeley, 1955).

a neighborhood?" One broker out of three felt that "there is a sizeable threat to the business of the broker who is thought to have arranged such a sale." [29] Presumably this would occur through local boycott by angered property owners in the offending broker's home territory. It follows that many brokers, regardless of their personal beliefs, would not handle a transaction that would bring the first nonwhite into a residential neighborhood.

But the broker's unwillingness to handle such business evidently is not the chief problem: when asked to specify the difficulties nonwhites run into in attempting to buy a home in an all-white area, half the brokers mentioned the owners' unwillingness to sell. About a third gave neighborhood opposition as the reason, with financing problems a close third. Only one broker in five said that the *broker's* unwillingness to sell was a major difficulty.[30]

On the other hand, brokers can set up obstacles to nonwhite purchase even if the sellers do not. To the question, "If the seller says he will sell to anyone, regardless of race, what do you do?" over 85 percent of the brokers replying said they try to avoid handling such sales, while 13 percent said they are willing to carry them through on an unrestricted basis.[31]

The study summarizes three main reasons that impel brokers to restrict nonwhites to a special housing market. To violate an established neighborhood pattern would, they believe, damage their business income and reputation, go against the wishes of most of the white residents, and depreciate property values.[32]

Some of the actual comments made by brokers point up the specific role that the property value question plays in their decisions:[33]

"What happens is that one person sells to a Negro for spite; then a whole block is ruined."

"Property values decline permanently; about 25 per cent in the case of Negroes, less for Orientals."

"When Negroes move into a block, adjoining property goes down in value $1,000 to $2,000

[29] *Ibid.*, p. 21.
[30] *Ibid.*, p. 23.
[31] *Ibid.*, p. 30.
[32] *Ibid.*, p. 35.
[33] *Ibid.*, pp. 44–49.

"If you flood the neighborhood, you cut your own throat. It lowers property values and doesn't help your reputation either."

Additional comments, gathered from interviews conducted during the present study, confirm this pattern among brokers:[34]

Insofar as we can, we try to control the character of occupancy in the neighborhoods in which we sell. The area between 25th and 31st, north of Noriega, is being reserved for high-type whites, and this policy will pay off over time by protecting neighborhood standards and values. By screening applicants we can keep out undesirables, although it isn't always easy to tell who is undesirable. Of course, minority groups aren't wanted out here, and most of them know better than to contact us. The other day the phone rang and it was an answer to our newspaper ad, which hadn't mentioned the location of the property. A dark woman's voice inquired about the location and when told it was in the Avenues she hastily said: "Oh, that's no place for us colored," and hung up. We sometimes have a Chinese or Japanese prospect walk in, but we get rid of them by saying that there is a deposit on the property they're interested in. We haven't yet had to prove we had a deposit, but could easily have one of our office staff make one up if needed.

We San Francisco realtors have adopted the National Code of Ethics which forbids us to be instrumental in introducing a use or character of occupancy which will clearly be detrimental to neighborhood values. It is under this instruction that we feel justified in turning away people who would be undesirable to the community and who would thus harm values.

Values fall about $1,000 or $1,500 in the vicinity of a nonwhite. That is how much the price has to be shaded in order to move it to white buyers. I don't think nonwhites pay more than market to get into a white neighborhood. In fact, in the case of Chinese, they drive a very hard bargain. They will offer perhaps $13,000 for a $15,000 home.

In a short housing market, there is no difference in income performance of white vs. nonwhite properties. But prospective buyers [of income properties] still demand a discount or refuse to buy, regardless of realistic analysis of income. Perhaps some justification exists for this, in view of possible future unemployment of nonwhites, but much of buyers' behavior seems irrational. Attitudes of whites are changing under pressure of circumstances of the last seven or eight years.

---

[34] Personal interviews with San Francisco Bay Area brokers during 1951 and 1955.

If nonwhites, especially Negroes, hit a white district, where they are not desired, they depress property values in the eyes of other whites. But nonwhites will pay more than whites after the area is entered.

Effect of nonwhite entry or presence is to drop prices about $1,500, on the average. Banks and other lending agencies hasten this process of value loss, since they make financing difficult if subject property is within one block of colored.

Prices drop fully 20 per cent due to colored coming in, because properties just aren't movable to whites. A realtor who sold to a nonwhite in the Sunset area now can't get loans on any property because of anger of financial people, real estate groups, and the community. He is going out of business.

One of the most interesting points made in these broker comments is the recurring theme that while sellers may not get their price from whites (who are reluctant to consider an area undergoing racial transition), they probably can from nonwhites. This is quite different from the unqualified prediction that all prices in an "invaded" area fall.

A public statement by the San Francisco Real Estate Board indicates that the foregoing comments reflect the practices followed by at least those brokers and salesmen who are Board members:

It is a matter of fact and experience that when a Negro or Chinese or Japanese or Filipino moves into a white district, the house values drop. . . . Other whites won't buy into the district. Owners can only sell to other Negroes and so value goes down and down. . . . We don't look at this as a social problem. That's not our job. For us this is an economic problem. Looking at it this way, the Board has asked that its members "not introduce" into a residential district "any occupancy or race" which will have the effect of lowering values.[35]

The Lender.—The impact of the property value question on lending policies is suggested by the response noted in the Jensen-Lindberg-Smith study in interviews with ten mortgage lending firms. Two-thirds of the lenders felt that "the encroachment of minorities upon a white neighborhood made it more difficult for prospective borrowers in that area to obtain loans." [36]

---

[35] "The Negro in San Francisco," *San Francisco Chronicle*, November 6, 1950.
[36] Jensen, Lindberg, and Smith, "The Minority Group Housing Market in San Francisco . . . ," p. 40.

Lenders, like brokers, especially avoid "first-entry" sales to nonwhites, and for the same reasons:

They were unanimous in giving business considerations as the justification for this practice. Eighty per cent stated that their depositors or policy holders in the neighborhood would threaten to withdraw their accounts, and at least one in three mentioned that the lowered property values would adversely affect their mortgages held on other properties in the neighborhood.[37]

Field interviews for the present study revealed further detail on lender beliefs and policies:[38]

A savings and loan association: We have about 4,000 depositors, most of whom live in the area in which we make loans. Almost all are Caucasian. At least 150 of them have plainly told me that they would not tolerate the use of their funds to install nonwhites in this area, and that they would withdraw their deposits if we adopted such a policy. If the time ever comes when nonwhites in this area make appreciable deposits with our association, we may be able to make loans to them here.

A savings and loan association: Nonwhite entry destroys property values only to whites, not to nonwhites. That is, sellers will lose only if they are determined to sell to whites. They can get their price from colored.

Another savings and loan association: We make loans to colored in established areas only. If they were introduced into a new area, values would fall 50 per cent. There are lots of things we would like to do personally, such as treating everybody equally, but we are responsible for millions of dollars and we cannot jeopardize our reputation and business standing by going against community wishes. We will lend on properties up to three blocks away from colored areas, but no closer, because we anticipate such areas will spread, and when they do the values fall to the point where we might be loaning 100 per cent or more of the value.

A large bank: There definitely is a detrimental value impact following establishment of nonwhite residence in a white neighborhood. We refused to finance a 180-unit all-Negro development because of the anticipated value repercussions on surrounding white areas, and have turned down similar smaller projects for the same reason.

---

[37] *Ibid.*, p. 41.
[38] From personal interviews with San Francisco Bay Area mortgage lenders during 1951 and 1955.

A large life insurance company: The effects of racial infiltration are often discussed among the lending agencies and, although we have no factual evidence to present, we are unanimous in the opinion that it harms values. It depresses the neighborhood and thus decreases the amount we will loan on any particular property. A single Negro in a block in the Sunset area would be like a caution flag to us to note the trend of the neighborhood and would probably be sufficient to influence our loans downward in that area.

The Builder.—The apprehension of lenders about property values in areas of racial change is echoed by the builders, who fear marketing difficulties will arise out of mixed racial patterns. A spokesman for one of the largest home building corporations in the San Francisco Bay Area typifies the general position of most builders:

Nonwhite entry has unfortunate effects. In the Richmond area, white owners let their property run down because they lost interest in the standards of the neighborhood after colored came in. It doesn't matter whether colored entrants are "good" or "bad" in type; their color is the thing, and their color stagnates the affected area because white people don't want them as neighbors. . . . We hold many vacant lots throughout the city for future development—perhaps enough for as many as 3,000 new single family units. But our development of those is sensitive to existing and developing racial patterns. If colored have come too close to some of our lots we will sell them and not build, because we couldn't market anything on them.[39]

It is evident, then, that brokers, lenders, and builders—those who create, sell, and resell homes—often believe that nonwhite occupancy is not good for property values. This belief influences their decisions to build, finance, sell, and buy in ways that restrict the opportunities of nonwhites to acquire housing and limit them to certain districts.

PROFESSIONAL STUDENTS OF HOUSING

Experts in sociology and urban land economics have typically taken the position that more knowledge was needed concerning the actual effects of nonwhite entry on an all-white neighborhood. Until sufficient empirical evidence should become available, they have urged the avoidance of fixed opinions in the matter,

---

[39] Personal interview, San Francisco, November, 1951.

and have pointed out the theoretical reasons why a number of price behavior patterns are possible.

In his classic study, however, Gunnar Myrdal painted a somewhat pessimistic picture of the economic aspects of "invasion" in the large cities of the North:

> When white residents of a neighborhood see that they cannot remove the few Negro intruders and also see more Negro families moving in, they conjure up certain stereotypes of how bad Negro neighbors are and move out of the neighborhood with almost panic speed. For this reason Negroes are dangerous for property values, as well as for neighborhood business, and all whites are aware of this fact. . . . If white property owners in a neighborhood rush to sell their property all at once, property values naturally are hurt. After the transition to Negro occupancy is made, however, property values rise again at least to the level justified by the aging and lack of improvement of the buildings.[40]

Myrdal's view that prices first dipped, then recovered to their old level or nearly so, was voiced at about the same time that the professional real estate literature was beginning to suggest the same thing.

In 1948, Robert Weaver undertook the most comprehensive survey of facts and theories about the race and value question that had been done up to that time, devoting a chapter of his book, *The Negro Ghetto,* to the topic. After reviewing the scarce and conflicting evidence, Weaver suggested some general theories about the possible economic consequences of nonwhite entry— theories that provide a framework for a variety of empirical findings:

> The effect of Negro occupancy upon property values varies from one section of the city to another and from one time to another. Within a given area, the initial result of the arrival of a few colored people may be imperceptible or it may lead to panic among white occupants; the arrival of a few Negroes may be the signal for a great decline in selling prices or it may lead to an appreciable increase. Much depends upon the state of the total housing market and the manner in which colored people enter an area. Or, again, prices may fall with large-scale Negro introduction only to recover again as the

---

[40] Gunnar Myrdal, *An American Dilemma* (New York: Harper and Brothers, 1944), p. 623.

transition is completed. Out of all of these possibilities . . . a separate and obviously incomplete theory of the relationship between racial occupancy and property values could be formulated. No such theory would be sound. *There is no one universal effect of Negro occupancy upon property values.*[41]

The manner in which nonwhites affect values in particular areas depends, in Weaver's view, on what is happening to four factors: (1) nonwhite income distribution; (2) general business conditions at the time of nonwhite entry; (3) long-run trend of values in the areas before entry; and (4) how nonwhite occupancy actually occurs.[42]

Charles Abrams, author of many works on housing, agrees with Weaver in suggesting that many different price patterns may follow "minority infiltration":[43]

The statement that one race or group inevitably affects prices favorably and another unfavorably disregards the complex of factors which play a part, such as the social and economic status of a particular minority at a particular time; its numbers in relation to the numbers in the majority group; the latter's social and cultural level; the minority's capacity for social improvement and assimilation; the size of the city and the physical condition of its neighborhoods; the particular pattern of minority distribution; the nature of the then current minority stereotype; the type of social and educational leadership and maturity in the community; the social and economic role of the minority in the community; the relationship between the groups in employment, and a host of other factors. . . . There are no fixed rules as to when minority neighbors raise or lower values; examples may be cited both ways and much study is still needed.[44]

These scholarly approaches to the problem leave the door open to a range of factual answers. They point out that the factor of race is only one of many that affect real estate prices, and that quite often it may by no means be the most important one.

THE FEDERAL HOUSING ADMINISTRATION

The Federal Housing Administration has altered its earlier adherence to racially homogeneous neighborhoods. Its old view was

---

[41] Weaver, *The Negro Ghetto,* p. 293. Italics in original.

[42] *Ibid.,* pp. 297–298.

[43] Abrams, *Forbidden Neighbors,* pp. 285–286. See also, by the same author, "The New 'Gresham's Law of Neighborhoods'—Fact or Fiction," *The Appraisal Journal,* XIX, no. 3 (July, 1951).

[44] Abrams, *Forbidden Neighbors,* pp. 286, 292.

put forth in the following provision of its *Underwriting Manual* for 1938: "If a neighborhood is to retain stability it is necessary that properties shall continue to be occupied by the same social and racial classes." [45]

Consistent with this theory, the FHA, because of its conviction that declining property values would result from a mixed neighborhood, thus endangering the long-range financing involved, formerly insisted that residential projects desiring FHA-insured financing draw up restrictive covenants against nonwhites. In recent years FHA has adopted the opposite position, refusing to insure projects where a written racially restrictive covenant exists. Concerning property values and race, the *Underwriting Manual* now states: "The tendency of user groups to seek compatible conditions can sustain and enhance, diminish or destroy neighborhood desirability. . . . If a mixture of user groups is found to exist, it must be determined whether the mixture will render the neighborhood less desirable to present and prospective occupants." [46]

THE SELF-FULFILLING PROPHECY

The beliefs, policies, and practices that have been briefly reviewed thus far interweave with each other, and with other real estate market factors, to produce many patterns of price behavior. In the interweaving process, a circular kind of "belief-cause-effect-and-belief" phenomenon often takes place, which operates to magnify and reinforce the barriers affecting nonwhites.

For example, if many white homeowners believe that their new Negro neighbor will cause neighborhood property values to drop, they may "panic," frantically list their homes for sale, and compete with each other for buyers. Such a sudden rise in the supply of homes in a small market area may well mean that not enough buyers can be found, whether white or nonwhite. Homes may not sell for weeks, even months, and when they do it may be at prices that have had to be discounted sharply to attract buyers from a wider radius. The result is that prices have fallen, just as the homeowners expected, and their faith in the formula that "Negroes hurt value" is made stronger than ever.

---

[45] Federal Housing Administration, *Underwriting Manual*, 1938, sec. 937.
[46] *Ibid.*, Rev. 1952, sec. 1320.

Again, mortgage lenders in a certain city may all feel the same way about a particular white neighborhood that has recently experienced the entry of one or two nonwhite families: "Its days as a first-class residential area are numbered; values will inevitably drop." Consequently, lending policies for that area will be modified. The percentage of loan to appraisal will be reduced, and appraisals themselves may gradually move downward because of subjective value judgments influencing the appraisers' objective approach. As a result, effective demand for homes in that area will be lower than it would be under ordinary circumstances, because potential buyers cannot get as large loans as before. Prices will fall, relative to other areas where lending policies remain the same, and the lenders' predictive judgment will be vindicated by events.

Probably, neither the homeowners nor the lenders in these examples realize that their own beliefs have influenced them to act in ways that bring about the results they have predicted. It is this very unawareness of their own role in predetermining history that makes the process effective. Considering that the beliefs themselves are open to question, the process demonstrates its capacity for making an unreal definition of a situation produce real results. As Robert Merton's analysis puts it: "The self-fulfilling prophecy is, in the beginning, a *false* definition of the situation evoking a new behavior which makes the originally false conception come *true*." [47] He regards the process as a tragicomic one: tragic in the sense that false or questionable predictions are sanctified by prediction-induced consequences; comic in that "the prophet will cite the actual course of events as proof that he was right from the very beginning."

From these observations on beliefs about race and value, representing many points of view, at least three general conclusions emerge:

1. The fear that property values are seriously damaged by nonwhite neighbors has been very generally felt among both real estate business circles and individual property owners.

2. This widespread fear has for many years contributed heavily to the confining of nonwhites to narrow housing markets. Restric-

---

[47] Robert K. Merton, "The Self-fulfilling Prophecy," *The Antioch Review*, VIII, no. 2 (Summer, 1946), 208. Italics in original.

tive selling, building, and lending policies have combined to produce this result.

3. Some questions have recently been raised concerning the precise effects of nonwhite occupancy on property values. These questions have emphasized the contrast between sweeping pessimistic generalizations and the lack of evidence to support them, and have drawn attention to the interplay of socioeconomic factors.

III

Plan and Scope of Study

The objective of this study is to bring into focus all the available evidence on the question of what actually happens to real estate prices when nonwhites move into an all-white neighborhood. Three classes of evidence are considered. The first of these—a review of what writers in the fields of real estate, property appraisal, and finance have said over the years about the relation of race and property values—has already been presented in chapter ii. Most of this material is based on professional experience and observation rather than scientific research. Nevertheless, the judgments of real estate authorities, regardless of their basis, could hardly be neglected in a study attempting comprehensive treatment.

Second, and contributing the bulk of the statistical evidence, is an original study conducted by the writer in a series of neighborhoods in San Francisco and Oakland, California, and Philadelphia, Pennsylvania.

Third, the findings of studies carried out by real estate investigators in selected neighborhoods of Chicago, Kansas City, Detroit, and Portland, Oregon, are summarized and evaluated.

The original part of this study presents data gathered in San Francisco, Oakland, and Philadelphia according to a uniform research design. The evidence for these three cities is, therefore, consistent and comparable. For the four other cities, there are five separate studies, conducted at different times by different investigators and utilizing somewhat different research procedures.[1] Therefore, only broad comparisons can be made among the results for these four cities and between any one of them and the three

---

[1] Studies by Paul F. Cressey (Chicago, 1930); E. F. Schietinger (Chicago, 1953); Thomas L. Gillette (Kansas City, 1954); Richard S. Wander (Detroit, 1953); Urban League of Portland (Portland, 1956). Titles and publication status of these studies are given in chapters ix and x below.

included in the "original" study. Comparisons are made to the extent warranted by the data, and an attempt is made to summarize the general findings from all sources.

The discussion of research method which follows refers primarily to the "original" study of neighborhoods in San Francisco, Oakland, and Philadelphia. Research procedures of the other studies are described as each study is reviewed.

RESEARCH METHOD: GENERAL CONSIDERATIONS

Whether prices rise, fall, or remain stable in a neighborhood experiencing racial change would, as an isolated observation, tell us little. Changes in general economic activity, shifts in the local demand for and supply of housing, and altered trends in neighborhood land use and residential desirability (to mention but a few possibilities) could easily explain any such price movements, independently of the changing racial pattern.

To measure the economic performance of a racially mixed area, its property price behavior must be checked against some standard that is free from the racial influence being analyzed. There are but two feasible standards:

1. A broadly based price index indicating the average behavior of the real estate market for homes in all-white neighborhoods in the same general area.

2. The prices of comparable houses in a neighborhood that duplicates the racially mixed one in every significant respect, except that it remains all-white.

There are several reasons for preferring the second standard. Most important, it comes closer to the research ideal of "holding other factors constant," and therefore permits a sharper isolation of race of occupancy as a real estate market influence. Furthermore, even though it confronts the investigator with knotty problems of site selection and data gathering, it is more manageable as a technique than the construction of a general price index representing market activity in all-white areas. While some of the areas analyzed in this report are in cities where a general price index has been developed, such indices typically reflect ranges of price and neighborhood diversity that detract from their usefulness as a standard. They may also have the crippling disadvantage of being based in part on market data from areas either experiencing, or on the verge of, racial mixture. Such "laboratory impurities" could not be eliminated without an exhaustive check of the residential pattern in every locality covered by the index. It is much more convenient to select a manageably sized, all-white neighborhood with characteristics comparable to the mixed neighborhood.

As a research technique, then, this study depends primarily on a price comparison of two residential neighborhoods, both formerly all-white, but only one of which has remained so. The steps involved in this technique are:

1. Find a residential neighborhood that has changed from an all-white to a mixed racial pattern. This is defined as a "test area."

2. Locate another neighborhood closely comparable to the test area in all of the important price-determining respects, except that it has remained all-white. This is defined as a "control area."

3. Collect sales price data in each area for the same time period.

4. Compare the behavior of average test area prices with that of average control area prices over time.

Most northern cities with growing nonwhite populations display two broad types of residential neighborhoods having mixed racial patterns:

Type I: *Central city neighborhoods.*—These are the older urban areas, built and lived in by wealthier families during the bustling days of urban birth and rapid central growth fifty to seventy years ago. Once past the peak of their popularity as living areas for the more successful elements in the community, these neighborhoods entered a period of rapid change: *in land use,* from residential to mixed commercial-residential, through shifts in the functioning of central city areas; *in type of dwelling unit,* from largely single-family homes to a high proportion of multiunit structures, mostly through conversion; *in attractiveness,* from high-class to slum area, as density and poverty increased; *in type of occupancy,* from owners who were upper-income professional and business people to tenants from the low-income semiskilled and manual-labor occupational groups, as successive waves of migrants from farm, town, and other countries swept into the cities.

Nonwhites naturally were among the incoming groups. They

became a particularly significant city population factor following 1918, when large-scale Negro movement from the South developed with increasing momentum. Hemmed in by segregation as well as by their disadvantaged economic position, their concentration in the older (usually slum) areas built up more and more, until city after city had its "black belt." As the in-migration pressure mounted, this belt expanded into surrounding blocks. This process still goes on in many northern cities. It has resulted in continuously expanding areas of racially mixed blocks containing high proportions of nonwhites.

Type II: *Neighborhoods outside the central city area.*—Much more recently created than most Type I neighborhoods, these tend to be located toward the city's edge and may even be outside city lines. Typically, they are single-family residential neighborhoods with a middle-income population of owner-occupants. They have experienced and are experiencing nonwhite entry because many nonwhites are unwilling to go to or remain in the crowded urban centers and now have both the motivation and the means to obtain better housing. Furthermore, the Supreme Court decision forbidding legal enforcement of race restrictive covenants drained segregation efforts of much of their effectiveness.

The neighborhoods selected for analysis in this report are Type II. The reasons given in the following paragraphs appear to justify such a selection:

Racial changes in Type I areas are closely intermingled with other developments that directly affect real estate values. Chief among these are the high rate of conversion from single-unit to multiunit structures, the change from owner-occupancy to tenant-occupancy, and the broad shifts in land use among residential, commercial, and light industrial patterns. Attempting to isolate the racial factor under these circumstances can hardly produce conclusive results. By contrast, it is relatively easy to find Type II areas where racial change is the only important variable.

It is rarely possible to find an all-white area with which the Type I neighborhood can be compared. Most areas in the city's interior with similar physical and evolutional characteristics have experienced nonwhite entry or are close to heavily nonwhite areas.

In either case, they are disqualified as standards of comparison. By contrast, comparable areas for Type II neighborhoods are not too difficult to find.

Type I areas typically include a very high proportion of rental as against owner-occupied units. Selling prices of rental properties are a function of the net income derived from rents. The operation of rent control during the war and early postwar period interfered with the market pricing mechanism for such properties, and it did this at a time when racial changes were extensive and rapid. This is not a problem with Type II areas, which predominantly have single-family, owner-occupied units.

While most whites living in still all-white sections of the central city are apprehensive about the economic damage that nonwhite "invasion" may cause them, whites living farther out seem to hold even more fearful views on the subject. The probable explanation for this stronger fear is that neighborhoods toward the city's edge and in the suburbs are usually made up of single-family, owner-occupied homes, where one might expect deep concern over possible damage to a relatively large family investment. Then too, residents of neighborhoods more removed from existing concentrations of nonwhites are psychologically less prepared to face the prospect of nonwhite entry; it is an entirely unexpected thing. Thus, focusing upon price behavior in Type II neighborhoods, where concern over the problem is deeper, may yield more useful results.

Type II areas merit special attention for still another reason: they are being sought out as places to live, in preference to central city areas, by an ever-larger proportion of nonwhites. In this, nonwhites are following the general trend of white home buyers. These areas provide more amenities for family life; and also the improving income situation of nonwhites enables many of them for the first time to consider such areas.

Finally, most Type II areas have been free of the "nonwhite invasion threat" (as it is often called) until the moment that the first nonwhite family moved in. Usually, a fortuitous combination of factors results in the home of a white owner becoming available to a nonwhite buyer—unexpectedly, as far as the white neighborhood is concerned. Thus it cannot be argued—as it so often is with Type I areas—that property values have been damaged *in advance* of the first nonwhite entrant. For this reason, Type II neighborhoods give a more clean-cut "laboratory situation" for testing the effects of race on value.

Value and Price

Actual selling prices are the basic data for this study, consistent with its objective of measuring the effects of nonwhite entry upon real estate price trends in formerly all-white neighborhoods. If one is attempting to detect the economic consequences of changing racial patterns, the prices at which homes change hands in the market are—it is here maintained—the best indicators available. Market prices, in fact, are the only *objective* evidence at hand. *The various kinds of appraised value introduce predictive, and necessarily subjective, elements that may obscure the very effects this study seeks to measure.*

In adopting this procedure, it is nevertheless recognized that for several purposes market price is not by itself the final answer to the question, "What is the value of a home?" The buyer who purchases for investment, the lender who regards the house as loan collateral, the local assessor who sets a value on it for tax purposes—each of these will place a somewhat different value on the same home. It is highly unlikely that any value they arrive at will equal, or even be very close to, actual market price. While they regard market price as an important factor in their calculations, each is concerned with trying to estimate value in a way that meets his specific purposes.

The investor is trying to find the figure representing the present worth of all future benefits that the property will yield. Obviously, his value estimate depends on his forecast of economic trends, analysis of the neighborhood's probable life history, estimate of the property's life span, and other variables impossible to anticipate with accuracy. Market price would equal his value estimate only if buyers and sellers analyzed the market in exactly his way, which seldom happens.

The courts have long accepted a definition of value as the price that a fully informed buyer, who is not compelled to buy, will pay and that a fully informed seller, who is not compelled to sell, will accept. Since buyers and sellers are rarely fully informed and are usually under some pressures to act, the market price that satisfies them both will only by chance be equal to value in this purely defined sense. It follows that property values, as they may be determined by professional appraisers who are advising buyer-investors, are distinct from actual market prices. By definition, appraisal values deëmphasize immediate market considerations as contrasted with long-term factors that affect the appraised property over its life span. But it is the immediate market situation that is of most concern to those interested in the economic effects of neighborhood racial change. The long-term reactions are not predictable on the basis of past experience, since there is no such experience with respect to racial change and property values.

Much of the preceding reasoning applies with equal force to the concept of long-term value used by the real estate lender. Appraisals for lending purposes are based on the long-range view and are therefore affected by all the hazards of forecasting. In a situation involving racial change, an appraiser's personal views about the long-term effects on property values can obviously affect the current appraisal value that he sets. For example, he may feel that nonwhites inevitably depress values, that current prices are completely unrealistic, and that therefore the loan value of the property should be set perhaps 20 percent lower than the current market to protect the lender against the eventual "unavoidable" deterioration in value.

The tax assessor in valuing a property for taxation purposes is chiefly concerned with the problem of treating comparable properties alike, not in arriving at an appraisal that is closely related to the market at any given time.

When one speaks of "value" therefore, it is always necessary to ask: "value—for what purpose?" For the same property there exists a whole array of values, each arrived at in a manner that can be defended according to the evaluator's objective.

But to rely on any value data other than market price in this study would be hazardous. The future economic behavior of neighborhoods experiencing racial change is not predictable on the basis of past experience. Considerable changes have occurred —and they are continuing—in the nonwhites' economic and social position. Together with altered attitudes on the part of many whites, these changes create new conditions in real estate markets, the effects of which no one can predict with much confidence. Actual market price behavior must be closely studied for signs of long-run trends that may eventually serve as reliable bases for predictions of value. But in looking for "the facts" of a situation it is important to bear in mind that a selling price is a fact while value is an estimate of what the price ought to be. This study is based on the analysis of observed selling prices.

Financing as a Market Factor

How much will lenders lend, and on what terms? For every local housing market the lending policies in operation during any given period have significant price effects. Three variables are involved: the rate of interest, the length of the payoff period, and the ratio of loan to appraised value. Other things remaining constant, a larger number of buyers will be able to register effective demands for housing as interest rates move down, payoff periods lengthen, or loan-value ratios increase, and house prices will tend to rise. Similarly, a reversal in all or any of these three variables that would reduce effective demand would have a price-depressing reaction.

However, because this study relies entirely on checking price behavior in racially changing neighborhoods against price behavior in comparable all-white neighborhoods, the *general* market impact of varying lending policies need not concern us. As long as lending policies exert equal market effects in the neighborhoods compared, they can be considered as neutral factors. If, on the other hand, the lending policies applying to areas into which nonwhites move, or to nonwhite loan applicants, are less favorable than the policies applying to all-white areas or white loan applicants, they will bias the respective price behavior in those areas. From all the evidence examined for this study, it appears that financing can be treated as a neutral factor in the comparative price analysis of white versus racially changing areas. The reasons why this is so deserve comment.

For all nonwhites in the United States, the 1950 Census data on residential financing present a mixed picture. Nonwhites appear to get financing on about the same terms as whites—income group by income group and price range by price range—*when they are granted loans from the same lenders.* Often, however, nonwhites cannot obtain a loan from the same institutional sources for one or more of the following reasons: age and condition of property; neighborhood condition and location; inadequate or unstable income; race. They must then turn to less favorable financing sources to a greater extent than do whites and thus face higher interest rates, shorter amortization periods, and lower loan-value ratios.[2] Less favorable first mortgages lead buyers to turn to second mortgages (junior liens) to make up the full purchase price. In 1950, whereas only 5.5 percent of white-owned properties were subject to conventional junior liens, 9.4 percent of nonwhite-owned properties were so encumbered.[3]

The general picture concerning financing differentials related to race of purchaser is worth noting, but for our purpose the immediately relevant questions are: (a) To what extent did financing differentials related to race show up in the areas studied? (b) If there were such differentials, how did they affect market price behavior in the mixed areas as compared to the all-white areas?

As to the first question, complete information on financing, by race, could be compiled for only a few of the areas studied, but it may be presumed to be fairly representative. It indicates that, *for loans that were made,* nonwhites were generally able to obtain *first* mortgages similar to those secured by whites.[4] The tendency toward uniformity of financing, regardless of race, is probably explained by these factors:

1. From a lender's point of view, the condition of most of the areas studied, and the dwelling units in them, can be rated as "good," with several in the "very good" and "fairly good" categories. Therefore the "hands-off" or distinctly unfavorable loan policies that are operative in many deteriorated areas with mixed residence patterns are not found here.

---

[2] See Davis McEntire, *Residence and Race: Final and Comprehensive Report to the Commission on Race and Housing,* chapter xiii, "Mortgage Financing" (Berkeley: University of California Press, 1960). For an analysis of comparative white-nonwhite residential financing in San Francisco see chapter xi of the present report.

[3] *United States Census of Housing: 1950,* Vol. IV, *Residential Financing,* Part 1, "United States," chap. 3, tables 4 and 18. "Conventional junior liens" refers to second mortgages held by individual lenders. VA-guaranteed second mortgages are the only other significant category of junior liens.

[4] See chapter xi below.

2. Nonwhites moving into these average and better-than-average neighborhoods appear to be at a slightly higher economic and social level than that typifying the white residents.[5] This may influence lenders to rate them as equally good credit risks in comparison with whites who are at a lower income level.

3. Many areas qualify for FHA and VA loans, the VA-guaranteed loan's being the predominant financing instrument since 1945. Nonwhites who succeeded in obtaining either an FHA or VA loan very likely did so on the same basis as did whites.

Despite this tendency toward uniformity in the financing of home purchases in the areas studied, whether the purchase was made by a white or a nonwhite, the data do show that nonwhites had smaller average cash down payments than did whites. Even with comparable first mortgages, therefore, nonwhites had to resort to secondary financing to a greater extent than did whites.[6] As a contributing reason, there may have been a significant number of cases in which nonwhites paid a premium price to enter a particular neighborhood.

Whatever the reasons, the relatively more frequent resort to second mortgages by nonwhite buyers in the areas studied is considered by some real estate businessmen and observers to overstate the level of market prices from the sellers' standpoint. The argument runs as follows:[7] Assume a nonwhite is able to pay down $1,000 cash on a $12,000 home, obtaining a conventional first mortgage loan of $8,000. To cover this balance, the seller lends the buyer $3,000 on a purchase money second mortgage. The seller subsequently sells this in the second mortgage market, but can do so only at a discounted price of $1,800. Thus, he nets $10,800 (assuming he owned the house clear), and the market price is "artificially high" by $1,200.

Such transactions occur in about one case out of six, if the analysis of San Francisco neighborhoods has general applicabil-

---

[5] In studying such a transition area in Kansas City, Gillette found that background data on whites and Negroes indicated that the Negro group had higher family incomes, greater prestige by type of occupation, and more education than the whites. Thomas L. Gillette, "Santa Fe: A Study of the Effects of Negro Invasion on Property Values" (unpublished Master's thesis, Department of Sociology, University of Kansas City, 1954). Discussed in detail in chapter ix.

[6] See chapter xi.

[7] Selling expenses are omitted from the argument, summarized from chapter xi.

ity.[8] Yet they differ significantly from the predominant finance pattern of an institutionally held first mortgage accompanied by a sizable down payment, and it is clear that the resulting prices are higher than they would be in the absence of secondary financing.

This being the case, should not observed market prices be adjusted so as to eliminate any upward bias in measuring neighborhood price trends in this study? For the following reasons it is here held that adjustments are unnecessary:

1. Similar "discounted second" transactions are made by purchasers in the all-white areas, and constitute the same proportion of total neighborhood sales, so far as *seller*-held financing is concerned.[9] (Only seller-held financing is in point since institutionally held secondary financing does not push market price up in anticipation of discounting the second mortgage; it merely fills the gap between the existing market price and all other funds available to the purchaser.) Not only do the all-white areas show an identical *proportion* of such transactions, as compared with the test areas, but the modal *size* of seller-held second mortgages is quite close: $2,530, as against $3,041.[10] Assuming these mortgages were sold by the sellers at an average discount of 50 percent, sellers in all-white areas would lose $1,265, as compared with a $1,520 loss to sellers in the test areas.[11] The average differential of $255 is not sufficiently large in relation to average selling price to necessitate an involved adjustment procedure. Comparing the level of market price observed in both types of areas can therefore be assumed to reflect essentially the same financing considerations.

2. As a separate point it may be noted that *buyers always pay the full sales price.* This is true regardless of the amounts actually realized by the sellers, who may receive considerably less than the listed exchange price because of the discounting procedure already described. "Net price to the seller" has no particular significance when price levels for two neighborhoods are

---

[8] See table 6.

[9] *Ibid.*

[10] See table 9.

[11] Interviews with buyers of second mortgages did not indicate that higher discount rates are applied to properties in mixed, as against all-white, areas.

being compared, if the structure of financing and discounting is essentially similar in both. This is especially true if, as in this study, attention is focused on the *relative* price performance displayed by test and control areas, rather than on the absolute level of prices. For the purposes of this study, then, a defensible measure of the comparative market worth of real estate would seem to be what buyers pay in one area as against what they pay in another.[12]

RESEARCH METHOD: SPECIFIC CONSIDERATIONS

Sources of Price Information

To investigate the effects of racial change on property prices requires reliable information on selling prices, dates of sale, financing arrangements, basic features of properties sold, assessed valuations, physical and social characteristics of the neighborhoods involved, and changes in racial composition over time. No single source provides all this information. For all its size and significance, the real estate market is remarkable for the paucity, decentralization, nonstandardization, and ambiguity of its records.

For neighborhoods in the San Francisco Bay Area, the most centralized and organized source of market data covering the first four items listed above was found in files maintained by multiple listing offices.[13] These are central clearing houses with which brokers list properties for the purpose of reaching more prospects. Selling commissions are shared with any member broker who can find a customer for the property. Only a portion of all sales in the areas studied was handled through multiple listing channels. For the periods involved, this portion averaged about 40 percent, ranging from around 30 percent in earlier years to 50 percent and above in recent years.

---

[12] Even if these considerations did not support the use of observed market prices in test and control areas, the practical problems of discovering and analyzing the financing details for every transaction in this study, and of then making indicated adjustments to observed prices, would have meant tracing the sales individually through the records of county courthouses and title companies—an involved and highly expensive project. Fortunately, this task could be avoided without affecting the significance of the test area–control area comparisons.

[13] See Appendix A for a fuller discussion of research problems and procedures.

There is reason to suspect a degree of bias in the determination as to which properties are placed with a multiple listing service, in that member brokers are not likely to list a property that they believe they can readily sell. They may therefore be more inclined to list the less desirable properties. Such a bias would tend to understate slightly the average price level in each neighborhood studied, but would not distort neighborhood comparisons as long as it operated "across the board." Member brokers who were interviewed believe that no significant difference in listing practices is operative between mixed and all-white areas.[14]

Individual real estate offices furnished considerable price information; this was used to supplement the data from multiple listing files. This brought the sample of sales up to about 50 percent of all area sales.

Financing arrangements were fully recorded only by the multiple listing office for San Francisco, but there is no reason to suppose that the analysis of financing based on the information available there would not apply generally to the other similar areas studied.

Philadelphia has no multiple listing offices, but an alternative source was found in published real estate directories, compiled for and leased to brokers, appraisers, and other interested parties. The directories give selling prices for every transaction in the areas covered. This source does not provide complete details on financing arrangements; on the other hand, it includes assessed valuations, which had to be separately obtained from assessors' offices for the other areas. Selling prices listed in the Philadephia Directory may be considered quite accurate since, under state law, they must be sworn to by the transacting parties.

Information about the physical and social characteristics of the neighborhoods studied, as well as the racial changes occurring in mixed areas, was gathered from several sources, including direct field inspections and interviews, local government agencies, private social and cultural organizations, and real estate offices and agencies.[15]

---

[14] Field interviews, July to December, 1951, and August to December, 1955.
[15] See Appendix B for a listing of sources.

Selection of Test Areas

In this study, a "test area" is a residential neighborhood composed of single-family homes, largely owner-occupied. Its boundaries are those commonly accepted by its residents and real estate brokers. It starts out as an all-white neighborhood but experiences nonwhite entry at some time during the observation period.

Choosing such areas for this study of selling prices involved several steps:

First, it was essential to find where nonwhite families lived in the urban area, especially with regard to single-family type neighborhoods. This information was obtained from a combination of sources: the 1950 Census; government agencies concerned with such functions as planning, community relations, and health; and local real estate brokers and appraisers.

Second, specific test neighborhoods were identified which satisfied the necessary criteria:

(a) The change from all-white to mixed racial occupancy should have taken place within the period covered by the price data available;[16]

(b) the area should conform to local definitions of the boundaries of the neighborhood real estate market;

(c) the area should be neither "too large" nor "too small." If too large, any localized price effects would probably be obliterated by the price-averaging process; if too small, there would be too few transactions to build up the necessary volume of selling price data. In practice, an area of ten to fifteen blocks was found to be the best neighborhood size for price research purposes;

(d) it should be possible to match the test area with a closely comparable control area;

(e) test areas ought to represent as wide a range as possible in price class and in degree of nonwhite entry.

---

[16] This proved to be a major limitation, because reliable price data were not available for years before 1940. Thus, neighborhoods which had nonwhite entry before that year could not be included. Philadelphia, for example—despite its size and heavy nonwhite in-migration—had only eight areas with sufficiently recent nonwhite entry to make price research possible, and only three of these met other selection criteria.

Since the economic reaction of neighborhoods to the factor of racial change could conceivably differ according to the price range of homes and the relative number of nonwhites who move in, the analysis is made more searching if neighborhoods differing in these characteristics are chosen.

As to *price class,* three categories are used:

> Low, $3,000–$ 7,500.
> Medium, $7,500–$14,000.
> High,   above $14,000.

This classification is arbitrary, but it applies with considerable accuracy to the broad price groupings of residences sold during the periods covered. A number of neighborhoods displayed price ranges not entirely contained in any one of these three categories, but were labeled according to the main cluster point for prices.

As a practical limitation, only two distinctly "low"-priced neighborhoods and two clearly "high"-priced neighborhoods could be found which experienced racial change since 1945. The remaining sixteen test areas fall within the "medium" price class.

The degree of nonwhite entry is described according to the number of nonwhite families living within a six-block area in the neighborhood at the time the neighborhood was studied. This measurement unit was chosen because interviews with whites in transition areas revealed that white residents usually become "sensitive" to nonwhite occupancy when it moves to within one or two blocks of their own home.[17] The resulting terminology can be summarized as follows:

Degree of nonwhite entry	Number of nonwhite families living within a six-block area	Approximate percent range of nonwhite population in six-block area
Very light	1 or 2	Less than 1.7
Light	3 to 6	1.7 to 3.9
Medium	7 to 20	4.0 to 11.9
Heavy	21 to 50	12.0 to 28.9
Very heavy	over 50	29.0 and over

While it was not always possible to get precise counts on the number of nonwhite families living in a neighborhood at various dates, information was generally available to form a picture of the

---

[17] Field interviews, August to December, 1951; September to November, 1955.

extent and tempo of entry sufficient for the investigator's purposes. The racial history of many of the areas puts them in the "heavy" and "very heavy" categories, as of the fall of 1955. However, since their price behavior is studied for a period of years, most are found to pass through the range of density from "very light" toward "very heavy." For some, it is possible to analyze their price movements during a period when they could be classified as "threatened by nonwhite entry."

In using these various criteria to select the test areas, the counsel of leading local real estate authorities was an extremely important guide. Each potential test area was checked with at least three authorities; if they did not agree that it met the criteria it was dropped from consideration.

The twenty areas finally settled upon represent the judgment of real estate experts most familiar with their detailed histories. For San Francisco and Oakland, several test areas lie next to one another. This is because the pattern of nonwhite occupancy gradually moved across several contiguous neighborhood market areas.

Selection of Comparable All-White Neighborhoods

Because the research approach used in this study depends on the comparison of price behavior in two neighborhoods, one all-white and the other with nonwhite entry, it is essential that the neighborhoods resemble each other as closely as possible. Comparable all-white control areas were matched with test areas on the basis of these criteria:

Age, type, and market value of dwelling units.
General topography.
Pattern of land use.
Relationship to central city, shopping areas, and transportation
    facilities.
Income class of occupants.
Social status class of occupants.
Pattern of neighborhood development.

Sifting through a large number of all-white residential areas eventually yielded control neighborhoods closely similar to the test areas. Comparability was established by matching control areas and test areas according to the key features listed above. The comparability was tested and confirmed by consulting with real estate brokers, appraisers, lenders, and assessors—each of whom was well acquainted with the particular areas on which he was asked to comment.[18] Repeated field inspections were carried out to double-check the similarity of control to test areas in all significant respects.

By definition, the control areas had no nonwhite entry at any time during the observation period. Further, no area was acceptable as a control if nonwhites came near enough during the observation period to lead the white residents to feel "threatened" by possible future entry.

Comparing Test and Control Prices

The final procedure in this analysis compares the price behavior observed in the test and control areas over as long a time period as the data permit. Where properties in both areas are very similar, and area price ranges are not large, average (arithmetic mean) sales prices for each quarter are compared for the observed period.

Such direct price averaging is not feasible for certain neighborhoods which display considerable diversity of type and size of dwelling unit, and therefore in price range. For these, the test area–control area comparison is carried out by means of the average ratio of price to assessed valuation, by quarters.

The assessed valuation figures for such ratio comparisons are those used by the county assessor's offices for taxation purposes, and are taken for a base year *preceding* the date of first nonwhite entry in each particular test area. This is to avoid the possibility of using an assessed valuation figure that might have been influenced by altered racial patterns.[19]

Dividing selling prices by assessed valuations for a base year

[18] See Appendix B for a list of these authorities.

[19] Such a possibility is highly unlikely, because valuations for taxation purposes are altered only gradually and at intervals of several years. Local government assessors pay more attention to physical changes in the property, such as additions, than to the going level of market price or the changing social character of the neighborhood. (Interviews with San Francisco Bay Area tax assessors, September to October, 1951; October to November, 1955.)

yields ratios that may be averaged, then used to reflect the general movement of prices in a neighborhood. If, for example, a neighborhood shows 1950 selling prices which average four times the 1950 assessed valuations, while its 1954 prices average five times the 1950 assessed valuations, it is clear that prices have moved up by an average 25 percent. It is this kind of relative movement that is compared between a test area and a control area, when actual selling prices cannot be directly compared.

By noting the relationship that prevails between test area and control area prices *before* entry, a reference point is established from which the price relationships *after* entry may be judged. It is the *relative* change between test area and control area that is significant. If, for example, the average price level for a test area is $500 above that for the control area during the pre-entry period, the maintenance or enlargement of that $500 margin after nonwhite entry took place could be taken as evidence that nonwhite entry did not cause prices to decline, relative to the level that existed before entry.

Great sensitivity in the arithmetic of the comparisons will not be found—nor should it be expected. The process of averaging, unless very large numbers of sales are involved, does not remove the "roughness" of real estate market prices—even when highly comparable properties are considered.

It should also be realized that neighborhood price trends do not move smoothly up or down, but respond to highly localized market influences. These influences include many factors other than race of occupants. Thus, it often happens that a test area may encounter a slackening or quickening in sales during the same period that a control area experiences the opposite. Such variations in local market conditions cannot be smoothed out of the analysis in any precise way. One can only try to obtain as accurate a picture as possible of the relative price levels in the test and control areas, over time, and then see whether the timing and intensity of nonwhite entry in the test area appears to be related to such relative changes as may show themselves.

By the foregoing procedure, twenty test neighborhoods were selected and compared with nineteen control neighborhoods, distributed among San Francisco and Oakland, California, and Philadelphia. A total of thirty-four test price–control price comparisons were made, with time periods falling in the general span of 1943 to 1955.

The paired maps (1 and 2, 3 and 4, and 5 and 6) in Part Two depict two main things: maps 1, 3, and 5 show the percent of population nonwhite by census tracts, as of 1950; maps 2, 4, and 6 show precise boundaries for the test and control neighborhoods.

By comparing the maps, an impression may be gained as to the study area locations in relation to the general patterns of non-white population. It is evident from such a comparison that hardly any of the test neighborhoods were near areas with significant concentrations of nonwhites before they began to become racially mixed. This is an important point which is more closely analyzed as each area is discussed. Care should be taken in interpreting maps 1, 3, and 5; it should not be assumed that nonwhites are distributed *throughout the census tract areas,* even though each tract containing nonwhites is uniformly shaded. It was beyond the resources of this study to accumulate and plot nonwhite population distribution by blocks. The maps therefore give only a generalized picture of the locations and densities of nonwhite population in 1950.

For each city, analysis of the test neighborhoods is presented in order of descending "degree of entry," that is, the neighborhoods that had the highest nonwhite concentrations as of the fall of 1955 are discussed first. Each neighborhood is covered in the same fashion: first comes its general description, both physically and sociologically; next follows a description of the control area or areas with which the transition neighborhood is compared; next, the quarterly price averages, or averages of price/assessed valuation, are compared; and finally, the analysis summarizes what appear to be the significant features of the test versus control area price behaviors.

IV

General Conclusions: I

The major statistical finding of the present study is that during the time period and for the cases studied the entry of nonwhites into previously all-white neighborhoods was much more often associated with price improvement or stability than with price weakening. A corollary and possibly more significant finding is that no single or uniform pattern of nonwhite influence on property prices could be detected. Rather, what happens to prices when nonwhites enter a neighborhood seems to depend on a variety of circumstances which, on balance, may influence prices upward or downward or leave them unaffected.[1]

These conclusions are at variance with the belief that nonwhite entry always provokes a fall in property values. Instances of such decline have been observed. But so have cases of rising values—and, as noted, these have appeared in the data of the present study much more frequently than the cases of decline.

Influencing Factors

To set these conclusions in proper light, and before looking at them in more detail, it is first necessary to examine briefly the factors that may influence prices when nonwhites move into a neighborhood as well as special factors affecting this study.

The major variables interacting in these local situations appear to be: (1) strength of whites' desire to move out; (2) strength of nonwhites' desire to move in; (3) willingness of whites to purchase property in racially mixed neighborhoods; (4) housing choices open to whites; (5) housing choices open to nonwhites; (6) absolute and relative purchasing power of nonwhites; (7) absolute and relative levels of house prices; (8) state of general

---

[1] The reference to prices in this paragraph, it will be understood, is to neighborhood price movements which can be connected with the racial factor and which are measured relative to price movements in all-white areas.

business conditions; (9) long-run trend of values in areas involved; (10) time.

The first three variables, in addition to being influenced by the others, are affected by a number of further conditions, including at least the following: the way in which nonwhite entry is initiated and continued; the socioeconomic status of both groups; the "attitudinal flexibility" of both groups; the existing state of race relations in the community at large and in the particular area; the availability and character of leadership in the community, not only in religious and secular organizations, but in local government agencies.

One extreme: the glutted market.—A combination of the foregoing conditions which would lead to abrupt and large price declines can be easily visualized. If the resident white owners regard the coming of the first nonwhites as a disaster to be escaped quickly at all costs, a great many properties will probably be offered for sale at the same time. Then, if few or no other whites are willing to buy into the area, and if the demand from nonwhites is not sufficient to take up promptly the houses offered for sale, the market will be glutted. The owners, in their anxiety to leave, will be willing to accept "sacrifice prices" and probably will have to do so in order to attract a sufficient demand. Later, as whites achieve their desire to escape, the continued in-movement of nonwhites could operate to push prices up again, perhaps even to or above their pre-entry level.

This is the "classic" case. It sometimes happens, and is usually cited in support of the belief that nonwhite entry damages values. For the supposed outcome to occur, however, requires not only a "panic flight" psychological state on the part of the white residents, but an availability of alternatives. A generally "tight" housing supply, as existed during and for some years after World War II, will slow down racial transition independently of the attitudes involved, and probably operate to prevent prices from declining. On the other hand, an abundant supply of desirable alternative housing will stimulate whites to move out of transitional (usually older, less desirable) areas, even if the sellers are in no great anxiety to escape.

The other extreme: short housing supply.—A different combination of circumstances will produce not falling but rising house prices when nonwhite entry occurs. This will happen when the white owners, for whatever reason, are in no haste to leave a neighborhood, but many nonwhites are eager to buy homes within it. In these conditions, the white sellers may be able to obtain premium prices from the house-hungry nonwhites.

Market situations of this kind have frequently developed during the years since 1940, particularly in urban areas experiencing population increases, both white and nonwhite, that tended to outrun the housing supply. Whites may be reluctant to move out because they do not see where they could move to with advantage or because they may be willing to accept some nonwhites in their neighborhood, or for both reasons.

Intermediate: a variety of market conditions.—Between the extremes described, it is clear that there is room for a variety of market conditions and price effects depending on particular circumstances. One of the many in-between situations occurs when a rapid white exodus is offset by an equally rapid in-movement of nonwhites. Instances have been observed of virtually complete racial turnover in a neighborhood within a period of one or two years. Prices in these circumstances might drift either way depending on the precise "balance of forces," but the evidence suggests it is unlikely that they would move far from their original level.

Another fairly common case, which may well become more frequent in the future, is the neighborhood where a very few nonwhites gain entry but, for whatever reasons, are not followed by others. It seems logical to suppose that such a neighborhood would probably decline somewhat in attractiveness to the white market, relative to comparable all-white areas, but assuming no rush of the white residents to sell, there is no reason to expect any large price changes. A study of several dozen such "infiltrated" neighborhoods in San Francisco and nearby cities supported the conclusion that the presence of one or two nonwhite families in a neighborhood, after a period of time, usually went unnoticed.[2]

---

[2] Davis McEntire, "A Study of Racial Attitudes in Neighborhoods Infiltrated by Nonwhites," *Bay Area Real Estate Report, Second Quarter,* 1955, p. 127.

Housing Market Conditions Since 1940

Housing market conditions prevailing during the time period covered by the present study were generally such as to minimize the vulnerability of local markets to price dislocations associated with racial changes. This should be borne in mind in assessing the significance of the factual data and the conclusions based on them.

In general, the period was characterized by strong demand for housing and by rising real estate prices. The housing demand of nonwhites in northern and western cities was undoubtedly stronger than ever before, both because of improved economic condition and the nonwhite's heavy in-migration to those cities. At the same time, racial restrictions on residence continued to be fairly tight in most cities, resulting in the concentration of nonwhite house purchases in relatively few "open" areas. Finally, there seems reason to believe that along with the general movement toward racial equality of rights and the improving economic position of minority groups, white populations have become more "sophisticated" toward neighborhood racial change than in the past. While instances of violent resistance to nonwhite entry or panic flight from "invaded" neighborhoods have not been lacking, they appear to have been less frequent than in some past periods. More often than not, in recent years, racial transition of neighborhood occupancy has been a peaceful process.

SUMMARY OF FINDINGS

Price Behavior in San Francisco, Oakland, and Philadelphia

Basic information for the present original study came from these three cities. Price data over the period 1943–1955 were gathered for house sales in single-family, largely owner-occupied, residential neighborhoods.

A total of 5,417 individual sales prices was collected from 20 formerly all-white neighborhoods which underwent some degree of nonwhite entry during the time of observation. Another 4,495 sales prices were gathered from 19 closely comparable neighborhoods which remained all-white over the same period. Neighbor-hoods were deliberately selected to give as much diversity as possible in price class, degree of nonwhite occupancy, and other factors.

The movement of house prices in the neighborhoods entered by nonwhites (test areas) was compared with price movements in matching all-white neighborhoods (control areas). For each pair of neighborhoods, two types of price comparisons were made:

(a) *The relationship of test prices to control prices before and after nonwhite entry.* On the assumption that the relationship between test and control prices during the time when *both* areas were all-white is the normal one, it becomes significant to see whether that relationship continued in essentially the same fashion after nonwhite entry began in the test area. For this purpose, the percent ratio of average test prices to average con-trol prices for the last four quarters of the observation period is compared with the corresponding ratio for the entire period pre-ceding nonwhite entry.

(b) *The relative change in test versus control prices* from the average pre-entry level to the last four quarters of the observa-tion period. In order to adjust for differing durations of the obser-vation period, the percent change so obtained is divided by the number of quarters from the entry date to the end of the period. The result is a figure expressing the average rate of increase or decrease in price, per quarter, for the period following the date of nonwhite entry. For the control areas the figure is computed for the same time interval so that the test figure may be directly compared with it.

Studying these comparisons yielded the following principal conclusions on price behavior:

1. In 41 per cent of the comparisons, test prices stayed within 5 percent of control prices over the observation period. This is taken as indicating no significant difference in price behavior.

2. In 44 percent of the comparisons, test prices ended relatively higher than control prices, by margins ranging from over 5 to 26 percent.

3. In the remaining 15 percent of the comparisons, test prices

ended the observation period relatively lower than control prices, by margins ranging from over 5 to 9 percent.

4. From the date of first nonwhite entry to the end of the observation period, 59 percent of the comparisons showed larger percentage increases per quarter for test prices than for control prices. The remaining 41 percent showed larger increases per quarter for control prices.

5. Neither the price class of the test neighborhood nor its percentage of nonwhite occupancy showed any regular relationship to observed price movements. All ranges of price and nonwhite occupancy displayed both superior and inferior test price behavior, as compared with control prices.

Four of the twenty test neighborhoods had nonwhites living in them before the period for which adequate price data could be gathered. In these cases no "before-and-after entry" comparisons could be made. The price performance of these areas—compared with that in five control areas—was judged by using the first four quarters of available price data as a measurement base. The findings for these four test areas were found to be generally consistent with those for the sixteen for which pre-entry price data exist.

The findings for all areas place in doubt existing beliefs concerning the harmful effects of nonwhite occupancy on property values. Were such beliefs rooted in fact, the statistical evidence of this study would have shown downward shifts in test neighborhood price levels, relative to control prices, following changes in the racial pattern. Few such shifts took place in the areas studied, and where they did occur they were moderate.

Two broad conclusions stand out: *first,* price changes which can be connected with the fact of nonwhite entry are not uniform, as often alleged, but diverse. Depending on circumstances, racial change in a neighborhood may be depressing or it may be stimulating to real estate prices and in varying degrees. *Second,* considering all of the evidence, the odds are about four to one that house prices in a neighborhood entered by nonwhites will keep up with or exceed prices in a comparable all-white area. These conclusions are chiefly based on observations of real estate markets in a period of generally rising prices. This period, moreover, was characterized by unusually strong demand for housing, particularly by nonwhites who had been making relatively large gains in personal income. These conditions seem likely to continue into the foreseeable future, and therefore the main findings of the present study may be valid for many neighborhoods certain to experience the entry of nonwhites.

Price Behavior in Chicago, Kansas City, Detroit, and Portland

The findings for San Francisco, Oakland, and Philadelphia are generally consistent with those of other investigators studying similar situations in Chicago, Kansas City, Detroit, and Portland, Oregon. Because of procedural differences, none of these studies is strictly comparable with the San Francisco-Oakland-Philadelphia inquiry. All the former studies agreed, however, in the finding that nonwhite entry was usually associated with rising rather than falling prices. It should be noted, too, that all reported developments during periods when real estate prices were rising generally. It remains an open question in several of these studies whether prices rose as rapidly or to the same extent in the transitional areas as in comparable all-white neighborhoods, and in one (Portland) it definitely appears that they did not. Nevertheless, the general finding that prices in the transitional areas usually did not fall but rather increased is a significant one in the light of the common assertion that nonwhite entry brings large absolute declines in property values.

The highlights of the other studies are summarized below.

1. *Cressey's 1920–1930 study of Chicago's South Side.*—In this early approach to the problem, based on the comparative land values in racially mixed and all-white neighborhoods, no definitive findings emerged. Cressey[3] found that values in some mixed areas fell behind those in comparable all-white districts, while they stayed even or moved ahead in comparison with others. Because of limitations in the data and the considerable lapse of time since the study was made, its findings do not contribute much toward understanding the present-day problem of race and property values.

2. *Schietinger's 1940–1951 studies in Chicago.*—One of the

---

[3] Paul F. Cressey, "The Succession of Cultural Groups in the City of Chicago" (unpublished Ph.D. thesis, University of Chicago, 1930).

most industrious investigators is Dr. E. F. Schietinger,[4] whose studies have examined the behavior of sales prices for nearly 900 properties in seven areas of Chicago's South Side. No all-white control areas were utilized, the prices in racially mixed areas being compared with base year assessed valuations and test area price averages. The study sought to determine the effect of nonwhite occupancy and threat of occupancy on values, and also whether the degree or stage of racial succession had an observable price influence.

Schietinger's main finding was that prices in areas entered by nonwhites were generally improved, especially where the typical residential structures were of two units or more. The exceptions seemed to be predominantly single-family areas which were either threatened by nonwhite entry or saturated by nonwhites over a considerable time period. A second major finding was that the degree of use potential in terms of owner occupancy or income, rather than whether occupancy was all-white or racially mixed, was the major price determinant.

3. *Gillette's 1949–1953 study in Kansas City.*—Selling prices in two Kansas City neighborhoods were compared by Thomas Gillette[5] over a five-year period. One neighborhood was racially changing and had nearly 50 percent Negro occupancy by the end of the period; the other was a comparable all-white area. The major finding was that over the observation interval gross selling prices were higher for the test area in 67 percent of the comparisons, higher for the all-white area in 23 percent, and about equal in the remaining 10 percent.

4. *Wander's 1940–1950 study in Detroit.*—In this investigation, Richard Wander[6] compared selling prices and assessed valua-

[4] E. F. Schietinger, "Real Estate Transfers During Negro Invasion, A Case Study" (unpublished Master's thesis, Department of Sociology, University of Chicago, 1948); "Racial Succession and Changing Property Values in Residential Chicago" (unpublished Ph.D. thesis, Department of Sociology, University of Chicago, 1953); "Racial Succession and the Value of Small Residential Properties," *American Sociological Review*, XVI, no. 6 (December, 1951); "Race and Residential Market Values in Chicago," *Land Economics*, XXX, no. 4 (November, 1954).

[5] Thomas L. Gillette, "Santa Fe: A Study of the Effects of Negro Invasion on Property Values" (unpublished Master's thesis, Department of Sociology, University of Kansas City, 1954).

[6] Richard Stewart Wander, "The Influence of Negro Infiltration Upon Real Estate Values" (unpublished Master's thesis, Department of Sociology and Anthropology, Wayne State University, 1953).

tions in an area that reached 30 percent Negro occupancy during 1948–1950 with those in two similar all-white areas. The comparisons were carried through the entire 1940–1950 decade. He also examined test area prices between blocks with and without nonwhite residents.

The findings indicate that properties in the test area had been declining in value relative to the two all-white areas up to 1948, but that the entry of Negroes first checked then reversed this trend. However, up to the end of 1950 when the study period ended, the reversal had not been sufficiently strong to bring the average test area price level up to that of the two control areas.

For selling prices *within* the test area alone, values for mixed blocks reached higher levels than those for all-white blocks.

5. *City of Detroit 1946–1950 study.*—Observations were made by the Mayor's Interracial Committee[7] of selling prices in an area experiencing Negro in-migration as compared with those in an all-white area of comparable properties. The principal finding was that the racial transition area displayed consistently higher selling prices than did the all-white area.

6. *Portland, Oregon, 1944–1954 study.*—Conducted by the Urban League of Portland,[8] this study was limited to five small areas, each entered by just one Negro family. Selling prices were compared with those in similar all-white areas.

The findings are subject to some reservations as to sufficiency of price data and comparability of test and control areas. While all test area prices continued on an upward trend after the Negro family moved in, they did not rise as fast as those in the control areas. Out of four sets of comparisons, one set was about even, another showed a moderate advantage for the control area, and the other two displayed a markedly slower rise for the test areas.

Financing Characteristics

An analysis of financing data available for sales in the San Francisco neighborhoods revealed that:

---

[7] Richard Marks, "The Impact of Negro Population Movement on Property Values in a Selected Area in Detroit," City of Detroit, Mayor's Interracial Committee, January 16, 1950 (mimeo.).

[8] The Urban League of Portland, *Nonwhite Neighbors and Property Prices in Portland, Oregon* (1956).

1. Only half as many nonwhites paid all cash as did whites (one in sixteen as compared with one in eight).

2. Almost as many nonwhite buyers purchased for cash plus a first mortgage (no secondary financing) as did whites (48.4 percent as against 53.6 percent).

3. Resort to secondary financing was about the same: two out of five nonwhite buyers, two out of six white buyers.

4. For nonwhites, cash down payments were from 17 to 25 percent less than those made by white buyers.

5. First mortgages extended to nonwhites were as large or larger than those to whites and involved the same loan/price ratios.

6. Recorded interest rates were the same for nonwhites as for whites.

Property Maintenance

Evidence obtained while gathering neighborhood data for San Francisco, Oakland, and Philadelphia indicated that nonwhites were maintaining their properties at least as well as white homeowners in comparable areas. This conclusion is supported by Gillette's investigation of this point for Kansas City.

IMPLICATIONS FOR THE FUTURE

Discussions of race and property values usually assume that the demand for housing in a racially mixed neighborhood must come entirely or almost entirely from nonwhites—that few if any whites will consider buying property in such areas. Insofar as this is true (and it has doubtless been largely true in the past), it means that the price effects of racial changes in a neighborhood depend basically on the rate and urgency with which whites add homes to the housing supply in relation to the strength of nonwhite housing demand. The major threat to prices seems to be a too sudden and large addition to the neighborhood supply of housing available to nonwhites. Time, therefore, has a major influence on how racial change will affect values. Racial transition that is accomplished gradually is likely to have very different effects on house prices than a sudden shift.

In the neighborhood real estate markets investigated for the present study, the sellers were white and most of the buyers were nonwhite. The study findings signify, therefore, that in the time period and the areas covered, nonwhites were generally able to enter each local market fast enough to avoid the creation of a relative price slump.

As segregation barriers in housing continue to weaken, how-ever, the important question for the future is probably not the ability of nonwhite demand to equal white supply, but the will-ingness of whites to continue buying into neighborhoods which have become racially mixed. To the extent that nonwhites gain opportunity to acquire housing in a variety of neighborhoods, their demand will be dispersed and they can no longer be counted upon to take all the houses in a particular area. The prospects for housing desegregation and its implications for the real estate market are outside the scope of the present study, but a few ob-servations may be ventured.

There is evidence that resistance of white people to buying or renting in racially mixed neighborhoods is greatly reduced when the nonwhite group is not numerous and is not perceived as likely to become the numerically dominant element. Studies have revealed frequent instances of neighborhoods which have re-mained interracial over a period of years with a low percentage of nonwhites. In a significant number of cases private builders have successfully sold new tract houses on an interracial basis.[9] Several states and cities have adopted legislation prohibiting racial discrimination in housing developments built with public aid, and New York City has recently extended the prohibition to multiple unit and subdivision housing generally. To the extent that racial exclusion lessens, the number of neighborhoods con-taining small numbers of nonwhites will be multiplied. Oppor-tunities to escape living near nonwhites by choosing exclusive neighborhoods will become fewer, and, as this process continues, race should gradually lose its importance as a consideration in the real estate market.

---

[9] Chester Rapkin and William G. Grigsby, *The Demand for Housing in Racially Mixed Areas: A Study of the Nature of Neighborhood Change,* Special Research Report to the Commission on Race and Housing (Berkeley: University of California Press, 1960); Eunice and George Grier, *Privately Developed Interracial Housing: An Analysis of Experience,* Special Research Report to the Commission on Race an Housing (Berkeley: University of California Press, 1960); McEntire, *Bay Area Real Estate Report,* Second Quarter, 1955, p. 127.

V

General Conclusions: II

The preceding chapter has summarized the general findings that emerged from a rather large body of data. Details for each neighborhood and each city studied are presented in Part Two.

It is useful to present the findings in still a third way, that is, with the test areas grouped according to degree of nonwhite entry, without distinction as to city. Some of the neighborhoods studied, as previously indicated, had shifted from all-white to predominantly nonwhite composition. Others had received only a sparse scattering of nonwhite families; still others were in-between. The procedure of grouping the areas according to degree of nonwhite entry was followed to test whether price behavior in neighborhoods becoming racially mixed differs with the extent of racial change.

EIGHT NEIGHBORHOODS WITH ''VERY HEAVY'' NONWHITE ENTRY

Neighborhoods were classified as having "very heavy" entry when they showed nonwhite occupancy of 30 percent or more by November, 1955. By that date the observed range was from 30 to 75 percent nonwhite occupancy. The pre-entry observation period varied between three and six years, and the number of years observed after entry varied from one to ten. These test areas experienced first nonwhite entry sometime during the period 1945–1954, with 1950 the median entry year.

Although three of the eight neighborhoods remained relatively tranquil under the impact of nonwhite entry, the other five reacted with varying degrees of tension, hostility, and attempted blockade. In no case, however, does it appear that violence or extreme intimidation was used against prospective or actual nonwhite residents. Considerable selling pressure of varying degree and duration developed among white homeowners in the five test areas with adverse reactions. In all cases, however, it appeared that there were enough nonwhite purchasers to keep the market reasonably caught up on offered properties.

Four of the eight areas are in San Francisco, three in Oakland, and one in Philadelphia. There seems little question but that most, if not all, of these neighborhoods are on their way toward becoming wholly nonwhite. This is in contrast to some of the other areas which have lower proportions of nonwhite entry, particularly those of a higher socioeconomic class, which may stabilize as interracial neighborhoods. Therefore, one question in appraising the price behavior in these neighborhoods with very heavy entry would seem to be: How does a clear trend toward eventual complete, or near complete, replacement of whites by nonwhites affect real estate prices?

The measures of price changes in the eight neighborhoods and their control areas are summarized in table 1. The data permit fourteen test-control area comparisons of average prices both before and after nonwhite entry. In ten of the comparisons, test prices showed relative gains over control prices; in four cases, the opposite was true. Only six of the comparisons showed differences between test and control areas exceeding 5 percent. Five of these were favorable to the test areas; one was favorable to the control area.

In two of the San Francisco test areas no price data were available for the pre-entry period; hence comparisons are limited to the period after nonwhite entry had occurred. In one of these cases, the test area markedly improved its price status relative to the control area. In the other, prices increased slightly more in the control than in the test area.

Considering the *rate of change* in test versus control prices, the table shows nine comparisons with larger percent increases in the test areas and seven comparisons where the control areas had the larger percent increase. In those areas where price movements could be measured from the average pre-entry level to the end of the observation period, six test areas showed a combined average price increase of 1.28 percent per quarter compared with an average of 0.66 percent in the fourteen control areas.

TABLE 1

SUMMARY OF PRICE BEHAVIOR IN EIGHT NEIGHBORHOODS
WITH VERY HEAVY NONWHITE ENTRY

Neighborhood	Percent nonwhite occupancy	Average price: percent change from pre-entry level	Number of quarters	Average per quarter	Test price as percent of control price (averages)		Test area higher (+) Test area lower (−)
					For pre-entry period	For last four quarters	
Silver Terrace A........	70	+14.8	21	+0.71			
Control area 1.......		+20.5	21	+0.98	107.0	103.2	(−)
Control area 2.......		+25.1	21	+1.20	109.0	98.2	(−)
Columbia Gardens......	60	+13.8	19	+0.73			
Control area 1.......		+14.6	19	+0.77	94.5	94.0	(−)
Control area 2.......		+9.6	19	+0.50	85.5	89.4	(+)
Brookfield Village......	50	+15.4	19	+0.81			
Control area 1.......		+9.9	17	+0.58	88.0	90.8	(+)
Control area 2.......		+9.6	19	+0.50	85.9	90.8	(+)
Control area 3.......		+14.8	19	+0.78	93.6	93.9	(+)
Control area 4.......		+14.6	19	+0.77	94.7	95.5	(+)
Silver Terrace B........	50	+9.2	10	+0.92			
Control area 1.......		+11.9	10	+1.19	102.2	101.6	(−)
Control area 2.......		+10.8	10	+1.08	100.8	104.1	(+)
Control area 3.......		+9.3	10	+0.93	112.8	119.2	(+)
Elmhurst.............	40	+3.8	3	+1.26			
Control area 1.......		−1.4	3	−0.47	93.1	97.9	(+)
Control area 2.......		−2.8	3	−0.93	89.9	96.2	(+)
Strawberry Mansion....	30	+107.9	33	+3.28			
Control area........		+79.9	33	+2.42	101.8	118.2	(+)
Test area higher...............................				(+) 8 cases			(+) 10 cases
Test area lower................................				(−) 6 cases			(−) 4 cases
Average increase per quarter							
6 Test areas..............................				+1.28			
14 Control areas...........................				+0.66			
South of Ridge Lane....	75	+4.1[b]	26	+0.15			
Control area[a].......		−12.0[b]	26	−0.46	95.2[b]	108.8	(+)
North of Ridge Lane....	55	+7.0[b]	24	+0.29			
Control area[a].......		+11.5[b]	24	+0.48	110.8[b]	106.4	(−)
Test area higher...............................				(+) 1 case			(+) 1 case
Test area lower................................				(−) 1 case			(−) 1 case
Average increase per quarter							
2 Test areas..............................				+0.22			
2 Control areas............................				+0.01			

SOURCE: See chapters vi, vii, viii.
[a] No price data available for pre-entry period; comparisons limited to period after nonwhite entry.
[b] Average for first four quarters.

It is clear that in these eight test areas in three cities, a fairly rapid shift from white to nonwhite occupancy, under the economic and social conditions existing during the observation period, was predominantly associated with price increases relatively superior to those found in similar neighborhoods with populations remaining entirely white. Within this group of areas, however, the degree of nonwhite entry apparently had no consistent price effects.

SIX NEIGHBORHOODS WITH "HEAVY" NONWHITE ENTRY

This category includes neighborhoods with nonwhite occupancy between 12 and 29 percent in November, 1955. Three test areas are in San Francisco, two in Philadelphia, and one in Oakland. The pre-entry period was between two and nine years, and the number of years after entry ranged from two to seven. First nonwhite entry occurred sometime during the period 1948–1953, the median entry year being 1951. One or two areas with non-white occupancy as early as 1948 still show a relatively low pro-portion of nonwhite occupancy, suggesting that they may not become "saturated" neighborhoods. For most of the six, the tempo of entry was less rapid than typically occurred in the "very heavy" entry neighborhoods. They have been grouped in this way to see whether a lesser degree and slower rate of entry have a different impact on test price behavior than do other types of entry.

The two Philadelphia areas had considerable excitement at the time of nonwhite entry, and for a year or two later. The other test neighborhoods exhibited only moderate reactions to the changing racial pattern. While pressure to sell was not so strong as in the very heavy entry neighborhoods (except possibly for the Philadelphia cases), it was certainly above a normal level. Again, however, there was no scarcity of nonwhite buyers to ab-sorb the offerings.

The six test areas are measured against nine all-white control areas. Comparisons are summarized in table 2. For two test neighborhoods price data are available only for the period after nonwhite entry, and they are separately listed. The data for these two indicate a slight advantage for the test neighborhoods: of three comparisons, two show test prices improving relative to control prices over the period; one shows a moderate relative decline. For the entire observation period, test prices in these two areas increased by an average 0.74 percent each quarter, as compared with an average increase of 0.58 percent for prices in the three control areas.

The other four test neighborhoods are compared with six con-trol neighborhoods. Two comparisons show differences of less than 5 percent, not large enough to be significant. Of the four

TABLE 2

SUMMARY OF PRICE BEHAVIOR IN SIX NEIGHBORHOODS
WITH HEAVY NONWHITE ENTRY

Neighborhood	Percent nonwhite occupancy	Average price: percent change from pre-entry level	Number of quarters	Average per quarter	Test price as percent of control price (averages)		Test area higher (+) Test area lower (−)
					For pre-entry period	For last four quarters	
Cedar-Spruce..........	28	+19.6	12	+1.63			
Control area.........		+22.3	12	+1.86	104.3	101.8	(−)
Ogontz...............	24	+19.7	14	+1.40			
Control area.........		+13.1	14	+0.94	84.6	91.3	(+)
Ingleside Heights.......	20	+14.7	17	+0.82			
Control area 1.......		+19.7	17	+1.16	109.1	103.5	(−)
Control area 2.......		+15.0	17	+0.88	98.6	98.4	(−)
Seminary C...........	14	+10.2	8	+1.30			
Control area 1.......		−2.7	8	−0.34	100.7	114.1	(+)
Control area 2.......		−1.2	8	−0.15	98.5	110.0	(+)
Test area higher...............................				(+) 3 cases			(+) 3 cases
Test area lower................................				(−) 3 cases			(−) 3 cases
Average increase per quarter 4 Test areas................................				+1.29			
6 Control areas..............................				+0.72			
Lakeview[a].............	20	+22.6[b]	24	+0.94			
Control area.........		+11.5[b]	24	+0.48	95.5[b]	105.3	(+)
Oceanview[a]...........	18	+13.2	24	+0.54			
Control area 1.......		+18.8	24	+0.78	114.5[b]	108.4	(−)
Control area 2.......		+11.5	24	+0.48	103.7[b]	105.5	(+)
Test area higher...............................				(+) 2 cases			(+) 2 cases
Test area lower................................				(−) 1 case			(−) 1 case
Average increase per quarter 2 Test areas................................				+0.74			
3 Control areas..............................				+0.58			

SOURCE: See chapters vi, vii, viii.
[a] No price data available for pre-entry period; comparisons limited to period after nonwhite entry.
[b] Average for first four quarters.

remaining comparisons, three show test prices ending relatively higher than control prices, while the other places control area prices in the superior position.

The conclusion from these six comparisons is that, even with nonwhites present in fairly high concentrations, the test areas demonstrated relatively better price performance than did their matching control areas.

Looking at the rate of change, it appears that test prices had a greater percent increase per quarter after nonwhite entry in three comparisons, and a smaller increase in the other three comparisons. Measured from the average pre-entry level to the end of the observation period, four test areas had an average price increase of 1.29 percent per quarter, compared to a figure of 0.72 for the six control areas.

Altogether, heavy nonwhite entry in the cases examined showed no general tendency to depreciate selling prices in formerly white neighborhoods, either absolutely or relatively. Instead, it was more frequently associated with higher prices than prevailed in comparable all-white control areas.

THREE NEIGHBORHOODS WITH "MEDIUM" NONWHITE ENTRY

In three neighborhoods, nonwhites occupied 6 to 7 percent of the dwellings as of November, 1955, a proportion which may be considered "medium" as compared with other areas in the present study. Among these, the pre-entry period of observation varied between one and four years, while the postentry period was between one and five years. First nonwhite entry occurred during the years 1950–1954. The three neighborhoods are compared with five all-white control areas.

These neighborhoods displayed no disturbed reactions to nonwhite entry, either initially or as the nonwhite settlement continued. Two of them will probably continue to increase their nonwhite populations, eventually becoming heavy entry neighborhoods. The third, a higher economic class neighborhood, may arrive at a stabilized interracial occupancy. All three areas are located in Oakland.

Price comparisons, summarized in table 3, strongly favor the test areas. In four of the five comparisons, the ratio of test prices to control prices was higher after nonwhite entry than before, with two comparisons showing very marked superiority.

In four cases out of five, the test areas also demonstrated a greater percentage price increase per quarter than did the control areas. Average test prices increased by an average 0.2 percent per quarter over the pre-entry level. The corresponding figure for the five control areas was a negligible 0.03 percent.

THREE NEIGHBORHOODS WITH "LIGHT" AND "VERY LIGHT" NONWHITE ENTRY

As of November, 1955, three of the formerly all-white neighborhoods selected for this study were found to have nonwhite occupancy that ranged between 1 and 4 percent and so were placed in the "light" and "very light" entry categories. One neighbor-

TABLE 3

SUMMARY OF PRICE BEHAVIOR IN THREE NEIGHBORHOODS WITH MEDIUM
NONWHITE ENTRY AND THREE NEIGHBORHOODS WITH LIGHT
AND VERY LIGHT NONWHITE ENTRY

Neighborhood	Percent nonwhite occupancy	Average price: percent change from pre-entry level	Number of quarters	Average per quarter	Test price as percent of control price (averages)		Test area higher (+) Test area lower (−)
					For pre-entry period	For last four quarters	
Medium Entry							
Seminary A............	7	+24.9	22	+1.13			
Control area 1.......		+0.8	22	+0.04	92.9	117.2	(+)
Control area 2.......		+7.2	22	+0.33	94.4	115.8	(+)
Seminary B............	7	+4.6	8	+0.58			
Control area 1.......		−2.7	8	−0.34	102.1	109.4	(+)
Control area 2.......		−1.2	8	−0.15	100.0	105.7	(+)
Oak Knoll.............	6	−4.4	4	−1.10			
Control area........		+1.0	4	+0.25	103.8	98.2	(−)
Test area higher.............................				(+) 4 cases			(+) 4 cases
Test area lower..............................				(−) 1 case			(−) 1 case
Average increase per quarter							
3 Test areas..............................				+0.20			
5 Control areas...........................				+0.03			
Light and Very Light Entry							
Sunset................	3	+11.2	13	+0.86	102.4	100.0	(−)
Control area 1.......		+13.6	13	+1.05			
Control area 2.......		+4.5	13	+0.35	86.1	90.5	(+)
East Piedmont Heights .	2.5	−9.5	6	−1.58	122.7	112.0	(−)
Control area........		−2.2	6	−0.37			
Montclair.............	less than 1.7	+14.2	16	−0.89	88.8	109.9	(+)
Control area........		−11.7	16	−0.73			
Test area higher.............................				(+) 2 cases			(+) 2 cases
Test area lower..............................				(−) 2 cases			(−) 2 cases
Average increase per quarter							
3 Test areas..............................				+0.05			
4 Control areas...........................				+0.07			

SOURCE: See chapters vi, vii, viii.

hood is in San Francisco; the other two are in Oakland. The pre-entry period of price observation was about three years in all cases, while the period after entry varied from one to three years. Nonwhite entry first started sometime during the period 1952–1954. The three test neighborhoods are contrasted with four all-white control neighborhoods.

These neighborhoods are of the "exclusive" type with housing considerably more expensive than any of the neighborhoods previously considered. The residents are chiefly of the business executive and professional classes.

Price comparisons are summarized in table 3. In two of the four comparisons with matching control areas, the ratios of test control prices were higher after nonwhite entry than before, with one comparison showing very marked superiority. In the two other comparisons, the reverse was true, but by smaller margins.

Percentage price increases per quarter were larger for test prices in two cases and smaller in one. In the other comparison, the test price *decrease* per quarter was larger. As measured from the average pre-entry price level, test prices increased by an average 0.05 per quarter as against a corresponding figure of 0.07 for control prices. The percentage changes per quarter do not group themselves in a manner that suggests a definite margin for either test or control prices. Their combined averages are almost identical.

On the whole, the picture for these "light entry" neighborhoods is closer to being neutral than for any of the heavier entry groups. The data are fairly evenly balanced, so that no dominant tendency is apparent for test prices either to increase or decrease after nonwhite entry, relative to control prices.

In general, the foregoing comparisons do not show any consistent or significant differences in price behavior associated with degree of nonwhite entry. Generally, the test neighborhoods demonstrated price performance superior to that in the control areas regardless of whether the degree of nonwhite entry was heavy or light.

PART TWO

Detailed Analysis

VI

San Francisco

There are eight test areas available for study in San Francisco.[1] All experienced nonwhite entry between 1945 and 1953. The neighborhoods are characterized by single-family houses with middle-class occupancy. Most of the areas lie toward the outer reaches of the city. As shown by maps 1 and 2, few of the neighborhoods were near areas with concentrations of nonwhite population in 1950.

Four areas are classified as very heavy entry, three are heavy entry, and one area is light entry. Their average price levels lie in the range defined as medium—$7,500 to $14,500, with good representation over that range. Over 1,500 individual sales in these eight test areas are compared with some 1,200 sales in seven control areas.

VERY HEAVY NONWHITE ENTRY:
FOUR NEIGHBORHOODS

The Test Area: South of Ridge Lane (*T-1-SF*)

Location.—In the Ocean Avenue district, halfway between San Francisco Bay and the ocean, four miles southwest of the downtown center and three-quarters of a mile north of San Francisco's southern boundary. On the eastern edge of the single-family residence belt running across southwestern San Francisco.

Boundaries, topography, and features.—Bounded by Ridge Lane, San Jose Avenue, and Summit Avenue, this is a ten-block area on a rolling hillside sloped to the southeast. It is sharply cut off from surrounding areas by two ridgetops and a main arterial. About 90 percent built-up, with land use entirely residential except for two small food stores and two other modest

---

[1] See chapter iii for the criteria governing selection of these neighborhoods, and for definitions of special terminology.

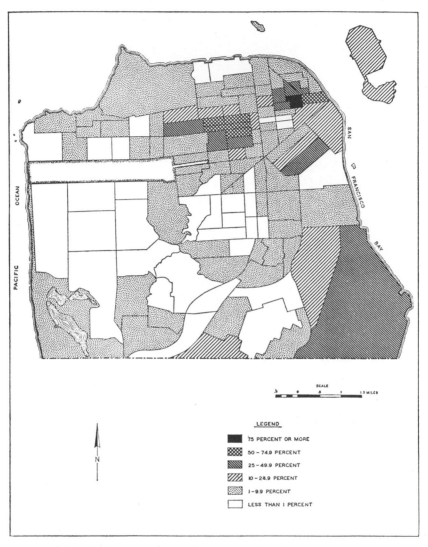

Map 1. Percent of population nonwhite by census tracts
in San Francisco, 1950.

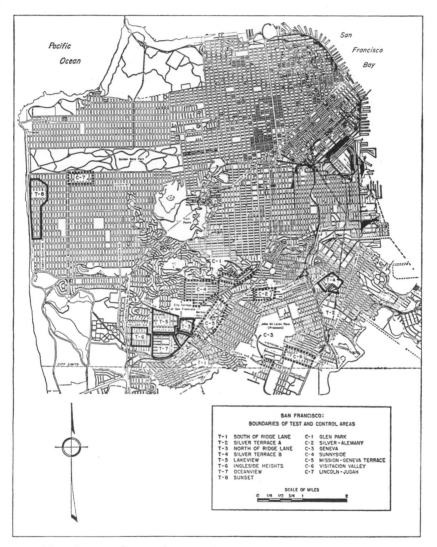

Map 2. Boundaries of test and control areas in San Francisco.

enterprises. About 280 homes in the area. Schools, parks, and large shopping areas are within three to five blocks of any residence, and good public transportation is available along San Jose Avenue. Of less than average desirability for a residential area of its price range, because of difficult terrain and a few homes not maintained at the prevailing standard.

Structures.—Almost entirely single-family, owner-occupied, two- or three-bedroom homes. Predominantly two-story frame construction, usually with stucco exterior, but shingle or board siding not uncommon.

Age distribution: One-fourth built 1940–1955; one-sixth built 1930–1939; two-thirds built 1929 and earlier. Many in the oldest age group have been renovated within the last ten years.

Condition (November, 1955): Fair to good, with several rather neglected properties scattered throughout the neighborhood.

Price range (November, 1955): Medium, $8,000–$12,000 (modal price about $10,500).

Socioeconomic characteristics.—Throughout its history this has been a middle-class and lower-middle-class neighborhood, with a mixture of white- and blue-collar occupations represented. There are some professional people among the nonwhites who have come into the area since 1945.

Racial changes: This was an all-white area until June, 1945, except for two Negro owner-occupant families dating from 1931. As is typical in such cases, the neighborhood accepted these two families, did not view them as community liabilities, and did not fear them as "spearheads" of a nonwhite "invasion." The neighborhood viewed itself, and was generally regarded, as all-white until the racial pattern began to change rapidly fourteen years later, in 1945.

In June, 1945, a home was sold by its owners to a Filipino family. Neighborhood residents were immediately and strongly disturbed, and a group of homeowners (by no means the majority) took what could be termed the "normal" steps for this situation: offers to repurchase the property, threats, hostile attitudes, and incidents. The Filipino household found this too unpleasant and sold out to a Negro family. Real estate men who know the area well feel that this started the general entry of nonwhites. Purchase and occupancy by nonwhites, primarily

Negroes, proceeded rapidly: by 1949 the area was 40 percent nonwhite; by 1955, 75 percent, or some 210 families. No white resistance was offered after the first incident.

Nonwhite entry occurred earlier in this area than in any other reported in this study. It seems to have been one of the first evidences of the nonwhites' "new direction" toward home purchase in the post-World War II period. At the time of entry (1945) the nearest concentrations of nonwhites were at Hunter's Point and the Bayview area, both over two miles away. The area thus had not been "threatened" by entry from an adjoining nonwhite neighborhood; the nonwhites "leapfrogged" in from considerable distances.

The Control Area: Glen Park (C-1-SF)

A neighborhood of fifteen square blocks (about 400 homes) located one and a half miles northeast of the test area, toward the Civic Center. Situated on a southeast slope of the Outer Mission district, Glen Park is bounded by Burnside Street, Surrey Street, Laidley Street, Miguel Street, Bernal Avenue, and Bosworth Street. Closely comparable to test area as to land use, size and type of dwelling unit, construction, condition, and access to facilities and services. Slightly higher price range (November, 1955): $9,000–$13,000. Slightly younger neighborhood, with three-fifths of the houses divided equally between the building periods 1940–1955 and 1930–1939, the remaining two-fifths having been built before 1930.

Price Analysis

Data on prices are available from the fourth quarter of 1949, when multiple listing sales records were first established. Real estate men familiar with both areas agree that prices in the test and control areas were closely comparable before 1945—that is, before nonwhite entry.

Over the 24-quarter period, there were 127 test sales (average: 5.3 per quarter) and 182 control sales (average: 7.6 per quarter).

Because sales in each quarter involved two- and three-bedroom properties of varying age, simple averaging of prices is not feasible. Instead, each price is divided by the assessed value of the property. Assessed valuations for 1944 are used. The San Fran-

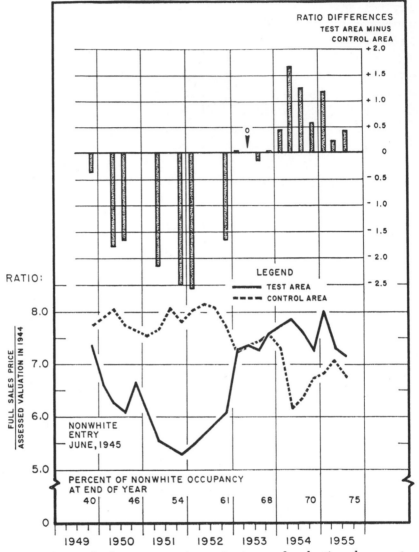

Fig. 1. Trend of average ratios, price/assessed valuation, by quarters, 1949–1955: San Francisco, South of Ridge Lane (test) and Glen Park (control). (Source: Data used in this figure and others in the San Francisco series compiled from Multiple Listing records and field investigations, 1951–1955.)

cisco Assessor's Office state that the 1950 figures are essentially unchanged from those for 1944, when both areas were all-white. The resulting ratios are averaged and compared, test area against control area. Figure 1 compares the ratios graphically.

During the six and a half year observation period, test area prices, as indicated by the plotted ratios, appear to have fluctuated around a nearly horizontal trend, falling below it before 1953 and rising above it afterwards. Control area prices, on the other hand, drifted down moderately but fairly steadily throughout the period. The percent change over the period, for each area, was as follows:

Area	Average ratio, first 4 quarters	Average ratio, last 4 quarters	Change	
			Amount	Percent
South of Ridge Lane (test)....	7.1	7.4	+0.3	+4.1
Glen Park (control)..........	7.8	6.8	−1.0	−12.0

Even though test area prices averaged only 7.1 times the assessed valuations at the beginning of the period, somewhat less than the 7.8 control ratio, they averaged 7.4 times assessed valuations, a percent increase of 4.1, at the end of the period. Test ratios finished above those for the control area, which actually dropped over the period.

The average differences between test and control ratios, and their relative size as a percent of the control ratio for each year, are shown in the following table.

SOUTH OF RIDGE LANE AND GLEN PARK

Year	Average difference (test ratio minus control ratio)	Test ratio as percent of control ratio (averages)
1949.............	−0.37	95.2
1950.............	−1.71	78.4
1951.............	−2.40	70.2
1952.............	−2.11	73.4
1953.............	−0.02	99.6
1954.............	+0.98	115.5
1955.............	+0.60	108.8

The first four quarters (1949) saw test ratios averaging 4.8 percent below control ratios. This was four years after nonwhite entry started, and 40 percent of the houses in the test area were nonwhite occupied. The ratios moved farthest apart during 1951, when the test figures averaged almost 30 percent less than the control level. At that time non-white occupancy was at 60 percent. From the end of 1951, however, test ratios started rising sharply, yielding average levels that caught up with control ratios in 1953 and moved ahead after that year. During the last two years, ending in the third quarter of 1955, nonwhite occupancy climbed to 75 percent. The final four quarters saw test ratios almost 9 percent higher than control ratios.

Thus, test prices gained both absolutely and relatively in comparison with control prices, over a period that saw nonwhites growing from 40 to 75 percent of the test area population. As shown by the ratios, test prices went from 4.8 percent below to 8.8 percent above control prices during the six and a half year observation period.

As discussed in the later section on financing (chapter xi), this comparison was the only one that showed a significant differential in the extent of seller-held secondary financing between the test area and control area. South of Ridge Lane had seller-held seconds in 30 percent of all transactions, with an average loan of $3,400. Glen Park had seller-held seconds in 17.6 percent of all transactions, averaging $2,700 each.

Assuming a market discount rate of 50 percent for second mortgages yields the conclusion that average test area prices are $510 higher and average control area prices are $238 higher than would be the case if no seller-held seconds existed. The net effect, then, is that average test prices are about $272 higher than they "should be" in relation to average control prices and should be adjusted downward by that amount. This is not a significant adjustment: the dollar amount is but 2.5 percent of the modal control price level.

If the comparison is adjusted for these financing differentials, it can be said that test prices went from 7.3 percent below to 6.3 percent above control prices during the observation period, a conclusion essentially the same as that reached before the adjustment.

The Test Area: Silver Terrace A (T–2–SF)

Location.—In the Bayview district, about a mile inland from the western shore of San Francisco Bay. Three miles south of the downtown center and just south of the city's main industrial area.

Boundaries, topography, and features.—Bounded by Topeka

Avenue, Thornton Avenue, and Bridgeview Drive. A five-block area on the southerly slope of a pronounced hill (the remainder of which makes up test area Silver Terrace B). Land use entirely residential. Fully built up, with about 200 homes, all having about equal access to schools, shopping, and public transportation. Regarded as a very desirable residential area because of excellent view, favorable climate, and easy access to main thoroughfares and freeway.

Structures.—Entirely single-family, predominantly owner-occupied. Structures are quite uniform, often identical, with five or six rooms, one bath, one-car garage being the typical space arrangements. Mostly two-level design, due to sloping ground, with frame construction and stucco finish.

Age distribution: Largely built up during the last fifteen years, nine-tenths of the houses being built in 1940–1949.

Condition (November, 1955): Good to very good.

Price range (November, 1955): Medium, $11,500–$14,000 (modal price about $12,000).

Socioeconomic characteristics.—A middle-class neighborhood, all-white until 1950. Many families of Italian stock among original owner-occupants, with strong attachments to homes and neighborhood. Heavy proportion of civil service employees, teachers, and professionals among nonwhites entering neighborhood.

Racial changes: First Negro family purchased a home on an interior street (Apollo) in February, 1950. This was a "grudge sale," in that sellers were embittered at what they considered an unfriendly neighborhood. They instructed the broker to sell only to a Negro. Followed by four more Negro families on the same street during the next six months, this meant a nonwhite occupancy of 3 percent by the end of 1950. During 1951 entry accelerated rapidly to 20 percent, and by the fall of 1955 stood at 70 percent, or some 140 nonwhite families. Among these are ten or twelve Filipino and several Oriental families. Entry did not result from nonwhite population pressure in surrounding blocks. In early 1950 no nonwhites lived closer than half a mile to Silver Terrace A.

White residents were considerably upset over the changing racial pattern during the first year, and moved away in large numbers. As many as fifteen to twenty homes were put up for sale at the same time. Nonwhites bought them. A more orderly transition followed during succeeding years, with less than half a dozen "For Sale" signs in evidence at any one time. White families now in the area are predominantly "original settlers" who, according to statements by several of their number,[2] will "never move away." They appear to enjoy the neighborhood's advantages so much that they are willing to continue on as a white "minority group."

It is significant that the neighborhood offered no organized resistance to entry, and there seem not to have been any threats or unpleasant actions by individual whites. Such a peaceful transition appears to have made it possible for the community to maintain its harmonious atmosphere despite a dramatic shift in racial composition. Many instances of friendly—and often close—interracial family relationships have come under the writer's personal observation, and others have been reported to him.

The Control Areas: Silver-Alemany and Geneva

Two closely comparable areas were found as controls for Silver Terrace A.

Silver-Alemany (C–2–SF).—A ten-block area of some 300 homes in the Outer Mission district, one mile due west of the test area and thus equally distant from the downtown center. Bounded by Alemany Boulevard, Cambridge Street, Silver Avenue, and Congdon Street. Lacks the view features of Silver Terrace A, but compensates by having more desirable land use and residential structure standards in surrounding areas.

Geneva (C–3–SF).—A six-block neighborhood of about 175 homes in the Visitacion Valley district, two miles southwest of the test area, just at the south boundary of San Francisco. Bounded by Geneva Avenue, Parque, Velasco Avenue, and Santos Street. Closely comparable to Silver Terrace A in all respects but three: no structures built earlier than 1940; less elevation and hence less view; two miles farther from downtown center. The last named item amounts to no more than a five-minute driving differential and, with the other two, is probably compensated for by the neighborhood's being closer to large open areas (including

---

[2] As made directly to the writer, or to local real estate men interviewed by him, Fall, 1951.

a park and a playground) and more removed from industrial-commercial zones.

Price Analysis

Price data begin with the fourth quarter, 1949, just a few months before the first nonwhite entry. Since entry occurred with no advance warning of any kind, however, it would be unjustified to assume the Silver Terrace A market area experienced any prior reactions that might have been produced by panicky home-owners.

Over the 23-quarter period there were 124 test-area sales (average: 5.4 per quarter) and 130 and 125, respectively, in Geneva and Silver-Alemany (averages: 5.7 and 5.4 per quarter).

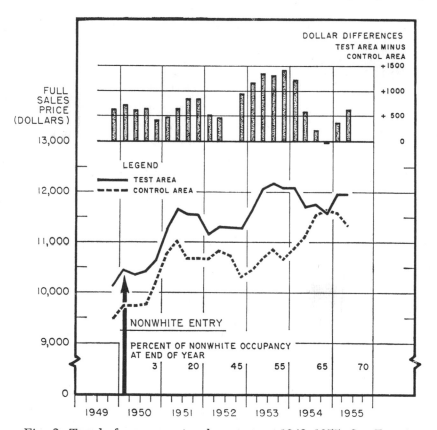

Fig. 2. Trend of average prices by quarters, 1949–1955: San Francisco, Silver Terrace A (test) and Silver-Alemany (control).

The very close comparability of the test area with both control areas, coupled with close price clustering with each quarter, permits price averages to be contrasted directly. This is done graphically in figures 2 and 3.

Both the test and control areas exhibited a rising price trend over the 23-quarter observation period. Price movements were roughly parallel, with test prices averaging from $219 to $1,412 above control prices. Only in the last quarter of 1954 did test prices briefly dip below control prices, by an average of $22. The percent change, as measured from before nonwhite entry to the end of the observation period, shows a somewhat steeper increase for the control area. This is chiefly the result of the lower starting point for control prices:

Area	Average price before entry (2 quarters)	Average price after entry (last 4 quarters)	Increase	
			Amount	Percent
Silver Terrace A (test)......	$10,283	$11,806	$1,523	14.8
Silver-Alemany (control)....	9,451	11,394	1,943	20.5

A comparison of price differences before and after nonwhite entry shows Silver Terrace A maintaining a fairly constant margin over the all-white Silver-Alemany area.

SILVER TERRACE A AND SILVER-ALEMANY

Period	Average difference in dollars (test price minus control price)	Test price as percent of control price (averages)
Before entry		
Six months ending in March, 1950.........	+672	107.0
After entry		
Year ending with first quarter of:		
1951...............................	+550	105.5
1952...............................	+707	106.6
1953...............................	+869	108.3
1954...............................	+1,328	112.4
1955 (five quarters ending June, 1955)...	+364	103.2

There appears to have been a slight drop in the average difference during the first postentry year (ending first quarter, 1951), but this was followed by a climb to price differences more in favor of the test area than before entry. A particularly strong price surge occurred during 1953, suggesting a "sellers' market" in the test neighborhood. The last five quarters showed an average difference considerably lower, but the ending positions of the two areas suggest that this relationship may swing back toward the earlier one.

In summary, the test area seems to have held its original lead over Silver-Alemany fairly steadily during a period when its nonwhite occupancy was rising to 70 per cent.

Figure 3 depicts price movements in Silver Terrace A as con-

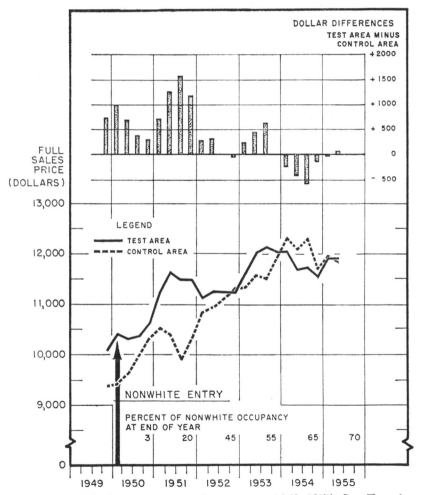

Fig. 3. Trend of average prices by quarters, 1949–1955: San Francisco, Silver Terrace A (test) and Geneva (control).

trasted with those in the second control area, Geneva. While the
general pattern of comparison is similar to that observed for the
first control area, it is apparent that the upward trend in the
Geneva neighborhood has been steeper than in Silver-Alemany.
Thus the test area shows up less favorably than in the first comparison. Over-all percent changes were:

Area	Average price before entry (2 quarters)	Average price after entry (last 4 quarters)	Increase	
			Actual	Percent
Silver Terrace A (test)......	$10,283	$11,806	$1,523	14.8
Geneva (control)...........	9,509	11,903	2,394	25.1

Control area prices increased 25 percent while those of the test
area increased only 15 percent. There were considerable fluctuations around the rising trend in both areas, with large differences
occurring when the fluctuations went in opposite directions.
This happened very noticeably in 1951, with test prices unusually
high and control prices in a sharp slump. It occurred in reverse
fashion in 1954, producing sizable negative differences. Price
differences before and after entry reveal an over-all gain in
control prices, with the test neighborhood gradually losing its
initial advantage, as shown in the following table.

SILVER TERRACE A AND GENEVA

Period	Average difference in dollars (test price minus control price)	Test price as percent of control price (averages)
Before entry		
Six months ending in March, 1950.........	+848	109.0
After entry		
Year ending with first quarter of:		
1951...................................	+512	105.1
1952...................................	+1,070	110.4
1953...................................	+164	101.5
1954...................................	+269	102.4
1955 (five quarters ending June, 1955).....	−219	98.2

While still an all-white area, Silver Terrace A showed a margin
of $848, or 9 percent, over Geneva. Except for the interrupting
gain during 1951 (reflected in the figure dated 1952 above),

test prices lost their lead while nonwhite occupancy began and steadily grew. Even though test prices ended the observation period $48 higher than control prices, the average difference for the five quarters ending June, 1955, was −$219, indicating that test prices averaged almost 2 percent less than control prices. This, of course, took place while nonwhite occupancy was rising from nothing to 70 percent.

In summary, then, it appears that the test area held onto a reduced lead over Silver-Alemany, the first control area, while it lost ground slightly as compared with Geneva.

The Test Area: North of Ridge Lane (T-3-SF)

Location.—In the Ocean Avenue district, one mile north of San Francisco's southern boundary. A midpeninsula neighborhood, four miles southwest of the downtown center, and just north of test area South of Ridge Lane.

Boundaries, topography, and features.—Bounded by Harold Avenue, Ocean Avenue, Tara Street, Niagara Avenue, San Jose Avenue, Ridge Lane. A twelve-block area, fully built up, containing some 350 homes. Northern half fairly level; southern half rises somewhat steeply to Ridge Lane. Land use entirely residential. Good access to schools, shopping, park, and transportation. Rated as higher than average in residential desirability, in its price class.

Structures.—Single-family, predominantly owner-occupied. Generally uniform size and appearance, with many identical homes. Typical space arrangements include living area over garage(s), most homes having five rooms (two bedrooms, one bath). There is a scattering of six-room (three-bedroom) units. Almost all are frame-stucco construction.

Age distribution: Almost 30 percent built before 1930; 30 percent in the 1930–1939 decade; almost 40 percent in 1940–1949; and 5 percent since 1950.

Condition (November, 1955): Good to very good.

Price range (November, 1955): Medium, $9,000–$13,500 (modal price about $11,500).

Socioeconomic characteristics.—Attractive middle-class neighborhood, all-white up to December, 1947. Reported to have been a thoroughly mixed ethnic area, with representation of Irish, Italian, Greek, and Jewish stock, among others. Better than average home and landscaping improvements by owners; this motivation also responsible for creation of the San Miguel Improvement Association to help preserve high property standards throughout the neighborhood.

Racial changes: First Negro family purchased and occupied a home on Louisburg (an interior street) in December, 1947. The sale was made by a broker who had an exclusive listing. General neighborhood reaction was one of moderate objection but not open resistance. The San Miguel Improvement Association tried to coördinate effective opposition to entry, including an owners' agreement to make no other sales to nonwhites, but not enough residents coöperated. Some residents were sympathetic toward the entry family, but did not reveal this until some time later.

Entry continued steadily, without incident, but at a leisurely rate: only 36 nonwhite families had moved in by mid-1952 (about 10 percent of the neighborhood). Nonwhite purchases picked up rapidly after 1952, however, with occupancy reaching 55 percent by November, 1955. The pattern of nonwhite residence has been a scattered one at all times, every street having roughly the same amount of entry.

While this area lies just north of another test area (South of Ridge Lane), which had nonwhite entry as early as 1945, there appears to have been very little nonwhite migration across Ridge Lane. The homes here have always been more expensive, relative to the area of older entry, and seem to have attracted nonwhite families of a slightly higher economic status, seeking to escape the congestion of established nonwhite areas such as the Fillmore and Hunter's Point districts. Entry came without warning, so that no "pre-invasion" market psychology should be presumed.

Paralleling the Silver Terrace A experience, the remaining whites seem to regard the integrated character of the area with calmness, and most real estate men interviewed believe there is a strong possibility that many will remain—unless they find themselves "too uncomfortably" in the minority during the next few years.

The Control Area: Sunnyside (C-4-SF)

An area of about 30 blocks, with some 850 dwelling units, one-half mile north of the test area. In the Outer Mission District, and completely insulated from test area by the City College of San Francisco campus and Balboa Park. Bounded by Gennessee Street, Melrose Avenue, Baden Street, Circular Avenue, and Havelock Street. Situated on a generally southerly slope, but this is a relatively unimportant difference as against the test area. The only other difference is in age distribution: Sunnyside has almost twice the proportion of homes in the oldest category (pre-1930) and commensurately fewer in the 1940–1949 building period. Its slightly greater average age is the only obvious explanation for its average price level's being about $1,000 less than that for North of Ridge Lane.

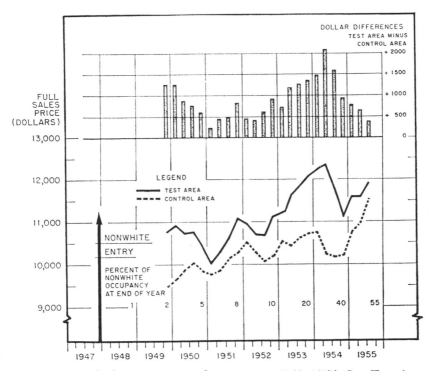

Fig. 4. Trend of average prices by quarters, 1948–1955: San Francisco, North of Ridge Lane (test) and Sunnyside (control).

Price Analysis

For the 24-quarter observation period (fourth quarter, 1949, to third quarter, 1955) there were 112 test-area sales (average: 4.7 per quarter) and 200 control-area sales (average: 8.5 per quarter). Price averages for each quarter may be directly compared, and are so shown in figure 4.

Nonwhite entry began at the close of 1947, almost two years before the availability of comparable price data. Local real estate men interviewed, however, state that the price relationships observable in 1949 and 1950 (with test area prices from $500 to $1,000 above control prices) existed as of 1947 and before. They do not feel that the 2 percent nonwhite occupancy at the end of 1949 had either raised or lowered test prices relative to control prices.

Test prices stayed above control prices for the entire period, although the difference varied considerably. The over-all gain for the 24 quarters was somewhat higher for the control area: 11.5 percent as compared to the test area's 7.0 percent.

Area	Average price, first 4 quarters	Average price, last 4 quarters	Increase	
			Amount	Percent
North of Ridge Lane (test)..	$10,797	$11,548	$ 751	7.0
Sunnyside (control).........	9,747	10,865	1,118	11.5

For in-between quarters, test prices were but 2.3 percent above control prices in the first quarter of 1951 ($10,022 versus $9,799), when nonwhite occupancy measured about 6 percent. They were at a maximum difference of 20.4 percent in the second quarter of 1954 ($12,327 versus $10,236), with nonwhite occupancy at around 35 percent.

In general, as nonwhite occupancy moved past 5 percent, up to early 1951, test prices weakened relatively. Then they pulled away from control prices between 1951 and mid-1954, during a rise in nonwhite occupancy to 35 percent. The last 18 months, during which nonwhite occupancy reached 55 percent, saw test prices moving closer to control prices. The situation year-by-year is shown in the following table.

NORTH OF RIDGE LANE AND SUNNYSIDE

Period	Average difference in dollars (test price minus control price)	Test price as percent of control price (averages)
Year ending with third quarter of:		
1950	+1,071	110.8
1951	+433	104.4
1952	+567	105.5
1953	+1,016	109.7
1954	+1,624	115.6
1955	+682	106.4

Following a dip during 1950–1952, price differences recovered to the 1949 level and higher during 1953–1954. From mid-1954, however, with entry seven years in the past and nonwhite occupancy up to 55 percent, test prices and control prices moved closer together. Examining the price trends suggests the conclusion, however, that this has probably come about through the relatively sharper climb in control prices since mid-1954, rather than because of any unusual signs of weakness in test prices. In any event, the price data for the period show neither a pulling-together nor a drawing-apart tendency as between test and control average prices: the fluctuations appear to continue in more or less random fashion.

The Test Area: Silver Terrace B (T-4-SF)

Location.—In the Bayview district, about one mile inland from the western edge of San Francisco Bay. Three miles south of the downtown center and just south of the city's main industrial area.

Boundaries, topography, and features.—Bounded by Silver Avenue, Quesada Avenue, Newhall Street, Topeka Avenue, Bridgeview Drive, and Ledyard Street. A ten-block area covering all but the southerly slope of a pronounced hill, on which is situated test area Silver Terrace A. Land use entirely residential; almost fully built up, with about 250 homes. Schools, shopping areas, and transportation within convenient access of the whole area.

Like Silver Terrace A, this is considered an outstanding residential area in its price class because of its many amenities, including view, climate, and nearness to fast-travel routes.

Structures.—Entirely single-family, predominantly owner-occupied. Much uniformity in size, style, and type of construction, with two-level design common because of generally sloping terrain. Evenly divided between five-room (two-bedroom, one-bath) and six-room (three-bedroom, one-bath) dwelling units, with one-car garage typical. Mostly frame-stucco construction.

Age distribution: In sharp contrast to Silver Terrace A, where postwar structures account for over 90 percent of all units, nine-tenths of the homes were built just before World War II. About 5 percent were built before 1930, with the remaining 5 percent in the 1950–1955 period.

Condition (November, 1955): Very good to excellent. This area has always displayed the highest standards of property maintenance, and the construction is of unusually good quality.

Price range (November, 1955): Medium to high, $12,000–$16,000 (modal price about $13,750).

Socioeconomic characteristics.—The all-white character of this neighborhood was unchanged until March, 1953. All evidence gathered adds up to a picture of a quiet, solid, middle-class neighborhood whose residents had strong feelings of attachment and pride for their home area. Unusually clean, well-maintained neighborhood, although the minor areas with construction since 1950 fall slightly short of the general standard.

Racial changes: First Negro purchase and occupancy occurred in March, 1953. Since this area touches Silver Terrace A on two sides, and no significant topographical or street barriers intervene, there was a distinct apprehension about the earlier entry pattern in this contiguous neighborhood. By March, 1953, Silver Terrace A was close to 50 percent nonwhite, and this rapidly growing concentration registered with some Silver Terrace B residents as a threat to their own neighborhood. There is little question that it was an important factor in the timing and extent of entry in Silver Terrace B.

Once begun, entry proceeded rapidly with no resistance reported. It reached 10 percent (25 families) by the end of 1953 and climbed steadily to 50 percent (125 families) by the third quarter of 1955. While such a rapid transition is obvious evidence that many former residents wished to move away, real estate opinion in the fall of 1955 was that most of those who wanted to leave had left. It is felt that the area may stabilize near its present 50-50 racial ratio, or that it will lose only a small additional group of whites.

Nonwhites now in the area—mostly Negroes—are characterized by neighbors and real estate men as "very steady family people" and "good citizens." A high proportion are civil service employees.

The Control Areas: Mission-Geneva Terrace; Visitacion Valley; Silver-Alemany

Mission-Geneva Terrace (C-5-SF).—A 25-block, 700-home area in the Outer Mission district, two miles west of the test area. Bounded by San Jose Avenue, Santa Rosa Avenue, Alemany Boulevard, and Mt. Vernon Avenue. Comparable to test area in all respects except two: it is situated in a gently sloped hollow rather than on a hill; it has an older age structure (20 percent built before 1930; 54 percent built in 1930–1939). The topographical difference is balanced by a more attractive surrounding land-use pattern, while the greater average age of structure appears to be unimportant in view of the excellent property maintenance observable throughout the area. Although five to ten years older, on a house-by-house comparison, original construction and present condition are fully equal to Silver Terrace B.

Visitacion Valley (C-6-SF).—A neighborhood of 20 blocks and some 500 homes, situated in the Visitacion Valley district at the extreme southeast corner of San Francisco. About a mile and a half south of the test area and thus that much farther from the downtown center. Bounded by Sunnydale Avenue, Sawyer Street, Leland Avenue, and Bayshore Boulevard. Its more remote location is compensated for by somewhat better environs (residential rather than industrial-commercial) and a younger age structure (20 percent built in 1950–1955, as compared with test area's 5 percent).

Silver-Alemany (C-2-SF).—Similar to test area (see p. 78).

Price Analysis

Test area prices may be directly compared with prices in each of the three control areas. For the 23-quarter period the observed sales in each area were as follows:

Area	*Total sales*	*Average per quarter*
Silver Terrace B	190	8.6
Mission-Geneva Terrace	184	8.4
Visitacion Valley	207	9.0
Silver-Alemany	125	5.7

Prices in the Silver Terrace B test area rose 9.2 percent by the end of the period, as measured from the average level prevailing for the pre-nonwhite-entry quarters. Measured over the same intervals, prices in the three control areas rose slightly more: 11.9, 10.8, and 9.3 percent, respectively:

Area	Average price before entry (13 quarters)	Average price after entry (last 4 quarters)	Increase	
			Amount	Percent
Silver Terrace B (test)	$11,756	$12,834	$1,078	9.2
Mission-Geneva Terrace (control)	11,484	12,856	1,372	11.9
Visitacion Valley (control)	11,707	12,668	961	10.8
Silver-Alemany (control)	10,426	11,394	968	9.3

The test area therefore displayed a rising trend of about the same character as in the all-white areas, while its nonwhite population grew to almost 50 percent over the last two and a half years of the period. The relative price movements are clearly shown in figures 5, 6, and 7, each of which is separately discussed.

While test area prices exceeded Mission-Geneva Terrace control prices in thirteen quarters, all but two of the positive differences were *before* nonwhite entry and all but one of the negative differences were *after* nonwhite entry. Average prices in both areas started within $100 of each other, at about the $10,900 level, and moved along reasonably closely for the first twelve quarters (up to the first quarter of 1953, when entry began). During this period, test prices exceeded control prices in each quarter except the first, with average price differences ranging between $13 and $850 (0.1 and 7.8 percent). The interruption

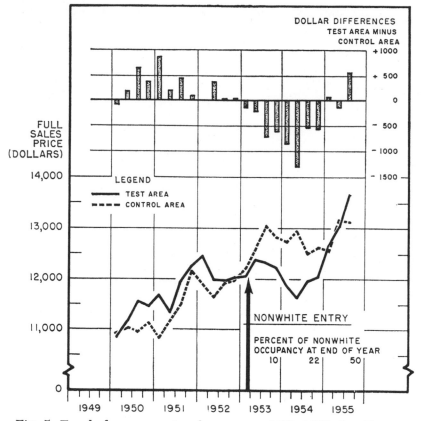

Fig. 5. Trend of average prices by quarters, 1950–1955: San Francisco, Silver Terrace B (test) and Mission-Geneva Terrace (control).

during 1952–1953 in the rising test price trend brought about a less favorable relative picture. As entry occurred, in March, 1953, test prices dropped an average of $151 (1.2 percent) below control prices, although both areas showed prices at the $12,000 level. During 1953 and midway into 1954, test prices continued to sag in absolute terms, falling to $11,640. Control prices weakened too, but not as much, so that the relative position of test area prices worsened. In the second quarter of 1954 they averaged $1,311 (10.1 percent) below control prices. Nonwhite occupancy at the time was approaching 20 percent.

Test prices recovered rapidly after mid-1954, both absolutely and relatively. By the end of the observation period (third quarter, 1955) they averaged $13,666, 4.3 percent higher than the control price average of $13,107. Average price differences, before and after nonwhite entry, are shown in the following table.

SILVER TERRACE B AND MISSION-GENEVA TERRACE

Period	Average difference in dollars (test price minus control price)	Test price as percent of control price (averages)
Before entry First quarter, 1950, to first quarter, 1953.	+246	102.2
After entry Year ending with first quarter of: 1954. . . . . 1955. . . . . 1956 (first half).	 −603 −589 +212	 95.3 95.4 101.6

Whereas test prices had been over 2 percent higher during the pre-entry period, they slumped to almost 5 percent lower in the first eight quarters after entry began. As the eight quarters ended, nonwhite occupancy stood at 22 percent, but at this point test prices turned sharply upward and quickly recovered the ground lost. By the end of the period, with nonwhite occupancy nearing 50 percent, test prices were in almost the same relationship to control prices that they had been originally.

As compared with the next control area, Visitacion Valley, the test area maintained about the same relative position for the period as a whole. Because the control prices themselves displayed more variability, the price differences are more erratic and larger. Figure 6 tells the story.

Test area prices, on the average, exceeded Visitacion Valley control prices in thirteen quarters and fell short in ten quarters. This fluctuation above and below control prices occurred equally before and after nonwhite entry, which took place just after the middle of the observation period. Starting out $709 (7 percent) above control prices in 1950, test area prices reached a maximum positive difference of $1,137 (10 percent) at the beginning of 1952 (test area average: $12,460; control area average: $11,323). This was exactly one year before the first nonwhite entry.

The situation altered rapidly during 1952, with test prices

falling sharply below control prices in the period mid-1952 to mid-1953. A maximum negative difference of $1,141 (8.6 percent) occurred in the first quarter of 1953, when entry began (test area average: $12,059; control area average: $13,200). Recovery

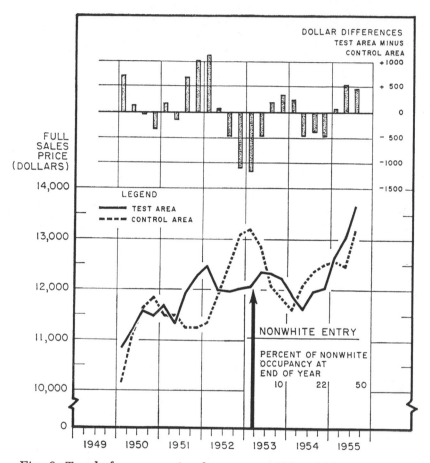

Fig. 6. Trend of average prices by quarters, 1950–1955: San Francisco, Silver Terrace B (test) and Visitacion Valley (control).

was equally rapid in late 1953, followed by another relative dip in 1954 and a second recovery into 1955. These fluctuations after entry, it will be recalled, took place as nonwhite occupancy rapidly grew to 50 percent by late 1955.

94   SAN FRANCISCO

Average price differences before and after nonwhite entry are
shown below.

SILVER TERRACE B AND VISITACION VALLEY

Period	Average difference in dollars (test price minus control price)	Test price as percent of control price (averages)
Before entry First quarter, 1950, to first quarter, 1953.	+57	100.8
After entry Year ending with first quarter of: 1954. 1955. 1956 (first half).	 +97 −306 +527	 100.9 97.5 104.1

Test prices were 0.8 percent higher than control prices for the
13-quarter pre-entry period. They did not keep up with control
prices during the two years from late 1952 to late 1954, resulting
in a noticeable relative drop. By the end of 1954, when nonwhite
entry stood at 22 percent, test prices were 2.5 percent below
control prices. Their sharp recovery, beginning in late 1954, again
took them higher than control prices, with their percentage advantage increasing to 4.1 by the end of the observation period.

This comparison shows relative price behavior roughly similar
to that for the test area as against Mission-Geneva Terrace. Taken
together, these two comparisons suggest that test prices fell,
absolutely and relatively, about a year *before* entry actually
occurred. In both comparisons, however, control prices continued
upward while test prices hesitated, thus emphasizing the relative
drop in test prices.

Comparison with a third control area, Silver-Alemany, which
"leveled off" over the same period that test prices did, offers a
more favorable interpretation of price behavior for Silver Terrace
B. While control prices are in a lower range throughout the period
(about $1,000 less, on the average) the control area is otherwise
closely comparable to the test area. What is significant are the
relative price movements.

Because Silver-Alemany prices also remained fairly stable during 1951–1953, the differences as compared with similar test prices

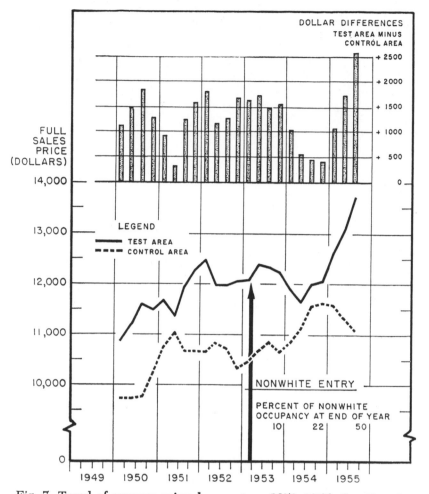

Fig. 7. Trend of average prices by quarters, 1950–1955: San Francisco,
Silver Terrace B (test) and Silver-Alemany (control).

were quite steady. A glance at figure 7 shows that average differences of between $900 and $1,800 occurred quite randomly up to
three quarters after nonwhite entry began.

A sharp relative drop occurred in 1954, with test prices only
$500 more than control prices. The strong rise in test prices after
mid-1954, coupled with a control price dip after 1954, brought
positive differences up abruptly to the former level and well
beyond. By years, the comparison is shown in the table following.

SILVER TERRACE B AND SILVER-ALEMANY

Period	Average difference in dollars (test price minus control price)	Test price as percent of control price (averages)
Before entry First quarter, 1950, to first quarter, 1953.	+1,330	112.8
After entry Year ending with first quarter of:		
1954..............................	+1,438	113.4
1955..............................	+615	105.4
1956 (first half)....................	+2,142	119.2

In contrast to the comparisons with the first two control areas, the first year after nonwhite entry shows a significant relative test price increase, as measured from the base of average pre-entry prices. The second year after entry displays a relative fall similar in proportion to that seen in the other two cases, while the third year after entry (late 1955) is one of even more dramatic recovery.

Except during 1954, test prices generally held their own in comparison to Silver-Alemany control prices. With nonwhite entry rising toward 50 percent during the last two and a half years of the period, test area prices ended 19 percent above control prices, compared to their 12.8 percent advantage during the period before entry.

In summarizing all three comparisons, it appears that test prices ended in as good a position as prevailed before nonwhite entry—and even attained a better position in the Silver–Alemany comparison.

The relative drop in test prices, as noted in the first two control comparisons, suggests some support for the view that the "threat" of entry temporarily disrupted local market functioning. Presumably, this would come about through an oversupply of homes placed on sale by perturbed owners, together with an undersupply of buyers (in this case, whites who hesitated to purchase in an area under threat of nonwhite entry). But the comparison with the third control area qualifies this view, since the control area itself showed the same leveling of prices over the 1952–1953 period. Nevertheless, the fact that the first two control areas had prices closer to those in the test area, and that there *are* two of them, requires that their evidence be given serious consideration.

HEAVY NONWHITE ENTRY:
THREE NEIGHBORHOODS

The Test Area: Lakeview (T-5-SF)

Location.—In the northern section of the Ocean Avenue district, in the central zone of the San Francisco peninsula, about a mile north of the city's southern boundary. Four miles southwest of the downtown center and just west of test area North of Ridge Lane. Oceanview test area is contiguous to it on the South, while Ingleside Heights and South of Ridge Lane touch its southwest and southeast corners, respectively.

Boundaries, topography, and features.—Bounded by Ocean, Harold, Grafton, Lee, Lakeview, and Ashton Avenues. With 28 blocks, the area has some 750 homes occupying all but a handful of the lots. Lakeview is on a high ridge forming the south boundary and the area slopes up to it fairly gently. Land use mostly residential, with some stores and small businesses along portions of Holloway and Ashton. Rated as average in desirability for a residential area of its price range.

Structures.—Single-family dwelling units, almost entirely owner-occupied. Structures fairly alike in design and construction; predominantly two-level, with living space over garage. Approximately two-thirds of the homes are five-room (two bedrooms, one bath) and the remainder are six-room (three bedrooms, one bath). Frame construction with stucco or rustic exteriors.

Age distribution: With 42 percent of its homes built before 1930, this rates as an older neighborhood. About 35 percent were built in 1930–1939, 16 percent in 1940–1949, and about 7 percent in 1950–1955.

Condition (November, 1955): Good to very good.

Price range (November, 1955): Medium, $9,000–$12,500 (modal price about $11,250).

Socioeconomic characteristics.—A middle-class neighborhood that has declined somewhat from its prime, about 1935. Has typically had a mixture of white- and blue-collar occupations represented. There is a considerable sprinkling of Irish and Italian names in transactions during the observation period.

Racial changes: First nonwhite purchase was by a Japanese family in March, 1948. By the end of the year about eight Japanese and Chinese families had become owner-occupants. The first Negro family moved in during early 1949, and nonwhite occupancy reached 2 percent by the end of the year. Negroes began to predominate in the continuing entry, which proceeded steadily, but at a leisurely rate. Some nonwhites already lived in two adjoining areas: North of Ridge Lane to the east, and South of Ridge Lane to the southeast. There were only a few Negro families in the former area, but about 80 or 90 in the latter. While few of these moved to the Lakeview neighborhood, their presence was felt by the whites there, and undoubtedly encouraged nonwhites from elsewhere in the city to seek homes in the vicinity, including Lakeview. By 1953, nonwhite occupancy was around 13 percent (some 100 families), and had reached 20 percent (150 families) by Fall, 1955. Some blocks had 70 to 80 percent nonwhite occupancy, others very little or none.

No organized opposition was made by white residents, but those with strenuous objections gradually left the area. No panic selling occurred. Real estate men believe the area may become integrated on about a 50-50 basis, but with little or no intermixing in many individual blocks. Nonwhites in the area are mostly civil service employees, with few professional occupations represented. Over half the nonwhite wives are employed full-time.

The Control Area: Sunnyside (C-4-SF)

This is the same control used for the North of Ridge Lane test area, and is described in the section on that area (p. 85). In every important respect it is closely comparable to Lakeview.

Price Analysis

For the 24 quarters observed, there were 189 test-area sales (7.9 per quarter) and 200 control-area sales (8.5 per quarter). These data are shown in figure 8.

Since no price data were available for the years before entry

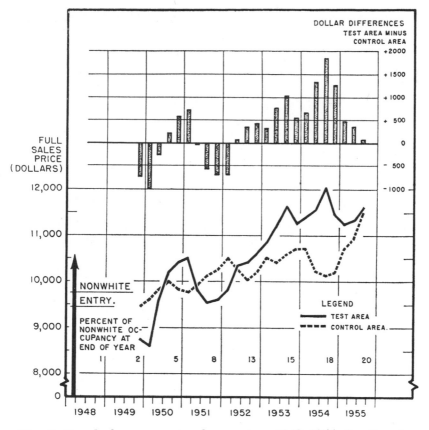

Fig. 8. Trend of average prices by quarters, 1949–1955: San Francisco, Lakeview (test) and Sunnyside (control).

occurred, the analysis cannot depend on a before-and-after comparison. On the basis of statements by real estate men familiar with both neighborhoods, it appears that prices in Lakeview did not exceed Sunnyside prices during the pre-1949 years, so that a safe assumption is that prices were about the same in the two areas before nonwhites came into Lakeview. The significant question, then, is how did prices perform in Lakeview, which was gradually building its nonwhite population toward 20 percent by 1955, as compared to the all-white Sunnyside neighborhood?

Test prices began the period well under control prices, but caught up with and passed them by 1952. For the remaining years, 1953–1955, they exceeded control prices by considerable margins in most quarters, with average prices almost identical in the ending quarter. Both neighborhoods had a generally rising price trend over the period, but test prices rose much more sharply.

Area	Average price, first 4 quarters	Average price, last 4 quarters	Increase	
			Amount	Percent
Lakeview (test)........	$9,318	$11,425	$2,107	22.6
Sunnyside (control).....	9,747	10,865	1,118	11.5

The test price percent rise of 22.6 was almost double the 11.5 increase for control prices. The relatively much more rapid gain in test prices is brought out in the year-by-year comparison shown below.

LAKEVIEW AND SUNNYSIDE

Period	Average difference in dollars (test price minus control price)	Test price as percent of control price (averages)
Year ending with third quarter of:		
1950............................	−429	95.5
1951............................	+185	101.9
1952............................	−233	97.8
1953............................	+639	106.1
1954............................	+1,111	110.7
1955............................	+560	105.3

The sharp relative test price drop during 1951 resulted in an interruption to the otherwise smooth climb in average Lakeview prices, but the general picture remains clear: the presence of non-whites in ever increasing proportions did not prevent Lakeview prices from catching up with and surpassing prices in the all-white Sunnyside neighborhood.

It is too soon to judge whether the relative dip in test prices at the very close of the observation period is a temporary condition or indicative of a return to the earlier price relationship between the two areas. The relative test price dip is partially accounted for by the unusually rapid upsurge in control prices, beginning with the last quarter of 1954. The final answer to this late development depends on further observation of prices in the two areas.

The Test Area: Ingleside Heights (T-6-SF)

Location.—In the western portion of the Ocean Avenue district, just east of State Highway 1 and within a half mile of the southern city limits. Four and one-half miles southwest of the downtown center. Its eastern side is contiguous with another test area, Oceanview, while Lakeview is just to its northeast.

Boundaries, topography, and features.—Bounded by Garfield Street, Head Street, Shields Street, Orizaba Avenue, Randolph Street, and Byxbee Street. An 18-block area with some 350 homes, occupying the top and sides of a moderately sloped hill. All residential land use except for shopping and commercial uses along Randolph Street. Of slightly better-than-average desirability as a living area, in its price class, because of pleasant neighborhood conditions and the expansive views to be had from almost every property. About 80 percent built up, with considerable building activity in the last ten years.

Structures.—Predominantly owner-occupied, the single-family homes of Ingleside Heights are quite homogeneous as to construction and design. Many two-level structures, with living space over garage area. Five-room houses (two bedrooms, one bath) outnumber six-room houses (three bedrooms, one bath) about two to one. Construction is frame, with stucco or rustic exteriors.

Age distribution: A young residential area with more than 90 percent of the dwellings built since 1940 and only 3 percent before 1930.

Condition (November, 1955): Good to very good.

Price range (November, 1955): Medium, $11,000–$14,000 (modal price about $12,500).

Socioeconomic characteristics.—Much that was said of Lakeview test area applies here. The main difference is that this is a much younger area and is still adding new structures at a significant rate. It is at a much healthier stage of the neighborhood life cycle, which at least partially explains a price structure about $1,200 higher than Lakeview's. It is a middle-class neighborhood. Sellers' names suggesting Irish or Italian ancestry occur more frequently than any other groups in the transaction records for the period of observation.

Racial changes: Ingleside Heights is the most westerly residential neighborhood so far reached by the broad westward progress of nonwhite occupancy in this general area. Beginning in the South of Ridge Lane neighborhood in 1945, nonwhites bought and occupied homes in the residential belt lying between Ocean and Alemany Avenues, moving gradually toward Junipero Serra Boulevard, a little over a mile away. Nonwhites crossed two significant boundaries: Plymouth Avenue in 1948, and Orizaba Avenue in late 1951, the latter being the eastern boundary of the present test area. Breaking through each of these lines carried important psychological weight with the white residents and speeded up the rate of racial succession in the entire area.

The first nonwhite purchase and occupancy in the Ingleside Heights test area was by a Negro family, in September, 1951. This involved a home on the west side of Orizaba, although the eastern side of the street had nonwhite residence a year earlier. White homeowners west of Orizaba, therefore, were aware of the trend of nonwhite occupancy. By late 1951, the areas just to the east of Ingleside Heights had nonwhite occupancy ranging from 8 to 12 percent, so this test area is properly classified as one subject to threat of entry for a year or two before the first nonwhite family actually moved in.

Nonwhite occupancy reached 2 percent (seven families) by the end of 1951, and increased steadily but gradually to 20 percent (75 families) by the end of the observation period (third quarter, 1955). Real estate men state that 90 percent of all sales now being made are to nonwhites. As in all other test areas observed, Negroes made up the bulk of the nonwhites, but about one family in ten was Chinese or Japanese. The westerly half of the test area, as of October, 1955, had no nonwhites.

As in the case of the Lakeview area, there has been no organized resistance, or even unpleasant demonstrations, by whites. Only minor panic selling took place, and none after the first year of entry. Similarly, too, some blocks have gone heavily nonwhite while others have remained all, or nearly all, white. Real estate men expect Ingleside Heights to stabilize with an integrated interracial pattern segregated by blocks.

Civil service employees and professional people are heavily represented in the nonwhite group.

The Control Areas: Geneva (C-3-SF)
and Visitacion Valley (C-6-SF)

Each of these has already been described (pp. 78, 89). They are both highly comparable to the test area, Geneva having a moderately lower price level.

Price Analysis

Over the 25-quarter observation period the following sales data were available:

Area	Total sales	Average per quarter
Ingleside Heights (test)	270	10.8
Geneva (control)	142	5.7
Visitacion Valley (control)	228	9.1

Average sales prices per quarter for the test area and each control area, respectively, are shown in figures 9 and 10. General price changes for all three areas were as follows:

Area	Average price before entry (8 quarters)	Average price after entry (last 4 quarters)	Increase	
			Amount	Percent
Ingleside Heights (test)	$10,859	$12,460	$1,601	14.7
Geneva (control)	9,944	11,903	1,959	19.7
Visitacion Valley (control)	11,019	12,668	1,649	15.0

As measured from the average price level for the pre-entry period, Ingleside Heights test prices had about the same percent increase as did Visitacion Valley, but were outdistanced by Geneva. These movements took place while nonwhite occupancy moved toward 20 percent. In absolute terms, although test prices ended the period in almost precisely the same relationship to both sets of control prices, there seems to have been a slowing down in the upward price trend after nonwhite entry in mid-1951. Due to the variability present in all three areas, it is difficult to detect a pattern in the year-by-year comparisons of price difference, but the broad conclusion appears warranted that, despite the irregu-

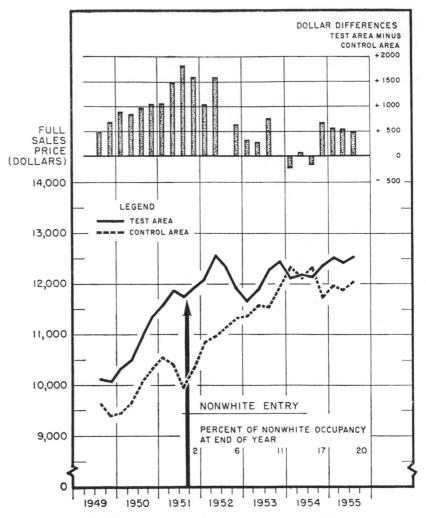

Fig. 9. Trend of average prices by quarters, 1949–1955: San Francisco, Ingleside Heights (test) and Geneva (control).

larities, average prices in all areas were moving along in fairly parallel fashion.

Comparing Ingleside Heights with Geneva, it is evident that the test area operated within a generally higher price range, producing positive price differences in most quarters, but the *fluctuations* in price differences are quite significant. Test prices increased steadily over control prices until nonwhite entry occurred in mid-1951, held up for the next three quarters, then declined relatively (and sometimes absolutely) until the third quarter of 1954. The last year of observation displayed a strong recovery to the pre-entry relative level.

In dollar terms, average test prices started out $481 above control prices ($10,138 as against $9,657) and reached a maximum positive difference of $1,797 in the third quarter of 1951, just at the first nonwhite move-in. While nonwhite occupancy swelled to some 15 percent, test prices steadily declined relative to control prices, the difference becoming negative in 1954. The low point was in the first quarter of that year, when test prices were $217 below the control area average ($12,108 as against $12,325). For the four quarters beginning with the last in 1954, test prices averaged $500 to $600 above control prices (about 4 percent).

When price differences are averaged by years, results are as shown below.

INGLESIDE HEIGHTS AND GENEVA

Period	Average difference in dollars (test price minus control price)	Test price as percent of control price (averages)
Before entry		
Third quarter, 1949, to second quarter, 1951	+916	109.1
After entry		
Year ending with second quarter of:		
1952	+1,477	114.1
1953	+402	103.5
1954	+201	101.8
1955 (ending in third quarter)	+410	103.5

Part of the large positive difference in the pre-entry period is due to the 1951 dip in control prices. The final percent difference (+3.5) is much closer to the average difference existing during 1949–1950, which seems to represent a more normal relationship between the two areas. The very large differences during 1952, reflected in the 114.1 percent figure above, result from the combination of the Geneva control price dip and the Ingleside Heights continued sharp climb. These differences are probably larger than they should be because of the way in which opposite price movements happened to coincide during that period. In any

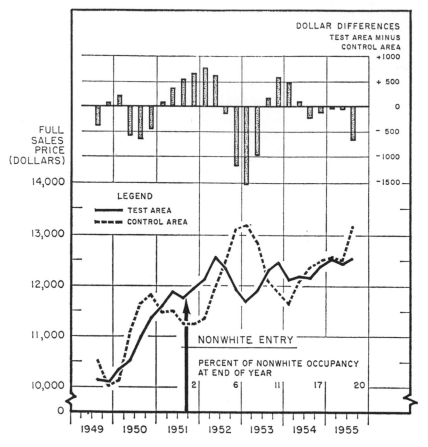

Fig. 10. Trend of average prices by quarters, 1949–1955: San Francisco, Ingleside Heights (test) and Visitacion Valley (control).

event, figure 9, together with the price differences averaged by years, suggests the possibility that the rapid opening rise in test prices may have been slowed down because of the market impact of nonwhite entry. This view is weakened, however, when it is observed that Ingleside Heights prices, for the period as a whole, ended very close to prices in both control areas, just as they had been at the outset of the observation period.

The comparison with Visitacion Valley, the second control area, yields results rather similar to the first comparison, as shown by figure 10. Test and control prices moved together fairly closely over the entire period, rising from the $10,000–$10,500 level to about $12,500–$13,000. Test prices were under control prices at both ends of the period: 3.6 percent less in the beginning quarter and 4.9 percent less in the last quarter. They exceeded control prices in twelve quarters and were below them in eleven quarters.

Relative to nonwhite entry, figure 10 shows the test area improving its comparative position until early 1952, when its relative price position worsened. Test prices fell in absolute terms during the last half of 1952 and into 1953, whereas control prices were rapidly increasing. This produced large negative price differences for that period, while nonwhite occupancy was growing from 5 to 8 percent of the area population.

During 1953, test prices recovered sharply, while control prices fell, yielding positive price differences in favor of the test area. The observation period closed with prices moving together very closely, except for the final quarter.

The wide swings in both test and control prices yield an erratic pattern of price differences averaged by yearly periods, but there is a tendency for these oscillations to cancel each other.

INGLESIDE HEIGHTS AND VISITACION VALLEY

Period	Average difference in dollars (test price minus control price)	Test price as percent of control price (averages)
Before entry Third quarter, 1949, to second quarter, 1951	−160	98.6
After entry Year ending with second quarter of:		
1952	+653	105.7
1953	−941	92.8
1954	+349	103.0
1955 (ending in third quarter)	−209	98.4

Apparently, the very large negative difference in 1953 was a result of the high peak in Visitacion Valley control prices coming simultaneously with a dip in test prices. Similarly, the moderately large positive differences in 1952 and 1954 resulted from the opposite combination. Because the trend lines suggested by figure 10 appear to run along together, it seems fair to conclude that despite these oscillations the underlying price pattern was largely the same in both areas. In any event, test prices were no worse off at the end of the period, when nonwhite entry had reached almost 20 percent, than they were at the outset, when both areas were all-white.

It is worth commenting that the nonwhite occupancy existing in the neighbor areas to the east evidently did not have any price effects in the test area. Not until mid-1952, when Ingleside Heights had some fifteen to twenty nonwhite families within its own boundaries, were there any price changes that might be associated with racial factors.

Viewed as a whole, these two comparisons suggest that non-white occupancy in 1951 may have interrupted that test area's tendency to pull away from both control areas. It might be argued that test area prices, in the absence of nonwhite entry, would have ended at much higher absolute levels, judging by their initial rate of growth in the period studied. While possible, this eventuality seems unlikely, since a continuation of the test area's opening price trend would soon have carried it far beyond a price level attainable by this type of neighborhood. Another reason for this conclusion's being unlikely is that all three areas maintained their relative positions over the period. Thus, a more acceptable explanation is that the strong rise in test prices during the first third of the period was due to a surge in market demand for that particular locale; that nonwhite entry may have inter-rupted this market trend; but that stabilization has occurred at a level very close to what would have resulted in the absence of racial changes. The data do not support the conclusion that non-white entry brought about any serious or lasting deterioration in test area prices.

The Test Area: Oceanview (T-7-SF)

Location.—In the southern section of the Ocean Avenue district, just north of U.S. Highway 101 and within a quarter mile of the southern city limits of San Francisco. Five miles southwest of the downtown center. Contiguous to three other test areas: Ingleside Heights on the west, Lakeview on the north, and South of Ridge Lane on the east.

Boundaries, topography, and features.—Bounded by Lakeview Avenue, Summit, San Jose Avenue, Alemany Boulevard, and Orizaba Avenue. An area of 20 blocks, containing some 600 homes, and sloping southerly from Lakeview Avenue to Alemany Boulevard. Except for some light commercial development along Alemany Boulevard, and the Ocean View School and Playground, land use is entirely residential. About average in general condition and desirability for its price class, its strongest feature is probably favorable climatic conditions due largely to its southerly exposure. Relatively few vacant lots remain in the area.

Structures.—Mostly single-family, owner-occupied dwelling units, but with considerable diversity in size, age, and type of construction. There are a few multiunit structures, consisting of a primary five- or six-bedroom unit with one, two, or three small rental units. About four-fifths of the structures have five rooms; the rest are equally divided between the four- and six-room categories. Frame construction is the rule, with exteriors finished in stucco, composition shingle, or rustic.

Age distribution: Generally a younger neighborhood, 70 percent of its homes having been built since 1940. Some 14 percent fall in the 1930–1939 decade and the remaining 16 percent were built before 1930.

Condition (November, 1955): Good to very good, but roughly one house in each block is below the neighborhood standard of maintenance.

Price range (November, 1955): Medium to high, $10,000–$14,500 (modal price $11,500).

Socioeconomic characteristics.—A middle-class neighborhood with many resemblances to Lakeview and Ingleside Heights (see preceding descriptions). Names indicating Irish, Italian, and Jewish backgrounds predominate in the transfers during the study period.

Racial changes: The westward movement of nonwhites as they settled in this general vicinity has already been described in connection with Ingleside Heights. Oceanview experienced entry in January, 1948, at about the same time as Lakeview just to the north. Existing nonwhite residence in the South of Ridge Lane area to the east, which had reached some 30 percent by that time, no doubt interested other nonwhites in settling in Oceanview, even though a high ridge forms a physical barrier between the two areas.

The first nonwhite family in the area was Negro and came

from the crowded and blighted downtown area known as the Fillmore district.[3] Only one neighbor objected, and no hostile actions resulted. By year's end there were some ten Negro families in the area (2 percent), and the entry process has continued steadily to the present time. By November, 1955, non-white occupancy, primarily Negro, had reached 18 percent (about 100 families). While some white families have left because of nonwhite entry, there has been no panic selling. But the rate at which properties have come on the market, according to local real estate men, is considerably higher than a normal turnover would produce. Nonwhites entering the area appear to be of comparable economic status with the white residents, as in the other test areas.

The Control Areas: Glen Park (C-1-SF) and Sunnyside (C-4-SF)

Each of these has already been described (see pp. 72 and 85). Both are closely comparable to Oceanview, although their price levels are $500 to $1,000 lower.

Price Analysis

Over the 24-quarter observation period the following sales data were gathered:

Area	Total sales	Average per quarter
Oceanview (test)	274	11.5
Glen Park (control)	182	7.6
Sunnyside (control)	200	8.3

Figures 11 and 12 show prices, averaged by quarters, for the test area as compared with each control area. While price data for the years immediately before and after nonwhite entry (in 1948) were not available, real estate men well acquainted with all three areas agree that in 1948, and for some years before, Oceanview prices were about $300 to $500 higher than in Sunnyside, and $800 to $1,000 higher than in Glen Park. As the charts show, these differences maintained themselves after entry, with some

---

[3] Many details are available on this first entry, since the *San Francisco Chronicle* later ran a feature story about it, under the title "How One Negro Found a Home for his Family," July 22, 1951.

fluctuations. General price movements during the observation period were as follows:

Area	Average price, first 4 quarters	Average price, last 4 quarters	Increase	
			Amount	Percent
Oceanview (test)..........	$10,112	$11,446	$1,334	13.2
Glen Park (control)........	8,886	10,561	1,675	18.8
Sunnyside (control)........	9,747	10,865	1,118	11.5

Over the observation period, the percent increase in test neighborhood prices fell between the increases shown by the two control areas. In absolute terms, Oceanview began and ended with higher prices, and displayed a more even upward trend than did either control area. Over the period of observation, nonwhite occupancy increased from 6 percent to almost 18 percent.

As compared with the Glen Park control area, test prices tended to average about $1,000 higher over the period, as shown by figure 11. There were considerable fluctuations, however, as revealed by the data on price differences by years.

OCEANVIEW AND GLEN PARK

Period	Average difference in dollars (test price minus control price)	Test price as percent of control price (averages)
Year ending with third quarter of:		
1950.............................	+1,285	114.5
1951.............................	+888	108.8
1952.............................	+551	105.3
1953.............................	+1,543	115.6
1954.............................	+1,432	114.3
1955.............................	+886	108.4

The abnormally large positive differences in 1953 and 1954 were due to the fall in control prices rather than to any marked upswing in test prices. On the other hand, the low figure for the period ending in 1952 resulted from a control price peak. Allowing for these irregularities leaves a general picture of a gradual reduction in test price percent margins over control prices. Whether Glen Park prices will continue to draw closer to the Oceanview level is unpredictable. However, it can be stated that

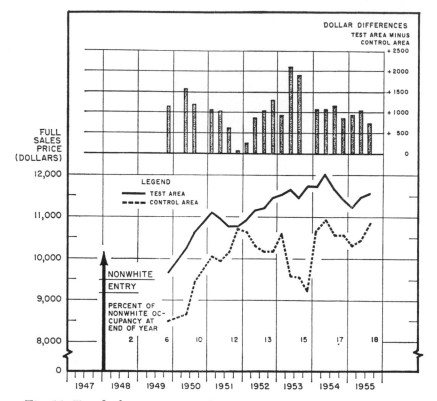

Fig. 11. Trend of average prices by quarters, 1949–1955: San Francisco, Oceanview (test) and Glen Park (control).

the presence of nonwhites in steadily increasing numbers did not appear to injure prices to any serious extent in the Oceanview neighborhood, as compared with the all-white Glen Park area.

A generally similar conclusion is suggested by the comparison of test prices with those in Sunnyside, the second control area. The picture is clearer in this case, however, since control prices are steadier in their behavior. Figure 12 presents the average price data.

Both test and control area exhibited rising price trends over the period, starting and ending very close to each other. In general, both began at around the $9,500 level and ended at $11,500, with test area prices higher in every quarter. Control prices dipped in late 1950 and during 1954, somewhat exaggerating the positive price differences for those quarters.

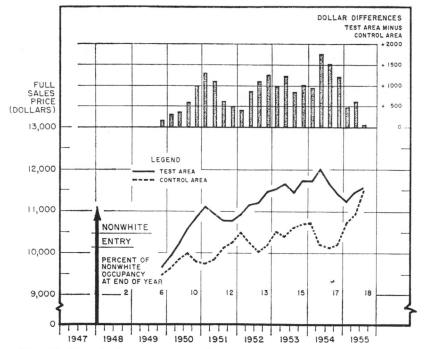

Fig. 12. Trend of average prices by quarters, 1949–1955: San Francisco, Oceanview (test) and Sunnyside (control).

Up to the middle of 1954, test prices seemed to be pulling farther away each year, on the average, but after that time they took an absolute drop of some $800. Almost simultaneously, control prices climbed remarkably fast, increasing by about $1,400. These opposite movements caused average prices in the two areas to be right together at the period's close. Average price differences, by yearly periods, are portrayed in the table below.

OCEANVIEW AND SUNNYSIDE

Period	Average difference in dollars (test price minus control price)	Test price as percent of control price (averages)
Year ending with third quarter of:		
1950	+365	103.7
1951	+1,014	110.3
1952	+728	107.1
1953	+1,098	110.5
1954	+1,315	112.6
1955	+581	105.5

The movement of price differences suggests a strong market upsurge in the Oceanview test area, lasting until mid-1954. As it lost momentum after that date, the relative change was accentuated by the late rise in control prices mentioned above. Even so, test prices ended 5.5 percent above control prices, as compared to their 3.7 percent margin at the outset. Possibly the nonwhite demand for homes in Oceanview was strong enough to steepen a rising price trend, but demand may have lessened in intensity after mid-1954.

In summary, the price analysis for Oceanview does not indicate that prices in the area have deteriorated in comparison with the two control areas. Nor do the price movements show any pattern that can be related to the nonwhite entry or increase.

LIGHT NONWHITE ENTRY: ONE NEIGHBORHOOD

The Test Area: Sunset (T-8-SF)

Location. In the northwestern part of the Sunset district, beginning one block south of Golden Gate Park and extending for nine blocks along the Pacific Ocean shoreline. Five miles west of the downtown center, in the largest single residential expanse in San Francisco.

Boundaries, topography, and features.—Bounded by Irving Street, a line from Irving and Forty-Seventh to Judah and Forty-Third, Forty-Third Avenue, a line from Forty-Third and Lawton to Forty-Sixth and Moraga, Forty-Sixth Avenue, Rivera Street, and Great Highway. Contains 30 blocks, with about 900 houses, all on level terrain. A shopping section exists along Judah Street, but the area is otherwise in residential land use. About 90 percent of the lots are built upon.

Structures.—Almost exclusively single-family, owner-occupied, a few homes have a two- or three-room rental unit. Mostly five- and six-room houses with one bath and either one- or two-car garage. Overwhelmingly frame-stucco construction.

Age distribution: A younger neighborhood, with 16 percent of the structures built in 1950–1955 and 59 percent in 1940–1949. The remaining 25 percent are evenly divided between the 1930–1939 and the pre-1930 building periods.

Condition (November, 1955): Good to excellent, although a few of the older homes are not up to that standard.

Price range (November, 1953: Medium to high, $10,500–$15,500 (modal price about $12,500).

Socioeconomic characteristics.—Predominantly a middle-class neighborhood, with some upper-middle-class families. Slightly less "standardized" socially than other parts of the Sunset district, where homes were typically built at the same time by one builder and were also more alike in size and design.

Racial changes: In June, 1952, the first Negro family bought and occupied a home in the northern portion of this test area. An additional score followed suit up to November, 1955, the pattern of purchases moving gradually southward in scattered fashion. Some eight or ten Chinese and Japanese families have entered during the same period, bringing the nonwhite proportion to a little over 3 percent. Because no other nonwhite concentrations existed in the Sunset district in general, the test area cannot be considered as threatened with entry prior to the move-in of the first nonwhite family. Although the Sunset district was long considered one of San Francisco's firmest white strongholds, no organized opposition or even individual action challenged nonwhite entry. Brokers report no panic moving, and few "For Sale" signs have been displayed since entry began.[4] This test area has the largest concentration of nonwhites in the vast 700-block Sunset-Parkside district. About twenty Chinese, Japanese, and Negro families are individually scattered through it, but none is in or near the Lincoln–Judah control area.

The Control Areas: Lincoln-Judah and Visitacion Valley

Lincoln-Judah (C-7-SF).—A 16-block, 400-house neighborhood situated at the north end of the Sunset district, about a half mile east of the test area. It is an older neighborhood, 43 percent of the homes dating back to 1929 and earlier, and 34 percent to 1930–1939. This is more than offset by a heavier representation

---

[4] As one very experienced broker put it, "Whites in this area are accepting the idea of colored living in their neighborhood. They are beginning to realize they can't run away from it—at least in San Francisco." Personal interview, September 8, 1955.

of six-room units, some of which have two bathrooms. Accordingly, control prices range higher than test prices by about $1,500, but local real estate representatives nevertheless recommend it as a good yardstick against which to measure the test area's price performance.

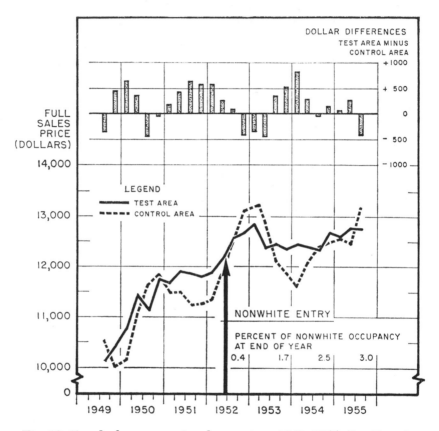

Fig. 13. Trend of average prices by quarters, 1949–1955: San Francisco, Sunset (test) and Visitacion Valley (control).

Visitacion Valley (C-6-SF).—This area has been described in a section on p. 89. It is situated on the opposite side of San Francisco, but otherwise is closely comparable. Its modal price level is very much in line with that for the test area in the pre-entry years.

Price Analysis

The following sales data were gathered for the 25-quarter observation period:

Area	Total sales	Average per quarter
Sunset (test)....................	287	11.5
Visitacion Valley (control).......	228	9.1
Lincoln-Judah (control)..........	195	7.8

Prices averaged by quarters are shown for the test area and each control area in figures 13 and 14.

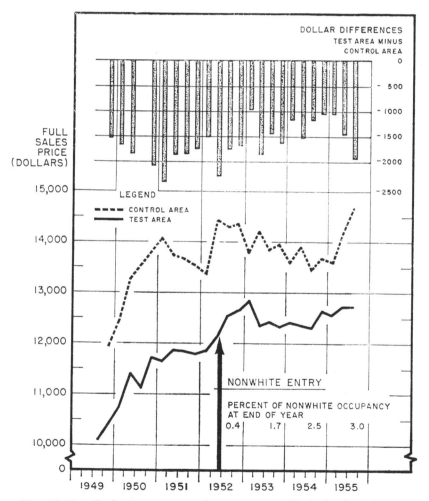

Fig. 14. Trend of average prices by quarters, 1949–1955: San Francisco, Sunset (test) and Lincoln-Judah (control).

As measured against the average price level prevailing during the entire pre-entry period, test prices after entry showed a percent increase slightly under that for Visitacion Valley but considerably higher than that for Lincoln-Judah:

Area	Average price before entry (12 quarters)	Average price after entry (last 4 quarters)	Increase	
			Amount	Percent
Sunset (test)..............	$11,408	$12,683	$1,275	11.2
Visitacion Valley (control)...	11,155	12,668	1,513	13.6
Lincoln-Judah (control).....	13,435	14,045	610	4.5

Prices went up 11.2 percent in the test area, as against increases of 13.6 and 4.5 percent for the control areas. The closeness of test prices to those in Visitacion Valley is brought out by figure 13. Price movements in these two areas were remarkably parallel. Differences exceed $500 in only five quarters (and then by very little), and appear to be randomly distributed in favor first of the test area, then of the control area. The largest fluctuations are largely attributable to control area price swings around the trend: a dip in 1951 and 1953–1954, and a sharp rise in 1952 to early 1953. The latter explains the negative price differences of those three quarters, which might otherwise be attributed to nonwhite entry in June, 1952.

Averaging the price differences confirms the visual impression offered by the chart. These averages are tabulated below.

SUNSET AND VISITACION VALLEY

Period	Average difference in dollars (test price minus control price)	Test price as percent of control price (averages)
Before entry Third quarter, 1949, to second quarter, 1952.............	+256	102.4
After entry Year ending with second quarter of: 1953.........................	−286	97.8
1954.........................	+487	104.1
1955.........................	+1	100.4

Test prices averaged 2.4 percent higher than Visitacion Valley prices before nonwhites moved in. In the first postentry year, they averaged about the same percentage below control prices, but moved to 4.1 percent above by the middle of 1954. When the observation period ended, they stood just even with control prices. These differences are so small that they can hardly be relied on as indicative of any real divergences between the test area and Visitacion Valley. In any event, they tend to cancel out over the period.

The comparison with the second test area, Lincoln-Judah, does reveal a change in the relationship between the two areas over the period of observation. This change is discernible in figure 14.

Although both areas experienced a general rise in prices over the period, test prices showed a steeper and steadier increase. They climbed, on the average, from $10,123 to $12,739, increasing by 25.8 percent; whereas control prices went from $11,956 to $14,678, a 22.8 percent increase.

Both areas showed rapid increases for the first eight quarters (into early 1951), but while test prices continued to climb until early 1953, control prices dipped sharply during 1951. During 1953–1954, prices held fairly steady in the test area, but moved downward slowly in the control area. The last five quarters saw a resumption of a significant upward trend in both cases.

Test prices generally moved closer to control prices over the period, with nonwhite occupancy apparently not affecting this development. Comparisons by individual quarters obscure this tendency, because of random fluctuations from quarter to quarter. Taking the average price differences by years, however, gives a clearer view of what happened.

SUNSET AND LINCOLN-JUDAH

Period	Average difference in dollars (test price minus control price)	Test price as percent of control price (averages)
Before entry Third quarter, 1949, to second quarter, 1952.............	−1,870	86.1
After entry Year ending with second quarter of: 1953..........................	−1,561	89.0
1954..........................	−1,435	89.6
1955..........................	−1,325	90.5

Test prices were under control prices by an average of $1,870 during the pre-entry period. By mid-1955, when nonwhite occupancy stood at between 2.5 and 3 percent, test prices were within $1,325 of Lincoln-Judah prices. Thus, test prices moved up relatively, from a level almost 14 percent under to one that was 9.5 percent under control prices. In this case it is clear that nonwhite entry was associated with a relative improvement in test area prices as compared to prices in an all-white comparable neighborhood.

Considering the two comparisons together, the net result is favorable for the Sunset test neighborhood. There is no indication of any kind that the presence of nonwhites in limited numbers in this higher-class residential area has harmed its price level in comparison with similar neighborhoods that have had no nonwhite entry.

SUMMARY: SAN FRANCISCO

Comparing the ratio of test area prices to control area prices in the last four quarters observed *after* nonwhite entry to the corresponding ratio for the base period *before* entry shows that test prices performed about as well as control prices. Out of the fourteen comparisons, six show test prices relatively higher than control prices at the end of the observation period, while eight show test prices relatively lower.

Half of the differences, however, are very small—4 percent or less—and for this reason cannot be taken as evidence of any significant difference in price behavior between test and control areas. It should be noted that the test areas with small differences in price behavior, relative to all-white areas, ranged evenly from 3 to 70 percent nonwhite occupancy. The seven comparisons with significant price differences are shown in the following table.

Test area and degree of nonwhite entry	Percent of nonwhite occupancy in test area	Test price as percent of control price (averages)		Percent change in test price–control price ratio
		For pre-entry period	For last 4 quarters	
South of Ridge Lane—Very heavy..	75	95.2[a]	108.8	+14.3
Lakeview—Heavy...............	20	95.5[a]	105.3	+10.3
Silver Terrace B—Very heavy.....	50	112.8	119.2	+5.7
Sunset—Light..................	3	86.1	90.5	+5.1
Ingleside Heights—Heavy.........	20	109.1	103.5	−5.1
Oceanview—Heavy..............	18	114.5[a]	108.4	−5.3
Silver Terrace A—Very heavy.....	70	109.0	98.2	−9.1

[a]Average for first four quarters; no pre-entry data available.

These results do not show a simple one-directional effect due to nonwhite entry. Apparently, where significant price differences did show up, nonwhite entry affected test prices favorably in four cases and unfavorably in the other three. The degree of nonwhite entry did not seem to be related to the direction or size of test price movements.

VII

Oakland

Nine test areas are analyzed in Oakland,[1] most lying near the city's southern boundary. Each experienced nonwhite entry between 1950 and 1954. Three had very heavy entry, one heavy, three medium, one light, and one very light. Average price levels range through the upper half of the medium bracket for seven areas, while two areas are in the high price bracket of $14,000 to $24,000. More than 1,400 individual sales in these nine test areas are compared with 1,200 sales in nine control areas.

VERY HEAVY NONWHITE ENTRY: THREE NEIGHBORHOODS

The Test Area: Columbia Gardens (T-1-O)

Location.—At the southwest extremity of Oakland, between the Municipal Airport and the East Shore Freeway, almost touching the southern city limits.

Boundaries, topography, and features.—About twelve irregularly shaped blocks, containing some 350 homes. Bounded by Coral, Gibraltar and Empire Roads, the land is fully built upon, quite level, and used entirely for residences.

Structures.—Entirely single-family design, predominantly owner-occupied. All built by one builder-developer as a tract development in 1943–1944, with many identical floor plans and close comparability throughout the area. Mostly three-bedroom houses, with one bath and garage. Some two-bedroom, but the sales data for these have been adjusted to make them comparable with three-bedroom units. Homes are modest "California ranch-type," one-story frame construction with no basement (a few

---

[1] See chapter iii for criteria governing selection of these neighborhoods and for definitions of special terminology.

two-story design), stucco or wood exterior, composition shingle roof, and floor furnace.

Condition (November, 1955): Good to very good.

Price range (November, 1955): Medium, $10,000–$11,000 (modal price $10,500).

Socioeconomic characteristics.—A middle- and lower-middle-class neighborhood, completely white until September, 1950. Initial purchase and occupancy were by white defense worker families. Most stayed on into the postwar period, many then moving to more expensive residential areas as their financial status improved.

Demand by new white buyers was insufficient to absorb all homes offered, so that pressure developed to find other buyer groups. Qualified Negro families, very eager for decent housing, were recognized as the most logical—and probably only—answer to this market.

Racial changes: The first sale to a Negro took place in September, 1950. By the end of the year there were fifteen Negro families in Columbia Gardens, or about 5 percent of all families in the neighborhood. Although no organized resistance or individual hostile acts occurred, the racial entry prompted many additional whites to move out, creating a still larger vacuum of homes for sale. All but a handful of these were bought by Negroes, and as this pattern persisted, the racial composition of the area shifted drastically. By 1952 there were 100 Negro families (30 percent) and the total reached 200 by the fall of 1955 (60 percent). About 90 percent of the sales now being made are to Negroes. A few Oriental families came in during the first year of nonwhite entry, but no others have followed. Real estate men feel that nonwhites now buying are not up to the socioeconomic level of the first nonwhite entrants. They say this is discouraging "better-class Negroes" from buying now, and may be a reason for some fall-off in sales over the past year.[2] Still, it is expected that this area will eventually become completely Negro-occupied.

The way in which nonwhite entry and subsequent "settlement" came about in this test area is sharply in contrast with the usual

---

[2] Other reasons mentioned: (1) New lower priced tracts opening up constantly in the general area of Southern Alameda County; (2) Less favorable selling terms under VA and FHA financing, as compared with a year or two ago. Interviews with local real estate brokers, August and September, 1955.

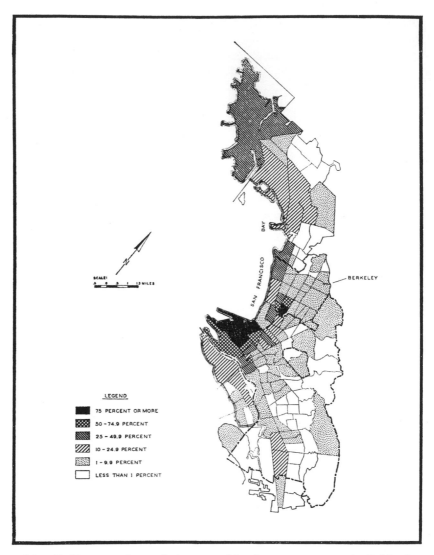

Map 3. Percent of population nonwhite by census tracts in Oakland,
California, and adjacent areas, 1950.

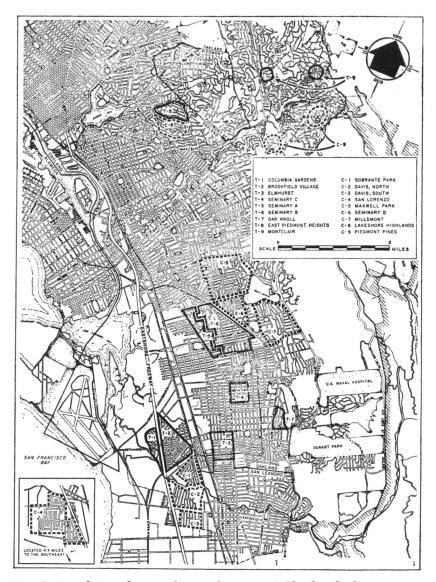

Map 4. Boundaries of test and control areas in Oakland and adjacent areas.

pattern, where nonwhite entry occurs despite the generally unfavorable attitudes and policies of the white residents and real
estate people. Here, nonwhite entry carried the tacit and, in some
cases, open approval of real estate men and some property
owners, who saw it as the only feasible way to clear the listings
coming on the market in the area. The decision to sell to nonwhites, however, was made only shortly before the first nonwhite
sale occurred (September, 1950), and Columbia Gardens cannot
be considered as a white area under threat of entry for any appreciable time before that date. No nonwhites lived nearer than
a mile at the time, and several major barriers, including a rail-
road, lay between Columbia Gardens and areas of nonwhite
residence.

The Control Areas: Davis South and San Lorenzo

There are two all-white areas that serve well as controls for
Columbia Gardens.

Davis South (C-3-O).—An area of fourteen blocks and some
510 houses, situated a mile south of the test area and in the
neighboring city of San Leandro. Bounded by Davis Street, Pacific
Avenue, Navy Street, Valley Street, and Pearson Avenue. Built up
at the same time (1943) as the test area, but with some 2 percent
of the homes dating back to 1930–1939, and 2 percent recently
built—since 1952. Closely comparable as to design and construction. However, being considerably closer to local shopping centers, as well as to downtown San Leandro, this control area has
consistently topped test prices by $500 to $800, on the average.
Bearing this difference in mind, real estate people concur in its
use as a control area for Columbia Gardens.

San Lorenzo (C-4-O).—Four miles south of the test area, San
Lorenzo is a very large residential community. Developed by a
single company, the houses are fairly uniform in design and construction, and comparable to Columbia Gardens in most features.
The planned nature of the development, coupled with important
amenities such as wide streets, numerous trees, and convenient
local shopping areas, accounts for a price level averaging $1,200
to $1,500 higher than for the test area.

For a specific comparison area, an area of fifty blocks straddling
the East Shore Freeway was singled out, having the following

boundaries: East Shore Freeway, Ginger Avenue, Hesperian Boulevard, Via Manzanas, Via Chiquita, Grant Avenue, Paseo del Campo, and Paseo Largavista. There are about 1,250 dwelling units in this area.

Price Analysis

As compared with each control area, average test prices make a generally favorable showing over the observation period. Comparable price data are available from 1948 on, two years before nonwhite entry occurred.[3] Over the 28 to 29 quarters studied, the number of observed transactions in all three areas was as follows:

Area	Total sales	Average per quarter
Columbia Gardens	234	7.8
Davis South	132	4.7
San Lorenzo	335	11.9

These data are shown graphically in figures 15 and 16.

The significant observation regarding Columbia Gardens vs. Davis South is that despite price fluctuations in both areas within individual years prices moved together in about the same relationship over the whole period. Test prices stayed about 5 to 7 percent under control prices, and the percent increase in average prices was almost the same for both areas.

Area	Average price before entry (11 quarters)	Average price after entry (last 4 quarters)	Increase	
			Amount	Percent
Columbia Gardens (test)....	$8,898	$10,134	$1,236	13.8
Davis South (control).......	9,427	10,808	1,381	14.6

These percent increases measure the rise in average prices from the level prevailing during the eleven quarters before entry began in the test area to the last four quarters for which data were

---

[3] Since all three areas contain practically no houses that are not tract-built, and therefore very comparable as to design and construction, it seemed desirable to adjust the sales price data to eliminate the only two physical differences that did exist: two versus three bedrooms and garage versus no garage. All sales figures were made equivalent to the price that would have been received for a three-bedroom home with garage. This is the predominant type of unit, so that a majority of the sales figures needed no adjustment. The consensus of informed real estate opinion was that, for these houses, one bedroom is worth $500 and a garage is worth $750.

available. During this time, nonwhite entry in Columbia Gardens steadily climbed toward 60 percent, yet test area prices showed a percent gain that, considering the variability of real estate price measurement, was the same as for the all-white control area.

During the year before entry, test prices gained both relatively and absolutely, producing the only *positive* price difference for the period of study (+$225 in the second quarter of 1950). Part of the relative improvement is ascribable to the rather sharp absolute price fall for the control area during 1950. In any event, the improved relative position for test prices persisted through 1951, by which time nonwhite occupancy was about 30 percent of all test area households. As the proportion of nonwhite occupancy increased toward 60 percent, test prices resumed their old pre-entry position relative to control prices. Absolutely, as figure 15 shows, both test and control prices moved upward fairly consistently over the period.

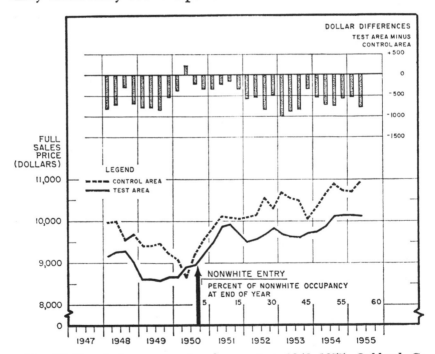

Fig. 15. Trend of average prices by quarters, 1948–1955: Oakland, Columbia Gardens (test) and Davis South (control). (Source: Data used in this figure and others in the Oakland series compiled from Multiple Listing records and field investigations, 1953–1955.)

The absolute dip of about $700 in test prices, which began two years before nonwhite entry, was paralleled by the even steeper fall in control prices. This "soft market" in Columbia Gardens has already been described in terms of a general depreciation of the area, as compared with similar homes elsewhere, occurring long before nonwhites moved in. There is no basis here for connecting the fall in prices to fear of entry, particularly when the circumstances of entry are reconsidered. Similarly, the sharp recovery in test prices from early 1950 to late 1951 was matched by control price increases and can hardly be uniquely related to the changing racial pattern.

Price differences for the before-entry and after-entry periods are shown below.

COLUMBIA GARDENS AND DAVIS SOUTH

Period	Average difference in dollars (test price minus control price)	Test price as percent of control price (averages)
Before entry		
First quarter, 1948, to third quarter, 1950..	−530	94.5
After entry		
Year ending with third quarter of:		
1951.................................	−268	97.3
1952.................................	−580	94.3
1953.................................	−805	92.4
1954.................................	−598	94.3
1955 (at end of second quarter).........	−643	94.0

Noteworthy is the sharp relative improvement in test prices during and immediately after nonwhite entry, when they increased from an average level 5.5 percent under control prices to one that was less than 3 percent below. During succeeding years the yearly averages show test prices running slightly lower than before entry occurred. A deviation of this size could easily be due to differences in the market desirability of the two neighborhoods. Whatever its cause, it is so minor that little significance can be attached to it.

Figure 16 depicts the same price line for Columbia Gardens, but this time in contrast with average prices for the second control area: San Lorenzo. Again, the general similarity in average price movements is striking. Although test prices dipped during

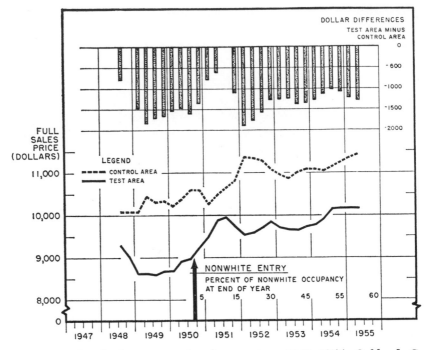

Fig. 16. Trend of average prices by quarters, 1948–1955: Oakland, Columbia Gardens (test) and San Lorenzo (control).

the pre-entry period while control prices held fairly steady, the general pattern after entry began in Columbia Gardens appears to have been quite parallel. Actually, test prices drew nearer to control prices over the whole period, as the following averages reveal:

Area	Average price before entry (9 quarters)	Average price after entry (last 4 quarters)	Increase	
			Amount	Percent
Columbia Gardens (test)....	$ 8,898	$10,134	$1,236	13.8
San Lorenzo (control).......	10,300	11,286	986	9.6

San Lorenzo evidently did not have the slower market that Columbia Gardens experienced during 1948 and 1949, but it appears to have had a comparably weaker demand situation in the years after 1950. The rapid rise in Columbia Gardens from 1950 on quickly altered the relative picture in the test area's favor, with test prices approaching to within $610 (6 percent) of control prices by June, 1951. At that time, nonwhite entry was moving toward 15 percent. Test prices for the last four quarters ended 13.8 percent higher than the nine-quarter average before entry. This was considerably above the 9.6 percent increase in average control prices over the same time period.

Subsequently, test prices dipped slightly during 1952, but later they again gained steadily to the end of the observation period. The comparative price behavior during the 1950–1955 period, while nonwhite entry was moving toward 60 percent in Columbia Gardens, shows the test area definitely improving its relative position as compared to pre-entry levels.

COLUMBIA GARDENS AND SAN LORENZO

Period	Average difference in dollars (test price minus control price)	Test price as percent of control price (averages)
Before entry Third quarter, 1948, to second quarter, 1950	−1,500	85.5
After entry Year ending with second quarter of:		
1951	−917	91.2
1952	−1,571	86.0
1953	−1,286	88.3
1954	−1,193	89.2
1955	−1,197	89.4

By mid-1955, Columbia Gardens had come closer to San Lorenzo by an average of $300, narrowing the percent gap from 14.5 below control prices in the pre-entry period, to 10.6 below for the last four quarters of the period, during which nonwhite entry was rapidly increasing. As in the comparison with Davis South, the first postentry year showed a dramatic relative improvement, due to the rapid rise in test prices.

It is very likely that the generally good showing by test prices is attributable to the steady buying pressure by nonwhites after entry began. That pressure was especially strengthened during 1954 and early 1955, when VA loans were more easily obtainable than before. The following statement by a leading local broker who has worked in the test area vicinity for many years is significant:

In late 1950, when Negroes first came in, the market went up because of their strong demand. At the present time [September, 1953] the market is at about the level it was when Negroes came in —perhaps a bit higher. Negroes haven't caused lower prices in this area. Actually they caused a boost that lasted at least a year. Before they came in, the market was very slow, properties often being listed for sale for six to eight weeks. They improved the market, and the average listing time decreased.[4]

The Test Area: Brookfield Village (T-2-O)

Location.—At the very southwest tip of Oakland, running along the east side of the East Shore Freeway. One mile east of the Bay and just north of Oakland's southern boundary.

Boundaries, topography, and features.—Bounded by Edes Avenue, 105th Avenue, and East Shore Freeway. Contains about twenty-seven blocks, many irregularly shaped, with some 900 homes. The land is quite level, almost entirely built on, and is all used for residences, except for portions of 98th Avenue. This street cuts through from east to west and has shopping and other business establishments. A light manufacturing and warehousing area lies in a narrow strip along Brookfield Village's east side, just across Edes Avenue.

Structures.—With the exception of a few scattered duplexes, this area has only single-family homes, predominantly owner-occupied. Mixed two- and three-bedroom homes, with two bedrooms in the majority. Sales data for two-bedroom units have been adjusted to make them comparable with three-bedroom units. Known as "California ranch-type," the houses are modest one-story frame construction with floor furnace and no basement. Most of this test area was built as a tract development in 1943–1944, to meet the housing needs of defense workers.

Condition (November, 1955): Good to very good.

Price range (November, 1955): Medium, $9,500–$11,000 (modal price $10,300).

Socioeconomic characteristics.—The descriptive comments made about Columbia Gardens apply precisely to this test area as well (see p. 125).

Racial changes: Precipitated by a similar set of conditions,

---

[4] Personal interview, September, 1953. These comments applied not only to Columbia Gardens but to the Brookfield Village test area as well.

nonwhite entry in Brookfield Village took place within three weeks of the first Columbia Gardens case, in late September, 1950. But the influx was not as rapid: by year's end there were only about ten nonwhite (Negro) families, or 1 percent of all families in the area, and even by the end of 1953, there were fewer than 100 families (10 percent). The tempo has gone up since then, with nonwhite occupancy reaching 20 percent in 1954 and jumping dramatically to 50 percent in 1955 (about 450 families). Over 90 percent of all sales now made are to Negroes.

At no time was there organized resistance or open hostility toward the incoming Negro families, although there is no question that many whites objected privately and then decided to move away. Real estate men say the area will become close to 100 percent Negro, but that the rate of transition from white to Negro may slow down from now on. This, they say, is because Negroes of somewhat lower socioeconomic status have been buying in recently, tending to discourage "better class Negroes" and thus slowing over-all sales activity.[5]

For reasons explained in the Columbia Gardens case, Brookfield Village was not under threat of nonwhite entry for any appreciable period before September, 1950, when the first sale to a Negro family took place.

The Control Areas: Sobrante Park; Davis North;
Davis South; San Lorenzo

Four closely comparable areas are available as controls for Brookfield Village. It is instructive to use them all. Since Davis South and San Lorenzo have already been mentioned in the Columbia Gardens case (p. 126), it is only necessary to add brief remarks about the other two control areas.

Sobrante Park (C-1-O).—Lies just south of the test area, but is clearly separated from it by a wide boundary street (105th Avenue) and an intervening strip of land. Bounded by 105th Avenue, Edes Avenue, Robledo Drive, and San Leandro Creek, it comprises a twelve-block area with 350 homes. These are highly comparable (often identical) to those in Brookfield Village,

---

[5] Personal interviews with local real estate brokers, August and September, 1955. See note 2 (p. 125) for other factors possibly accounting for the recent slow-up in sales.

except that the control area's generally more secluded atmosphere, lesser commercial development and traffic flow, and more pleasant appearance because of tree-lined streets, has caused home prices to be from $800 to $1,000 higher (about 9 percent) over the history of both neighborhoods. Age, style, construction details, size, and other structural details match almost identically with the test-area units.

Although Sobrante Park can be considered as exposed to a nonwhite entry threat, in the sense that Brookfield Village was increasing its nonwhite occupancy to 50 percent during the 1950–1955 period, it stayed all-white until February, 1955, with fifteen Negro families moving in by the following November. In comparison with San Lorenzo (another closely similar all-white area nowhere near any nonwhites) this control area shows the same pattern of price behavior, suggesting that whatever threat did exist had no discernible effect on prices. While it would not be wise to have it as the only control area, there is value in using it in company with three others under no threat of nonwhite entry.

Davis North (*C-2-O*).—Lies just south of San Leandro Creek and east of the East Shore Freeway. This places it inside the City of San Leandro and about a third of a mile south of the test area. It is a pleasant, entirely residential, level area of about nineteen blocks and 500 homes, closely resembling Sobrante Park in its environmental amenities. Due to these neighborhood factors, its price level has historically been about $600 to $800 (about 7 percent) above Brookfield Village, although the dwelling units themselves are very similar.

Price Analysis

Sales data are available over the period 1947–1955, for about 30 quarters in most cases. Transactions were as follows:

Area	Total sales	Average per quarter
Brookfield Village	228	7.4
Sobrante Park	199	6.9
San Lorenzo	347	11.6
Davis North	248	8.0
Davis South	137	4.6

Because the four control areas appear to divide themselves naturally into two slightly different behavior patterns, the price analysis is simplified by comparing Brookfield Village with a *pair*

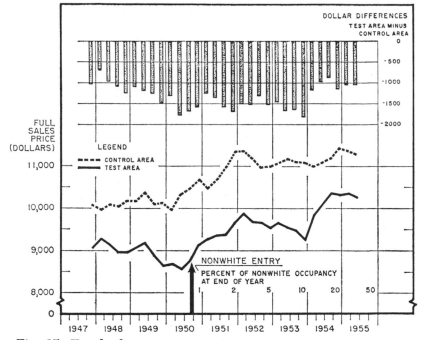

Fig. 17. Trend of average prices by quarters, 1947–1955: Oakland, Brookfield Village (test) and Sobrante Park (control).

of control areas at one time. Therefore, figures 17 and 18 show test price comparisons with Sobrante Park and San Lorenzo, while figures 19 and 20 present the data for Davis North and Davis South.

Compared with these first two control areas, Brookfield Village prices, on the average, moved closely parallel. Individual years obviously introduced some departures from this parallel movement, but inspection of the charts conveys a clear impression of similar price behavior.

Upward trends occurred in all three areas over the seven and a half year period, with the test area showing the largest increases, both absolutely and relatively:

Area	Average price before entry (12 quarters)	Average price after entry (last 4 quarters)	Increase	
			Amount	Percent
Brookfield Village (test).....	$ 8,935	$10,308	$1,373	15.4
Sobrante Park (control).....	10,135	11,160	1,007	9.9
San Lorenzo (control).......	10,300	11,286	986	9.6

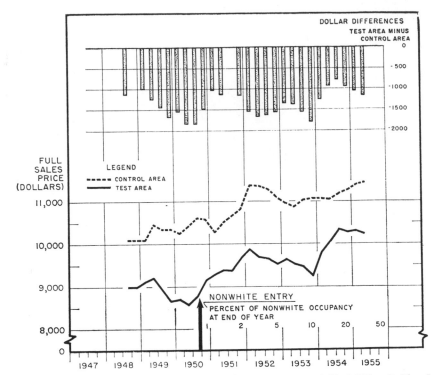

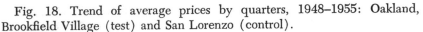

Fig. 18. Trend of average prices by quarters, 1948–1955: Oakland, Brookfield Village (test) and San Lorenzo (control).

For the test area, however, the trend did not turn up until mid-1950, shortly before nonwhite entry began. Up to that time, test prices fell by about $500 (from $9,000 to $8,500) as a result of the slow market in the general neighborhood, already discussed in the case of Columbia Gardens. The slow market affected Sobrante Park, too, but not as much as evidenced by the level price behavior up to the beginning trend rise in 1950. The greater attractiveness of Sobrante Park probably accounts for its some-what superior competitive performance.

Speaking broadly, test prices averaged $1,000 to $1,500 less than prices in either control area, and followed about this pattern throughout the period. From the beginning of the period to mid-1950 they dropped from $1,000 below to $1,500 below. During the year immediately following entry they recovered almost to the starting relationship. For the next two years (1952 and 1953) they stayed about $1,500 below, while nonwhite entry climbed to 10 percent. During the final six quarters they rose to within $800–$1,000 of control prices, while nonwhite entry was increasing to 50 percent.

The sharp price increase for Brookfield Village from mid-1950 to early 1952 was matched in each control area. Therefore, rather than being ascribable to any racial factor as such, it appears to have resulted from better demand conditions during the period. This would have to be the control-area explanation, too. The fact that the better demand situation in the test area came about through utilizing some of the pent-up *nonwhite* demand for shelter is worth noting, for it suggests that nonwhite entry can— under conditions such as these—raise prices. Obviously, *white* entry taking place in similar fashion would have similar economic effects (and evidently *did* in the two control areas).

Average price differences before and after entry are shown in the following table.

BROOKFIELD VILLAGE AND SOBRANTE PARK–SAN LORENZO

Period	Average difference in dollars (test price minus control price)		Test price as percent of control price (averages)	
	Sobrante Park	San Lorenzo	Sobrante Park	San Lorenzo
Before entry				
Fourth quarter, 1947, to second quarter, 1950	−1,218	....	88.0	....
Third quarter, 1948, to second quarter, 1950	....	−1,452	....	85.9
After entry				
Year ending with second quarter of:				
1951	−1,424	−1,200	86.7	88.5
1952	−1,484	−1,480	86.8	86.8
1953	−1,538	−1,439	86.1	86.9
1954	−1,191	−1,182	89.2	89.3
1955	−1,046	−1,043	90.8	90.8

These figures bear out what has already been said. During the years following nonwhite entry, test prices first fell from $200 to $300 lower than their average difference below Sobrante Park prices before entry, but later exceeded relative pre-entry levels. By contrast, they drew closer to control prices in San Lorenzo.

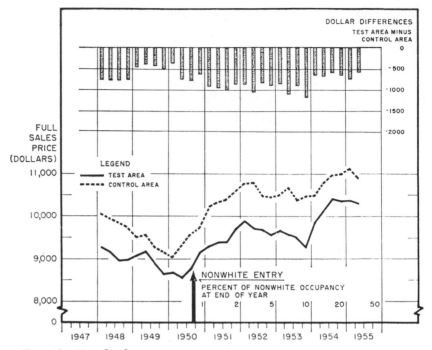

Fig. 19. Trend of average prices by quarters, 1948–1955: Oakland, Brookfield Village (test) and Davis North (control).

For the two closing years, test prices averaged only 9 to 11 percent less than control prices, compared with the 12 to 14 percent spread prevailing before entry occurred.

Turning to the comparison with the remaining control areas, figures 19 and 20 portray the data.

Practically everything said about the comparison with the first two control areas applies to this second pair. The most significant distinction involves control price behavior. Both these control areas seem to have experienced the local market slump already referred to at earlier points, so that their prices show absolute decreases until about mid-1950. Since this happened in the test area, too, but not as rapidly, the result is that price *differences* over this period became smaller. That is, test prices gained *relative* to control prices. The charts show this very clearly.

Once past the mid-1950 point, the relative price patterns are strikingly similar to those found in the first set of comparisons.

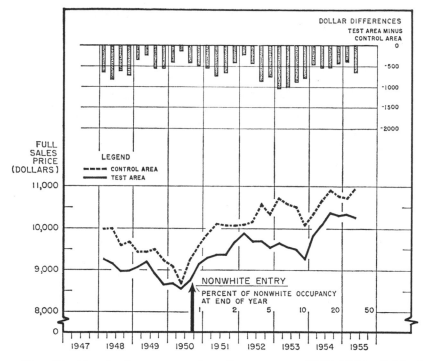

Fig. 20. Trend of average prices by quarters, 1948–1955: Oakland, Brookfield Village (test) and Davis South (control).

Presentation of the general trend figures and the price differences averaged by years follows:

Area	Average price before entry (11 or 12 quarters)	Average price after entry (last 4 quarters)	Increase	
			Amount	Percent
Brookfield Village (test).....	$8,935	$10,308	$1,373	15.4
Davis North (control).......	9,536	10,951	1,415	14.8
Davis South (control).......	9,427	10,808	1,381	14.6

Some minor fluctuations occurred, but the general pattern of average prices is one of almost complete conformity. The percent increase in average prices is practically identical for the test area —which experienced nonwhite entry approaching 50 percent in less than four and a half years—and the two all-white control neighborhoods. While control prices are about \$500 to \$600 higher than test prices, this difference was fairly steadily maintained throughout most of the 30 quarters of the observation period, as shown in the following table.

BROOKFIELD VILLAGE AND DAVIS NORTH–DAVIS SOUTH

Period	Average difference in dollars (test price minus control price)		Test price as percent of control price (averages)	
	Davis North	Davis South	Davis North	Davis South
Before entry First quarter, 1948, to third quarter, 1950...............	−610	−501	93.6	94.7
After entry Year ending with second quarter of:				
1951............................	−873	−612	91.4	93.8
1952............................	−909	−489	91.4	95.2
1953............................	−942	−958	91.0	90.9
1954............................	−769	−587	92.7	94.5
1955............................	−663	−489	93.9	95.5

Before any nonwhite entry, test prices were about 5 to 6 percent less than control prices in Davis North and Davis South. There was a minor tendency for this difference to become larger during 1953–1954, when test prices were about 7 to 9 percent under control prices. However, the last year of observation saw a return to the relationship that prevailed before nonwhite entry— in fact, test prices ended slightly closer to control prices than they were at the outset.

As in the Columbia Gardens case, Brookfield Village prices held their own with control prices over the period, probably because of the steady inflow of nonwhite buyers.

The Test Area: Elmhurst (T-3-O)

Location.—In the Elmhurst district, almost touching the boundary between Oakland and San Leandro, this test area lies at the southern edge of Oakland. It is situated just west of East 14th Street, halfway between the Bay and the San Leandro Hills. It is one mile east of the Columbia Gardens and Brookfield Village test areas.

Boundaries, topography, and features.—Bounded by 98th Avenue, East 14th Street, 107th Avenue, and E Street, this area takes in twenty-three blocks and about 600 homes. The interior land use is residential, but some business establishments exist along portions of the boundary streets. Area is level and fully built up.

Structures.—Mostly single-family units, 90 percent owner-occupied, but with considerable diversity in type, size, and construction. Equally divided between five- and six-room units (two and three bedrooms), with a few smaller and larger units scattered over the area. Frame construction, with stucco or rustic finish, average quality. Some two thirds of the homes were built in the 1942-1945 period, the rest in the interval, 1928–1935.

Condition (November, 1955): Good to very good.

Price range (November, 1955): Medium, $9,500–$12,000 (modal price $10,500).

Socioeconomic characteristics.—A middle- and lower-middle-class area, completely white until October, 1954. Provides convenient living area for many workers in the nearby industrial and warehousing areas of southern Oakland and San Leandro.

Racial changes: This area is in the general path of nonwhite settlement in the formerly all-white areas of South Oakland. Beginning in early 1950, the general picture is one of nonwhite entry and settlement moving southward from 55th Avenue and reaching Elmhurst by October, 1954. Entry—almost entirely Negro—proceeded rapidly, with no resistance or disturbance involved. Many white residents had already decided to move, in all probability to somewhat higher-priced homes in suburban areas, thereby making Elmhurst a more likely market for nonwhites. Entry impelled other whites to move out, so the nonwhite move-in was given great impetus. Nonwhites comprised 10 percent of all families by the end of 1954 (about 60 households) and reached 40 percent by September, 1955 (almost 250 families). Practically all current sales are to Negroes.

At the time of first nonwhite entry, the surrounding neighborhoods were all-white, so that no direct threat of entry existed. The extent to which Elmhurst residents were aware of the nonwhite settlement's gradually moving in their direction from the north is not known.

The Control Areas: Maxwell Park and Seminary D

Maxwell Park (C-5-O).— A large residential area in East Oakland, bounded by High Street, MacArthur Boulevard, 55th Avenue, and Fairfax Avenue. This takes in seventy-two blocks with some 1,800 parcels of property. Moderately hilly, with some duplexes and apartments scattered through the predominantly single-family area. Homes are two- or three-bedroom, stucco construction, and of the same general dimensions as those in Elmhurst. Owner-occupancy is about 75 percent. Condition and quality are good, with the year built varying between 1920 and 1935 in most cases (average age about 27 years as of 1955). Prices range higher than Elmhurst, running between $10,500 and $15,500 as of November, 1955, with a modal price of about $13,000.

Seminary D (C-6-O).—About half the size of Maxwell Park, this second control area lies just south of it, and is defined by 55th Avenue, Camden Street, and Foothill Boulevard. It has thirty blocks with some 600 homes. The description of Maxwell Park applies to this area as well, except that the price range is broader and at a slightly lower average. In 1955, the range was $9,500 to $16,000, with a modal price of about $12,500.

Price Analysis

Since the price ranges in the test area and both control areas are quite broad, and there is also considerable diversity in age and size of structures, the comparisons are better carried out on the basis of price/assessed valuation ratios, rather than direct price matchings.

For the 22 quarters furnishing both test and control data, each price has been divided by the 1950 assessed valuation figure for the property. The resulting ratios have been averaged by quarters and are shown in figures 21 and 22.

The following number of transactions were observed:

Area	Total sales	Average per quarter
Elmhurst	174	7.9
Maxwell Park	308	14.0
Seminary D	207	9.5

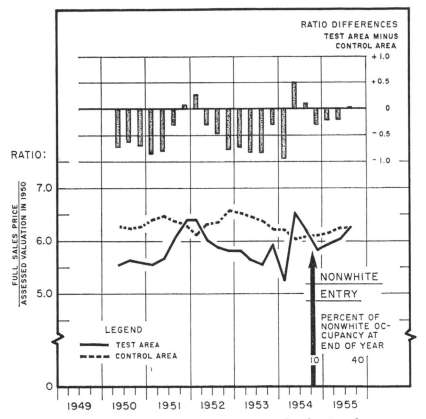

Fig. 21. Trend of average ratios, price/assessed valuation, by quarters, 1950–1955: Oakland, Elmhurst (test) and Maxwell Park (control).

Looking first at the broad price movements for all three areas together, it appears that the Elmhurst test area experienced a moderate percent increase (3.8) whereas the two control areas had minor decreases (1.4 and 2.8, respectively). These figures express the change between the average ratio for the last three quarters of the period and the average ratio for the 19 quarters before entry began. This is a somewhat unbalanced comparison in that data are available for only three quarters after nonwhite entry, but so long as the test and control neighborhoods are compared on the same basis the figures have some interpretive value.

Figure 21 shows the average ratios, by quarters, for the test area as compared with the first control area—Maxwell Park.

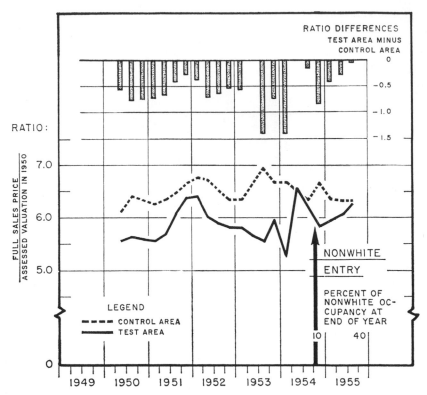

Fig. 22. Trend of average ratios, price/assessed valuation, by quarters, 1950–1955: Oakland, Elmhurst (test) and Seminary D (control).

Over the 22 quarters from early 1950 to late 1955, test prices rose at a faster rate than control prices, although with wider fluctuations. Both areas, at the period's close, showed prices averaging 6.3 times the assessed valuations for 1950. At the beginning, however, the test figure was only 5.6 as contrasted with 6.0 for the control area.

Although the test ratio did catch up by the end of the period, it was lower than the control ratio in all but four of the remaining quarters. The ratios moved together in parallel fashion during these periods: 1950 to mid-1951; late 1952 to mid-1953; and late 1954 to late 1955. At these times, the test ratio was typically 0.5 to 0.8 points below the control ratio.

The unusually sharp rise in the test ratio in the six months preceding nonwhite entry is not fully explainable. Some of it may be attributable to the boost given to the real estate market by easier VA terms during the year, but the control areas responded to this stimulus in a more restrained way.

Most significant is the unchecked, fairly rapid rise in test prices immediately after entry in October, 1954, as shown by the rise in test ratios. Within a year they went from 5.8 to 6.3—an 11 percent gain. Simultaneously, nonwhite occupancy was increasing to 40 percent in the area.

For the pre-entry period, test ratios averaged 0.44 points (6.9 percent) under control ratios, while the postentry period saw test ratios pull up to an average only 0.13 points below (2.1 percent).

While it is not feasible to extract much detail from the analysis of these ratios, it seems clear that test-area prices performed better after nonwhite entry than they did before. The briefness of the postentry period precludes a lengthy analysis of comparative test–control price behavior, yet the data that are available suggest that nonwhite entry did not harm and may have raised prices in the Elmhurst neighborhood.

Comparing Elmhurst with Seminary D ratios yields results very similar to those already presented, as figure 22 shows. Test and control ratios are seen to be in almost exactly the same relationship at the beginning and end of the observation period as they were for the first control-area comparison.

The chief difference here is that Seminary D has higher ratios than did Maxwell Park for many of the quarters in the years 1951–1955. Test ratios, therefore, are relatively lower more often in this second comparison.

Up to mid-1953, test ratios were typically about 0.6 points below control ratios—that is, about 9 percent under. From mid-1953 until late 1954 (just after entry) the average difference became larger, with test ratios dropping to nearly 1.5 points (20 percent) below control ratios in two quarters. After nonwhite entry, test ratios rapidly moved up to meet control ratios, while nonwhite occupancy was moving toward 40 percent.

For the pre-entry period, test ratios were an average 0.66 (10.1

percent) below control ratios, but they averaged within 0.24 (3.8 percent) of control ratios for the period after entry.

ELMHURST AND MAXWELL PARK–SEMINARY D

Period	Average differences (test ratio minus control ratio)		Test ratios as percent of control ratios (averages)	
	Maxwell Park	Seminary D	Maxwell Park	Seminary D
Before entry Second quarter, 1950, to third quarter, 1954.....	−0.4	−0.7	93.1	89.9
After entry Four quarters ending third quarter, 1955........	−0.2	−0.2	97.9	96.2

Comparison with both control areas, then, indicates that very heavy and rapid nonwhite entry and relatively better price performance occurred together in the Elmhurst test area.

HEAVY NONWHITE ENTRY: ONE NEIGHBORHOOD

The Test Area: Seminary C (T-4-O)

Location.—Toward the southern tip of Oakland, about one mile north of the city limits and halfway between the Bay and the San Leandro Hills. This test area is just east of East 14th Street and roughly a mile north and east of test areas Brookfield Village and Elmhurst.

Boundaries, topography, and features.—Bounded by East 14th Street and Birch Street, between 83rd and 88th Avenues, this area embraces eighteen blocks with about 500 homes. Land use is residential, with commercial development along East 14th Street. The area is fully built up.

Structures.—Houses are predominantly single-family, owner-occupied, varying in size from four to six rooms (two or three bedrooms). Some diversity in design is noticeable resulting from construction by a number of builders at several building periods. Frame construction, stucco finish, average quality. Definitely an older neighborhood, with two-thirds of the units built during 1925–1935, and the other third primarily dating from 1942–1945.

Condition (November, 1955): Good.

Price range (November, 1955): Medium, $8,000–$12,500 (modal price about $10,500).

Socioeconomic characteristics.—Similar to the Elmhurst test area in its middle- and lower-middle-class structure, but with more emphasis on lower-middle. All-white until October, 1953. A living area for many industrial workers employed in the general vicinity.

Racial Changes: Being closer to the starting point of the non-white settlement belt described under Elmhurst, Seminary C experienced entry earlier than Elmhurst. A Negro family purchased a home there in October, 1953, and some ten additional Negro families brought nonwhite occupancy to 2 percent by that year's end. Entry proceeded much more slowly than in Elmhurst, however, so that, in the two years to the end of the observation period, a total of about 75 nonwhite families (mostly Negro) brought the nonwhite occupancy figure to a moderate 14 percent. This is still "heavy entry" as defined for this study, but considerably lighter than observed in the other "heavy entry" test areas.

Scattered nonwhite residence existed to the north of this test area as early as mid-1952, but it was under 5-percent and could hardly be considered a threat to Seminary C in any mass invasion sense. Again, however, it is not known to what extent Seminary C residents feared nonwhite entry before it actually started. Judging by the relatively slow increase of Negroes in the area, homes were not put up for sale at the rate observed in Elmhurst, implying less disturbance among the white homeowners.

The Control Areas: Maxwell Park and Seminary D

These are the same controls used for the Elmhurst test area and are described on p. 142.

Price Analysis

Ratios of price divided by 1950 assessed valuation are used to depict price behavior because of considerable diversity in the price data.

Ratios averaged by quarters are shown in figures 23 and 24. Transactions numbered 164 for the test area during the 22-quarter period (7.5 per quarter), as aganst 308 and 190 for the control areas (14.0 and 8.6 per quarter, respectively).

General price trends in the three neighborhoods, as indicated by price/assessed valuation ratios, were as follows:

Area	Average ratio before entry (14 quarters)	Average ratio after entry (last 4 quarters)	Change	
			Amount	Percent
Seminary C (test)...........	6.40	7.05	+0.65	+10.2
Maxwell Park (control).....	6.36	6.19	−0.17	−2.7
Seminary D (control).......	6.49	6.41	−0.08	−1.2

The test neighborhood showed a 10 percent increase over the average level for the pre-entry period, whereas the two control areas displayed minor decreases. During the postentry period, nonwhite occupancy rose steadily toward a 14 percent proportion of the Seminary C households.

Figure 23 presents the average ratios for the test area as con-

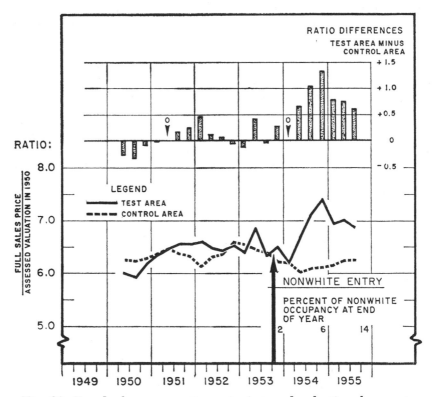

Fig. 23. Trend of average ratios, price/assessed valuation, by quarters, 1950–1955: Oakland, Seminary C (test) and Maxwell Park (control).

trasted with the first control area, Maxwell Park. It is at once apparent from the chart that test prices moved up relatively faster than control prices over the period as a whole. In the initial quarter compared (second, 1950), control area houses sold for prices averaging 6.3 times their 1950 assessed valuations, while the test ratio was 6.0. One year later, test ratios equaled control ratios at the 6.5 level, and moved higher than control ratios in all but three of the remaining quarters. Test ratios ended at 6.9, appreciably above the control figure of 6.3. Whereas control ratios stayed between 6.0 and 6.6 the entire time, exhibiting an almost horizontal trend, test ratios moved from 6.0 to about the 7.0 level and showed a definitely rising trend.

The increase in test ratios following nonwhite entry in October, 1953, is especially striking. While there was a fairly stable pattern in the two years before entry, test ratios moved up sharply afterward, resulting in large positive margins over control ratios.

The average ratio differences for the two postentry years, as measured against the average level obtaining for the period before entry, are shown below.

SEMINARY C AND MAXWELL PARK

Period	Average differences (test ratio minus control ratio)	Test ratio as percent of control ratio (averages)
Before entry Second quarter, 1950, to third quarter, 1953..............	+0.34	100.7

After entry
Year ending with third quarter of:
  1954.........................
  1955.........................
	+0.49
	+0.86
		108.1
		114.1

Test prices were practically identical with control prices before nonwhite entry, but pulled rapidly away during the two postentry years. By the end of the observation period, Seminary C test prices stood about 14 percent above control prices.

Figure 24 shows test vs. Seminary D control ratios. These behave in similar fashion, relative to each other, to those noted in the first comparison with Maxwell Park. Because Seminary D ratios are slightly higher than those for Maxwell Park in a num-

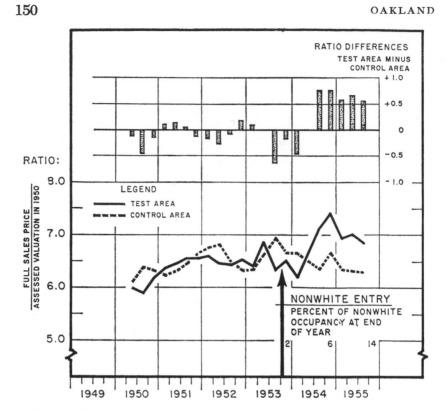

Fig. 24. Trend of average ratios, price/assessed valuation, by quarters, 1950–1955: Oakland, Seminary C (test) and Seminary D (control).

ber of quarters, test ratios do not exceed control ratios by as large margins.

Test prices at the period's beginning averaged only six times 1950 assessed valuations, as compared with an average control area ratio of 6.1. By the final quarter (third, 1955) the test figure was up 15 percent to 6.9, as against a control rise of 3 percent to 6.3.

During the observation period, test ratios were below control ratios more often than above, until the third quarter after non-white entry. After that, with nonwhite occupancy moving from 6 to 14 percent, test ratios exceeded control ratios by margins of 0.5 to 0.75 points.

Ratio comparisons for yearly periods, as measured against the average level for the pre-entry period, are shown in the following table.

SEMINARY C AND SEMINARY D

Period	Average differences (test ratio minus control ratio)	Test ratio as percent of control ratio (averages)

Before entry
  Second quarter, 1950, to
    third quarter, 1953.............
	−0.10	98.5

After entry
  Year ending with third quarter of:
    1954.........................
	+0.53	107.1

1955.........................	+0.64	110.0

Again, as in the first comparison, the dramatic upsweep for test area prices following nonwhite entry is clearly revealed. From a position 1.5 percent below the control ratio during the pre-entry period, Seminary C test prices rose to a level 10 percent above by the end of the observation period.

The Seminary C neighborhood therefore shows favorable relative price behavior associated with considerable nonwhite inflow at a moderate rate.

MEDIUM NONWHITE ENTRY: THREE NEIGHBORHOODS

The Test Area: Seminary A (T-5-O)

Location.—In the Seminary district, two miles north of Oakland's southern boundary. It forms a four-block wide strip for a mile along the eastern side of East 14th Street. Test area Seminary B adjoins it to the east and Seminary C is half a mile to the south.

Boundaries, topography, and features.—This area lies between 55th and 73rd Avenues, with East 14th Street as its west boundary. The east boundary moves irregularly over nine streets about four blocks from East 14th Street, beginning with Scoville Street at 55th Avenue and ending with Orral Street at 73rd Avenue. Fully built up, the area is fairly level and—except along East 14th Avenue—occupied by residential structures.

Structures.—While there are a few duplexes and apartments, the area is predominantly single-family dwelling units, with about

85 percent owner-occupancy. Five- and six-room units form the bulk of the structures, but a few four- and seven-room homes are scattered through the area. Houses are of frame construction, largely stucco exterior, of average quality. About 90 percent of the homes were built in the 1920–1930 decade, making the area definitely an older one. The rest were built during the 1942–1947 period. All were in good condition as of November, 1955, with many of the older homes having been remodeled or refurbished.

Price range (November, 1955): Low to medium, $6,000–$13,000 (modal price about $10,000).

Socioeconomic characteristics.—A middle- and lower-middle-class residential neighborhood. All-white until March, 1950, with a mixed white- and blue-collar population mostly employed in downtown Oakland businesses or industrial operations in south Oakland and San Leandro.

Racial changes: As discussed in connection with the Elmhurst test area, this area was the "origin point" for nonwhite (predominantly Negro) entry and settlement in the general region of southern Oakland. Starting at 55th Avenue in early 1950, nonwhites moved in gradually. The white residents accepted this development without discernible excitement. Three and a half years later, by the end of 1953, nonwhites were living at the south end of Seminary A, and constituted about 5 percent of all households.

It is somewhat surprising to find the rate of entry so gradual in an area where racial change for the large south Oakland region began. By the end of 1955, nonwhite occupancy had reached only 7 percent. A reasonable explanation might be that the absence of excitement and open hostility on the part of white residents signifies an underlying attachment to the neighborhood which made them reluctant to leave. Obviously, nonwhites can buy into a neighborhood only to the extent that homes are placed on the market.

Nonwhite entry into Seminary A took place unexpectedly in the sense that the nearest nonwhite residence area lay about a mile north. Thus no direct nonwhite entry threat existed so far as Seminary A residents in general were concerned. Of course, once entry began, in March 1950, it became known to white home-

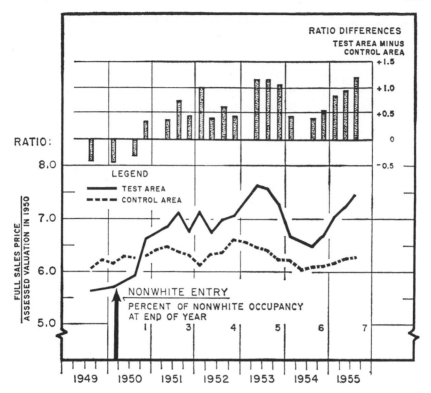

Fig. 25. Trend of average ratios, price/assessed valuation, by quarters, 1949–1955: Oakland, Seminary A (test) and Maxwell Park (control).

owners living just to the south, and this knowledge spread southward with nonwhite settlement.

The Control Areas: Maxwell Park and Seminary D

The control areas already used for test areas Elmhurst and Seminary C serve for this test area as well and have been described in the section on p. 142.

Price Analysis

Ratios of price to 1950 assessed valuation serve better than direct price comparisons, for the same reasons cited under Elmhurst and Seminary C. Over the 25 quarters for which sales data are available (mid-1949 to late-1955), there were 122 transactions for

Seminary A, as compared with 360 and 190 for the two control areas. Maxwell Park shows a much larger total, due to its three-fold greater area.

Price/assessed valuation ratios are plotted in figures 25 and 26. As compared with both sets of control ratios, test ratios showed a much larger percent increase over the pre-entry level:

Area	Average ratio before entry (3 quarters)	Average ratio after entry (last 4 quarters)	Increase	
			Amount	Percent
Seminary A (test)...........	5.67	7.08	1.41	24.9
Maxwell Park (control).....	6.14	6.19	0.05	0.8
Seminary D (control).......	5.98	6.41	0.43	7.2

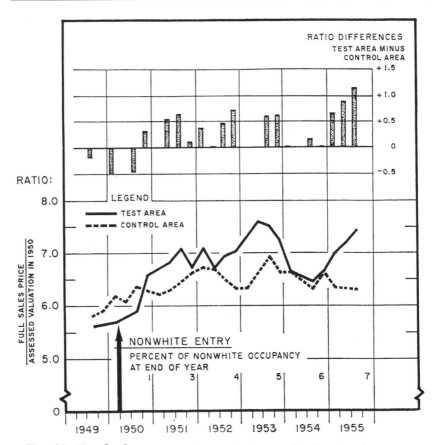

Fig. 26. Trend of average ratios, price/assessed valuation, by quarters, 1949–1955: Oakland, Seminary A (test) and Seminary D (control).

The ratio figures indicate that test prices started below control prices in the period before nonwhite entry, then rose almost 25 percent by the end of the period, far outdistancing control prices. During the five and a half year interval after entry, nonwhite occupancy in the Seminary A neighborhood rose to 7 percent. Both control areas showed minor price increases, with Maxwell Park maintaining practically a horizontal price trend for the same period in which test prices rose so sharply.

Figure 25 presents ratios averaged by quarters for the test area as compared with Maxwell Park. Test ratios climbed from 5.6 (selling price was 5.6 times the 1950 assessed valuation, on the average) to 7.4. Control ratios increased from 6.0 to 6.3. Close inspection of figure 25 shows that the *direction* of movement was the same for test and control ratios at any particular time, but that the *rate* was steeper for test ratios. Since 22 of the 25 quarters are after nonwhite entry, this suggests that Seminary A was quite "price sensitive" as it experienced racial change. Whether it was more sensitive than before entry cannot be demonstrated from the data available.

Despite its greater swings above and below its average upward movement, the test ratio pattern is one of strong superiority relative to control ratios. Averaged by years, the differences between test and control ratios are as follows:

SEMINARY A AND MAXWELL PARK

Period	Average differences (test ratio minus control ratio)	Test ratio as percent of control ratio (averages)
Before entry Third quarter, 1949, to first quarter, 1950..............	−0.43	92.9
After entry Year ending with first quarter of: 1951.........................	0.0	100.0
1952.........................	+0.63	110.0
1953.........................	+0.49	107.9
1954.........................	+0.95	115.0
1955.........................	+0.61	109.9
1956 (first half)...............	+1.08	117.2

From an average position 7 percent under Maxwell Park, test ratios climbed fairly steadily above control ratios, ending more than 17 percent above them. Allowing for some roughness in the use of price/assessed valuation ratios as area price indicators, this is a good sign of a price superiority for test prices over the period. The picture after entry, and steadily through the increase to 7 percent in nonwhite occupancy, is a positive one for Seminary A. Medium nonwhite entry, occurring in an orderly and gradual way, is associated with a strong upward price movement in this test area.

Comparison with the second control area (figure 26) yields very much the same picture. In general, the relative performance of test and control ratios was as described under the first control area analysis. The principal differences arise because Seminary D has generally higher ratios than Maxwell Park, so that test ratios do not lie quite so far above them.

Test ratios started out slightly below control ratios (5.6 versus 5.8). They moved above control ratios in the third quarter of 1950, six months after nonwhite entry began, and stayed above by an average margin of about 0.6 (8 to 10 percent) from then on. They closed at 7.4, compared with the 6.3 control ratio.

Averaged by years the ratio differences are as shown in the following table.

SEMINARY A AND SEMINARY D

Period	Average differences (test ratio minus control ratio)	Test ratio as percent of control ratio (averages)
Before entry Third quarter, 1949, to first quarter, 1950..............	−0.34	94.4
After entry Year ending with first quarter of:		
1951.........................	−0.10	98.5
1952.........................	+0.40	106.1
1953.........................	+0.40	106.1
1954.........................	+0.39	105.8
1955.........................	+0.27	104.3
1956 (first half)...............	+1.00	115.8

Examination of the average differences as percents of the control ratios reveals a pattern almost identical to that found in the first control area comparison. Test ratios started 5.6 percent under Seminary D ratios, pulled almost even during the first four quarters after nonwhite entry, and remained well ahead for the rest of the observation period. They ended almost 16 percent higher than control ratios.

The comparison with Seminary D strengthens the conclusion reached on the first comparison with Maxwell Park. For this test area of Seminary A it appears that nonwhite settlement over a five and a half year interval, occurring without excitement and reaching the moderate level of 7 percent of all families in the area, operated to raise average prices above the level attained in two similar all-white neighborhoods.

The Test Area: Seminary B (T-6-O)

Location.—In the Seminary district, midway between Mills College and the East Shore Freeway, and two miles from Oakland's southern boundary. It shares a boundary with test area Seminary A, which lies along its west side.

Boundaries, topography, and features.—Bounded by 55th Avenue, Foothill Boulevard, Bond Street, 73rd Avenue, and the common boundary with test area Seminary A. This is the largest Oakland test area, amounting to forty-six blocks and approximately thirteen hundred dwellings. The land slopes down gently from Foothill Boulevard, is fully built upon, and is predominantly used for residential purposes.

Structures.—Dwellings in this area have the same characteristics as those in Seminary A, described on p. 151. Actually, Seminary A and Seminary B together form one large residential neighborhood. They are separated for analysis only because nonwhite settlement was definitely confined to the western side of Seminary A until late 1953.

One distinction should be mentioned: selling prices are noticeably higher in the more elevated section just below Foothill Boulevard. This puts Seminary B's price range slightly higher than Seminary A's, as of November, 1955: $8,000–$15,000 (modal price about $11,500).

Socioeconomic characteristics.—Solidly middle class, with a sprinkling of professional people among the stable white- and blue-collar groups. Some variance in social status from street to street: Havenscourt Boulevard, for example, is an interior street with a prestige and price level somewhat above the streets around it.

Racial changes: The original nonwhite settlement in south Oakland occurred just to the west of this test area in Seminary A. Seminary B was merely a "witness" to this development during the three and a half years that the nonwhite pattern moved southward from 55th to 73rd Avenue. Not until October, 1953, did Negro settlement move across the Seminary A–Seminary B boundary. Over the next two years about 80 nonwhite families, predominantly Negroes, bought homes throughout Seminary B, although the higher prestige streets referred to remained all-white nearly to the end of the period. Nonwhite occupancy thus approached 7 percent by the fall of 1955, taking place with little or no excitement on the part of the white residents.

As in the Seminary A area, the gradual entry by nonwhites bears out the view that relatively few white homeowners became sufficiently concerned to put their homes on the market.

It can be argued that the presence of from 1 to 7 percent nonwhite occupancy in the adjoining Seminary A test area, over the 1950–1953 period, created an invasion threat for Seminary B. However, the price analysis does not show that fear of such a threat affected the level of selling prices.

The Control Areas: Maxwell Park and Seminary D.

The control areas used for Elmhurst, Seminary A, and Seminary C are also well suited for Seminary B. These two control areas have already been described in relation to Elmhurst (p. 142).

Price Analysis

For all three areas the price diversity due to varying structure size is such that ratios of price to 1950 assessed valuation are much more satisfactory than direct price averages.

During the 22-quarter observation period, from early 1950 to late 1955, data for 320 test area transactions were available, as compared with 308 for Maxwell Park and 190 for Seminary D. Price/assessed valuation ratios are plotted in figures 27 and 28.

Looking first at the general price trends in all three areas, as measured from the average pre-entry level, it appears that test prices moved up more than did control prices:

Area	Average ratio before entry (14 quarters)	Average ratio after entry (last 4 quarters)	Change	
			Amount	Percent
Seminary B (test).........	6.47	6.77	+0.3	+4.6
Maxwell Park (control).....	6.36	6.19	−0.17	−2.7
Seminary D (control).......	6.49	6.41	−0.08	−1.2

Both control areas showed practically horizontal price trends over the same time span for which the test trend rose moderately. All three neighborhoods had very much the same average ratio during the pre-entry period, but they diverged after the entry date, as indicated by the average for the last four quarters of the period. During the postentry interval, the test area experienced nonwhite entry that was growing toward 7 percent by the close of 1955.

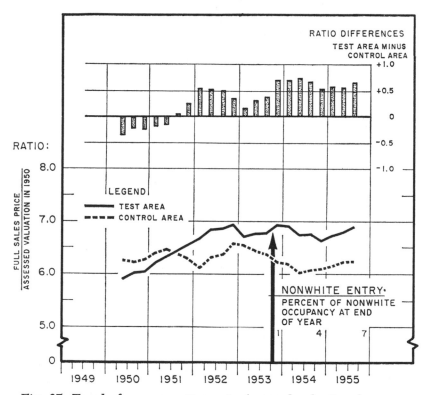

Fig. 27. Trend of average ratios, price/assessed valuation, by quarters, 1950–1955: Oakland, Seminary B (test) and Maxwell Park (control).

The divergence is larger between the test area and Maxwell Park because that control area showed a larger decrease in its price trend for the particular quarters considered. Quarterly averages of the ratios for this pair of areas are shown in figure 27.

Relative to Maxwell Park control area, Seminary B ratios behaved about as observed for Seminary A and C. Selling prices in the test area moved from an average 5.9 times 1950 assessed valuations at the outset to a ratio of 6.9 by the end of the period. The corresponding ratios for the control area were 6.3 and 6.3— no increase at all.

Test ratios first exceeded control ratios in mid-1951, and stayed well above from then on. This happened during the same three and a half years that nonwhite occupancy was increasing in adjoining test area Seminary A, suggesting that no adverse price reaction in Seminary B arose because of a fear of nonwhite entry. The differences between test and control ratios before and after nonwhite entry are shown in the table following.

SEMINARY B AND MAXWELL PARK

Period	Average differences (test ratio minus control ratio)	Test ratio as percent of control ratio (averages)
Before entry Second quarter, 1950, to third quarter, 1953.............	+0.14	102.1
After entry Year ending third quarter of: 1954...................... 1955......................	+0.71 +0.58	111.5 109.4

Before nonwhites came into Seminary B, it showed ratios averaging about 2 percent higher than those for the all-white Maxwell Park neighborhood. After entry, test ratios rose to a level about 10 percent above control ratios. Apparently, the entry of nonwhites was associated with a relative improvement in the price level of the test area as contrasted with all-white Maxwell Park. As figure 27 shows, the upward trend in test ratios stopped by the end of 1952, one year before entry began, and after that date test ratios maintained a fairly steady horizontal trend. While this might have been related to the changing racial pattern, it could also have resulted from a slowing down due to any number of

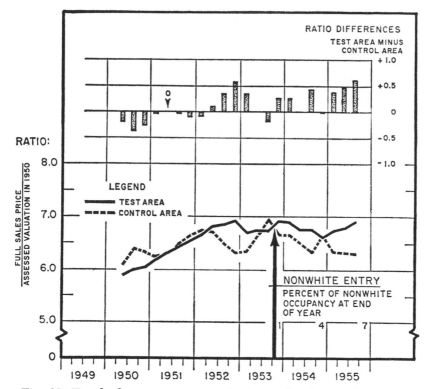

Fig. 28. Trend of average ratios, price/assessed valuation, by quarters, 1950–1955: Oakland, Seminary B (test) and Seminary D (control).

other causes. The only certainty in the situation is that test ratios stayed above ratios for the comparable all-white Maxwell Park neighborhood.

Figure 28 presents the quarterly averages of price-assessed valuation ratios for Seminary B and the second control area, Seminary D. As compared with this second control area, test prices performed in much the same way as they did in relation to the first: Figure 28 shows test ratios starting lower and ending higher than control ratios, but the relative climb is not as sharp as in the first comparison. Obviously, this is because Seminary D control ratios lie somewhat higher than do Maxwell Park's.

As the period began, the test ratio was slightly under the control ratio (5.9 as against 6.1). It drew equal at the 6.3 level in mid-1951 and climbed steadily ahead in early 1952. In the quarter just before entry occurred in October, 1953, the test ratio was slightly below, but this was due to a sudden control peak rather than to a test ratio dip. Staying above for the rest of the period, the test ratio ended markedly higher (6.9 versus 6.3). This took place while nonwhite occupancy moved toward 7 percent.

Test ratios minus control ratios yielded larger differences after nonwhite entry than before.

SEMINARY B AND SEMINARY D

Period	Average differences (test ratio minus control ratio)	Test ratio as percent of control ratio (averages)
Before entry Second quarter, 1950, to third quarter, 1953..............	0.00	100.0
After entry Year ending with third quarter of: 1954.........................	+0.31	104.8
1955.........................	+0.36	105.7

There was no difference between the test and control ratios when differences were averaged over the 14-quarter pre-entry period. After entry, ratio differences turned in favor of the test area by about 5 or 6 percent, while nonwhite occupancy moved toward 7 percent of the test-area houses.

It is apparent that Seminary B, adjacent to an area with 7 percent nonwhite occupancy, and itself experiencing a nonwhite inflow of similar proportions during the 1953–1955 period, showed selling prices moving up more strongly than those in the two all-white control areas.

The Test Area: Oak Knoll (T-7-O)

Location.—In the Oak Knoll district, at the base of the San Leandro Hills, one and one quarter miles from Oakland's southern boundary. Test areas Elmhurst and Seminary C are a mile to the west.

Boundaries, topography, and features.—Bounded by MacArthur Boulevard, Marlin Street, Burr Avenue, Stearns Avenue, and 98th Avenue. This is the smallest Oakland test area studied, containing seven blocks and some 185 dwellings. Moderately hilly, the land slopes down to the west and is entirely residential in use.

Structures.—A single-family home area, with 90 percent owner-occupancy. California style bungalows predominate and are equally divided between the two- and three-bedroom categories. Frame and stucco construction, of good quality. About half the homes were built in the 1920–1930 decade; the rest in 1943–1950. Condition was good to excellent as of November, 1955. At that time, the price range was $9,500–$16,000 (medium to high), with the modal price at about $13,500.

Socioeconomic characteristics.—Middle- and upper-middle-class neighborhood, having a more than average cohesiveness because of its almost self-contained street pattern.

Racial changes: The first Negro purchase in this area took place in September, 1954, just one month before Elmhurst also experienced entry. One year later there were about ten Negro families living in Oak Knoll as homeowners, amounting to 6 percent of all families. At present, further Negro entry is proceeding quite rapidly. No hysteria or open hostility has been evident at any time since entry started.

There was no threat of entry before September, 1954, because no concentration of nonwhites lived closer than Seminary C, a mile away. While the number of nonwhites is small, as is the test area itself, there is a special significance attached to this case. MacArthur Boulevard is a major thoroughfare (U. S. Highway 50) and separates the hill areas from the level residential neighborhoods to the west. Its crossing by nonwhites suggests new developments in the changing racial pattern in housing, with nonwhites beginning to enter the more desirable, more expensive residential areas. The East Piedmont Heights and Montclair test areas discussed below, are additional examples of this trend.

The Control Area: Millsmont (C-7-O)

A large residential area comprising forty-two blocks and about 840 homes, just south of the Mills College campus. Boundary streets are Seminary Avenue, Mountain Boulevard, Burckhalter Avenue, 73rd Avenue, and Monadnock Way. Comparable in all respects to Oak Knoll, but better situated in relation to shopping areas and downtown Oakland. The nearest nonwhites are located in the Seminary B test area, one-half mile to the west.

Price Analysis

Although the two areas to be compared are very similar, each displays a fairly wide price range because of the size and age diversity in dwelling units. Therefore, once again, the ratio of selling price to 1950 assessed valuation is used, rather than the selling price as such.

For the 22-quarter period, from early 1950 to late 1955, there were 71 test sales and 204 control area sales. These data were used to compute the ratios plotted in figure 29.

Test ratios dropped below their pre-entry level, whereas control ratios showed a slight increase over the same time span:

Area	Average ratio before entry (18 quarters)	Average ratio after entry (last 4 quarters)	Change	
			Amount	Percent
Oak Knoll (test)............	6.38	6.10	−0.28	−4.4
Millsmont (control)........	6.15	6.21	+0.06	+1.0

The before-and-after entry picture is one of reversed roles for the two areas. Whereas test ratios stayed above control ratios, on the average, during the 18 quarters that both areas were all-white, they fell below during the four quarters immediately after entry. Test ratios fell 4.4 percent while control ratios rose 1 percent. Figure 29 portrays these shifts.

A study of the chart reveals that while both test and control ratios ended almost precisely at their respective starting levels, test ratios did not quite maintain their initial superiority.

At the start, the test ratio was 6.1, slightly above the 5.9 control figure. Test ratios held or increased this lead until late 1953, when steeply climbing control ratios passed them. Out of the eight quarters following this reversal, test ratios were higher than control ratios in only two, one being the final quarter of the observation period.

Nonwhite entry occurred in September, 1954. In the two preceding quarters, the test ratio rose sharply, but declined in the two quarters after entry. So did the control ratio, for that matter, and without showing the upturn that occurred for the test ratio in early 1955.

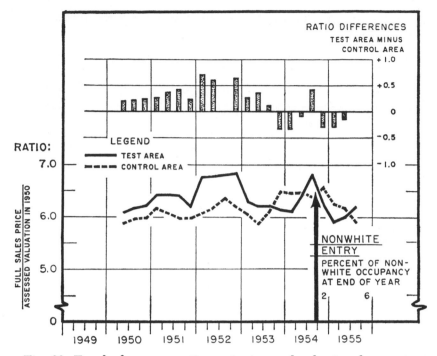

Fig. 29. Trend of average ratios, price/assessed valuation, by quarters, 1950–1955: Oakland, Oak Knoll (test) and Millsmont (control).

The impressions obtained by studying figure 29 are confirmed by the average of the differences between test and control ratios, before and after entry, as shown in the table below.

OAK KNOLL AND MILLSMONT

Period	Average differences (test ratio minus control ratio)	Test ratio as percent of control ratio (averages)
Before entry Second quarter, 1950, to third quarter, 1954..............	+0.24	103.8
After entry Year ending with third quarter of: 1955.........................	−0.24	98.2

While test ratios (and therefore prices) were about 4 percent higher than control figures before nonwhite entry, they were almost 2 percent lower after entry. The presence of nonwhites may have brought about this relative fall in Oak Knoll prices, but the shortness of the period following entry makes such a conclusion somewhat premature. As figure 29 shows, test ratios started up again during 1955, whereas control ratios were still heading downward. If these relative movements should persist, the unfavorable test area results would soon be reversed. Additional observation is called for before a final answer can be given in this matter.

LIGHT NONWHITE ENTRY: ONE NEIGHBORHOOD

The Test Area: East Piedmont Heights (T-8-O)

Location.—In northeast Oakland, between Lake Merritt and Piedmont, two miles east of the downtown center.

Boundaries, topography, and features.—A fifteen-block area bounded by Santa Ray, Balfour, Arimo, and Carlston Avenues, with about 450 homes. Situated on hilly terrain generally sloped to the south, with tree-lined streets for the most part following the contour lines. Entirely residential, this neighborhood is above average in attractiveness. Most homes have outstanding views and well-kept gardens.

Structures.—Predominantly a single-family home neighborhood, but with some duplexes. Most units are two-story design, because of the sloped ground, and have three or four bedrooms. Owner-occupancy is over 90 percent. Frame and stucco construction, of above average quality. Although structural condition is good to excellent, this is an older neighborhood, having been almost completely built up by 1935. Most homes were built in the late 1920's. The price range, at the end of 1955, was wide, and can be termed medium to high. The extremes were $13,500 and $24,000, with a clustering tendency evident around $17,500.

Socioeconomic characteristics.—A typical middle- and upper-middle-class area, having a natural identity due to the topography and street pattern. All white-collar and professional people, whose larger incomes are implied by a large proportion of two-car families.

Racial changes: A Negro family began the nonwhite entry of this area in March, 1954. The sale to a Negro buyer took place because the owner was at odds with his neighbor across the street and wanted to disturb him. Needing to move anyway, he seized the opportunity for a spite sale. Surrounding areas were—and still are—all-white.

While this sale provoked some neighborhood excitement, there was no organized opposition nor any individual act of hostility. This is significant, in view of the semiexclusive character of the neighborhood. The surrounding areas are also of this character— often more so—and the City of Piedmont, a local symbol of exclusiveness, begins just two blocks to the northeast.

Further Negro entry took place at an average rate of one family every six or seven weeks. By September, 1955, twelve Negro families had purchased and occupied homes throughout the area, and constituted 2.5 percent of all families. In most cases they bought properties at the upper end of the test-area price range.

Further Negro entry is expected by residents and real estate brokers alike, and nonwhite occupancy may eventually become fairly high. This is quite likely since the area is attractive to Negro families at professional income levels, who have less access to desirable residential areas within their means than do nonwhites who seek more modest homes.

As in the Oak Knoll and Montclair test area cases, entry of this area by nonwhites is part of their very recent movement into better-class neighborhoods in the San Francisco Bay Area, and has more significance than the small number of families involved might suggest.

The Control Area: Lakeshore Highlands (C-8-O)

Located just south of the test area, but definitely separated from it by the strong barrier formed by Mandana Boulevard and the steep ridge paralleling it to the south. An eighteen-block area of about 370 homes, bounded by Mandana Boulevard, Mandana Circle, Underhills Road, Hillcroft Circle, Northvale Road, and Rosemount Road.

Very comparable to the test area in terrain and with the same pattern of tree-lined contour streets. Properties are somewhat larger and more pretentious, and have more elaborate gardening and landscaping. Houses are generally five to ten years younger and maintenance is superior to that in the test area. All one-family homes, predominantly two-story stucco, and with nearly complete owner-occupancy. Prices range from $15,000 to $29,000 and cluster around $23,000.

Price Analysis

The use of price/assessed valuation ratios rather than direct selling prices is obviously indicated here, due to the diversity of prices in both areas, and also to the difference in the modal price level between the areas. Selling prices are divided by 1950 assessed valuations and the resulting ratios are averaged by quarters.

For the 22 quarters observed (early 1950 to late 1955) there were 60 test sales and 83 control sales—2.7 and 3.8 per quarter,

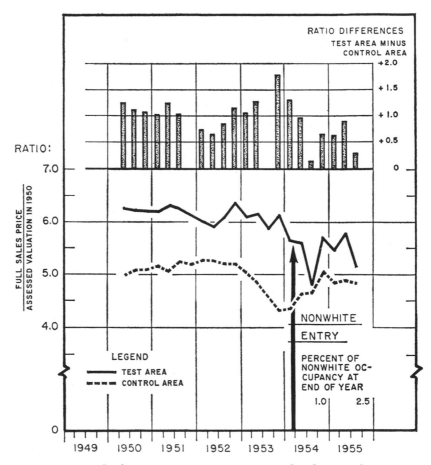

Fig. 30. Trend of average ratios, price/assessed valuation, by quarters, 1950–1955: Oakland, East Piedmont Heights (test) and Lakeshore Highlands (control)

respectively. These data were the basis for the ratios shown in figure 30.

Changes in price levels since the date when nonwhites came into the East Piedmont Heights neighborhood are as follows:

Area	Average ratio before entry (16 quarters)	Average ratio after entry (last 4 quarters)	Decrease	
			Amount	Percent
East Piedmont Heights (test)	6.11	5.53	0.58	9.5
Lakeshore Highlands (control)	5.02	4.91	0.11	2.2

Average ratios fell in both areas, when measured against the level prevailing during the pre-entry period, but the fall was more severe for the test area. Test ratios dropped nearly 10 percent by the last four quarters of the observation period, whereas control ratios declined only 2 percent. Examination of figure 30 suggests that test ratios maintained their gradual long-term downward trend throughout the period, whereas control ratios interrupted a similar tendency by turning upward from the end of 1953 on. During the postentry period, nonwhite occupancy was increasing toward 2.5 percent.

The illustration shows prices moving downward in both areas, for the period as a whole. The fall in test prices, however, was larger and more continuous than for control prices. Test prices averaged 6.3 times assessed valuations as the period started, as compared with the 5.0 control ratio. The final test ratio was 5.1, only slightly above the 4.8 control figure.

Ratios for both areas moved roughly parallel up to the end of 1953, just before nonwhite entry started in East Piedmont Heights. Thus, the absolute differences between the ratios remained fairly constant, fluctuating between 0.7 and 1.3, in favor of the test area. Because of the joint downward trend, the *relative* advantage of test ratios increased during this time.

Beginning with 1954, however, control ratios started up again, while test ratios kept moving down. Consequently, both the relative and absolute margins of test ratios over control ratios lessened. This happened during the eighteen months of nonwhite entry, with Negro families accounting for 1 percent of test area dwellings by the end of 1954, and 2.5 percent by late 1955.

Comparison of the average ratio differences, before and after entry, confirms the visual evidence of the relatively weaker test ratio performance.

EAST PIEDMONT HEIGHTS AND LAKESHORE HIGHLANDS

Period	Average differences (test ratio minus control ratio)	Test ratio as percent of control ratio (averages)
Before entry Second quarter, 1950, to first quarter, 1954..............	+1.12	122.7

After entry
Year ending with first quarter of:
    1955........................
    1956 (first half)...............
	
	+0.59
	+0.60
		
		112.5
		112.0

The average percent margin of test ratios over control ratios was cut almost in half after entry, decreasing from 22.7 percent to 12 percent. In the first four quarters, test ratios averaged 6.2, as against 5.5 in the last four quarters. This is about an 11 percent fall, implying an approximately equivalent drop in selling prices. Corresponding control ratio averages are 5.1 and 4.9, for a decrease of 4 percent.

These results check roughly with general observations by local real estate people. They estimate that the average price in East Piedmont Heights has fallen from $22,000 to $18,000 in recent years. This amounts to an 18 percent drop. The difficulty of estimating average prices when the range of prices is wide undoubtedly accounts for the difference between their estimate and the figure derived from the ratios.

There seems to be little doubt that the only significant variable between the test and control areas—the presence of Negroes—has lowered test prices relative to control prices. Whether this is a temporary or permanent price depression remains to be seen over the next few years.

The logical explanation for such a price sag is that not enough nonwhite families are able and ready to move into this higher-priced neighborhood to absorb the homes placed on sale, and white buyers do not wish to. This fits the experience of real estate people in the area, who report that properties are not selling fast enough to "clear the board." [6]

---

[6] Personal interviews, September, 1955.

VERY LIGHT NONWHITE ENTRY:
ONE NEIGHBORHOOD

The Test Area: Montclair (T-9-O)

Location.—In the Oakland Hill area between the City of Piedmont and the Oakland city line along the ridge of the East Bay hills.

Boundaries, topography, and features.—This test area is a composite one, formed by combining three small neighborhoods, each about one-third mile in diameter. Only by merging these areas, each of which has a resident Negro family, could barely sufficient sales data be gathered. About 240 homes are represented by the three areas. Because of the winding streets and the small neighborhoods involved, it is not feasible to attempt to list boundary streets. Instead, each neighborhood is defined by drawing a circle of approximately one-quarter-mile radius, with the center at the location of the Negro residence. These centers are: (1) Cabot Drive (5700 block); (2) Asilomar Drive at Saroni Drive; (3) Colton Boulevard at Arrowhead Drive.

These three neighborhoods are closely comparable, although the Cabot Drive one is not quite as young as the other two and has a slightly lower price level. All are hillside areas, heavily wooded, with beautiful views and irregularly shaped lots.

Structures.—Homes are spacious, three- or four-bedroom, single-family, frame and stucco construction. Quality is high, and style is divided between California bungalows and English design. Close to 100 percent owner-occupied. In general, homes vary between five and twelve years old, with a few on either side of this range. The areas are about 60 to 80 percent built up and include no tract houses. Prices range from $15,000 to $23,000, with a clustering at $19,000.

Socioeconomic characteristics.—These neighborhoods are toward the top of the residential scale in attractiveness and desirability. Few families can afford properties larger and more expensive. Obviously, these areas are lived in by successful business and professional people, with emphasis on the suburban way of life.

Racial changes: In September, 1953, a Negro undertaker bought a home in the Asilomar Drive section, and a Negro attorney bought on Colton Boulevard. Both purchases were made through white buyers who "fronted" for the real, nonwhite purchasers. Neighborhood resentment flared up in the Colton Boulevard section, manifesting itself over several months through unpleasant telephone calls and the regular throwing of garbage-filled bags on the front lawn. In recent months, peace has returned to the neighborhood.

One year later (September, 1954), a Negro family purchased a home on Cabot Drive, with no open resentment reported.

These three rather scattered purchases and move-ins by Negroes have not set off an avalanche of sales by whites. In fact, barely enough sales occurred to make a rough analysis feasible. Even so, real estate people do report a higher level of activity than for the hill areas as a group, suggesting some move-outs by disturbed whites. These move-outs have thus far resulted in sales to white rather than nonwhite families, but it is expected that more nonwhites will gradually buy in over a period of time.

The Control Area: Piedmont Pines (C-9-O)

In a fashion similar to that used for the composite Montclair test area, two sections of the Piedmont Pines hill area have been combined in order to accumulate enough control sales.

Piedmont Pines is just north of Redwood Regional Park, and south of the Montclair test area. The two sections chosen for their comparability with the test area are roughly described by circles of a quarter-mile radius centered on: (1) Camino Lenada at La Cuesta; and (2) Aitken Drive at Girvin Drive. About 190 homes are in these two sections. No difference worthy of comment exists between the composite control and test areas.

Price Analysis

Wide price ranges within the areas examined for this comparison dictate the use of price/assessed valuation ratios, as opposed to direct price average.

Over the quarters for which data could be gathered (23 for the test area, 15 for the control), there were 31 test sales and 25

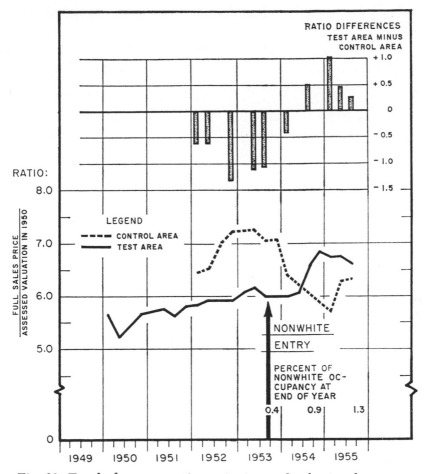

Fig. 31. Trend of average ratios, price/assessed valuation, by quarters, 1950–1955: Oakland, Montclair (test) and Piedmont Pines (control).

control sales. These were divided by 1950 assessed valuations and the resulting ratios plotted in figure 31.[7] The limited number of sales naturally reduced the smoothing-out effect obtained when many ratios are averaged, and the fluctuations inherent in the ratio method are therefore more pronounced than usual.

---

[7] Because nonwhite entry occurred a year later in the Cabot Drive test section than in the other two test sections, its sales are omitted from the calculations for the intervening year (September, 1953–September, 1954). This is to permit the effects of nonwhite entry in the other two sections to be reflected without influence from the price level in the still all-white section.

Test ratios showed a marked increase over the observation period, while control ratios declined. Using the seven-quarter pre-entry period as a reference base, test ratios climbed over 14 percent by the last four quarters of the observation period, while control ratios declined 12 percent.

Area	Average ratio before entry (7 quarters)	Average ratio after entry (last 4 quarters)	Change	
			Amount	Percent
Montclair (test).............	5.90	6.74	+0.84	+14.2
Piedmont Pines (control)....	6.92	6.11	−0.81	−11.7

From the figure it appears that control prices dipped all through 1954, just when test prices showed a sharp rise. The upturn in control prices that is evident in 1955 will probably bring ratios for the two areas close together. The reversed position of the two areas, after nonwhite entry, occurred while the test area was experiencing the move-in of three Negro families, amounting to 1.3 percent of the Montclair neighborhood population.

In figure 31, it can be seen that prices in the test area did relatively better than control area prices. Test prices, as indicated by the plotted price/assessed valuation ratios, rose in all but five of the 23 quarters, following an upward trend that was seemingly unaffected by nonwhite entry. Despite an absolute decrease in the last three quarters, the general ending level is in line with the over-all trend.

From an average ratio of 5.7 for the first four quarters observed, the test ratio rose 17 percent to an average of 6.7 for the last four quarters. This implies a roughly corresponding rise in selling prices.

Control ratios, by comparison, moved downward over their 15-quarter observation period, although there were large fluctuations around this trend. From an average ratio of 6.8 for the first four quarters observed, the control ratio fell 10 percent to an average of 6.1 for the final four quarters.

Average ratio differences, before and after entry, are shown below.

MONTCLAIR AND PIEDMONT PINES

Period	Average difference (test ratio minus control ratio)	Test ratio as percent of control ratio (averages)
Before entry First quarter, 1952, to third quarter, 1953..............	−0.94	88.8
After entry Year ending with third quarter of: 1954......................... 1955.........................	+0.04 +0.59	100.9 109.9

From a position 11 percent below control ratios in the pre-entry period, test ratios reached 10 percent above control ratios for the last four quarters of the observation period. Because the available data for this comparison were at a bare minimum, it would be unwise to try to refine the analysis too much. For the same reason, it would be unwarranted to place too much emphasis on the positive character of the findings.

As a tentative finding, however, it may be stated that test prices continued their previously established rate of climb without discernible interruption or setback as a result of light nonwhite entry. It may also be said that test prices performed relatively better than did prices for an all-white area having close comparability.

SUMMARY: OAKLAND

Of the seventeen test–control comparisons for Oakland neighborhoods, fourteen show test prices relatively higher than control prices at the end of the observation period, while three show test prices relatively lower.

Five comparisons yield test–control differences with changes of less than 5 percent plus or minus. As discussed in the summary of price comparisons for San Francisco neighborhoods, these are considered to signify no real difference in price behavior between the test areas and control areas. It is significant that these five comparisons involved test areas with from 50 to 60 percent nonwhite occupancy, yet test prices and control prices behaved very similarly.

There are twelve other test–control comparisons with percent change differences exceeding 5 percent. These are shown in the following table.

Test area and degree of nonwhite entry[a]	Percent of nonwhite occupancy in test area	Test price as a percent of control price (averages)		Percent increase or decrease in test price–control price ratio
		For pre-entry period	For last 4 quarters	
Seminary A (1)—medium	7	92.9	117.2	+26.2
Montclair—very light	1	88.8	109.9	+23.8
Seminary A (2)—medium	7	94.4	115.8	+22.7
Seminary C (1)—heavy	14	99.3	114.0	+13.3
Seminary C (2)—heavy	14	98.5	110.0	+11.7
Seminary B (1)—medium	7	102.1	109.4	+7.1
Elmhurst (1)—very heavy	40	89.9	96.2	+7.0
Brookfield Village—very heavy	50	85.9	90.8	+5.7
Seminary B (2)—medium	7	100.0	105.7	+5.7
Elmhurst (2)—very heavy	40	93.1	97.9	+5.2
Oak Knoll—medium	6	103.8	98.2	−5.4
East Piedmont Heights—light	3	122.7	112.0	−8.7

[a] Numbers in parentheses indicate test area compared with more than one control area.

Here is a heavy score in favor of the test areas. Ten neighborhoods with nonwhite entry showed significant percent increases over the all-white control neighborhoods with which they were compared. Two neighborhoods showed significantly large relative decreases in comparison with their control areas.

Quite clearly, for all but two test areas nonwhite entry did not depress selling prices. On the contrary, since other market factors were very nearly identical between test areas and control areas, nonwhite entry may be presumed to have had an upward influence on price behavior in at least ten test areas. The degree of nonwhite entry apparently had no consistent relationship to the behavior of test area prices.

VIII

Philadelphia

Philadelphia provides three test areas for examination.[1] Non-whites settled in these during the years 1947–1952. One is classified as a very heavy entry area, the other two as heavy. Two areas fall in the low-price category and one is in the medium range. There were over 2,400 individual test-area sales for use in the comparative analysis with 2,000 sales from three control areas.

VERY HEAVY NONWHITE ENTRY: ONE NEIGHBORHOOD

The Test Area: Strawberry Mansion (T-1-P)

Location.—In the southwest section of the Tioga district, about one-half mile east of the Schuylkill River and two miles northwest of the civic center.

Boundaries, topography, and features.—An approximately square area of about forty blocks, bounded by Lehigh Avenue, 29th Street, Gordon Street, and 33rd Street. The neighborhood is quite level and is primarily residential in character, although a few of the primary streets have scattered neighborhood stores and other services. There are about 3,000 dwellings in this neighborhood.

Structures.—Much conformity is evident in the style and design of homes in this area, as in many other residential areas of Philadelphia. Most of the houses were built 60 to 65 years ago and are two-story brick, straight-front, row-type units, with one-family occupancy. There are a few three-story homes of similar construction, but these, too, are for single-family occupancy.

---

[1] See chapter iii for the criteria governing selection of these neighborhoods and for definitions of special terminology.

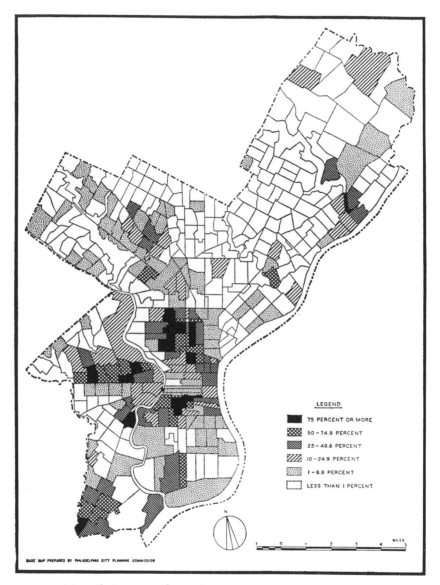

LEGEND

75 PERCENT OR MORE

50 - 74.9 PERCENT

25 - 49.9 PERCENT

10 - 24.9 PERCENT

1 - 9.9 PERCENT

LESS THAN 1 PERCENT

BASE MAP PREPARED BY PHILADELPHIA CITY PLANNING COMMISSION

Map 5. Percent of population nonwhite by census tracts
in Philadelphia, 1950.

Map 6. Boundaries of test and control areas in Philadelphia.

About 10 percent of the units are rentals, the rest being occupied by their owners.

Condition (November, 1955): Fair to good. These are old buildings, but the original construction was sound, and they are holding up well. About half appear to be in need of minor repairs and upkeep, so that the general appearance is one of a neighborhood on the verge of physical deterioration.

Price range (November, 1955): Low, $5,000–$7,000 (modal price about $6,000). Most of the price variation within the area results because a house is on either a primary or secondary-width street, since other factors such as size, condition, convenience, and the like are practically identical for all.

Socioeconomic characteristics.—The area is situated in the general region north of Market Street, which contains the largest part of the Negro population of Philadelphia (see maps 5 and 6). It was a heavily concentrated Jewish neighborhood.

Racial changes: The first Negro family came in during June, 1947. Since then, about 100 Negro families have settled in the neighborhood each year. By November, 1955, there were about 1,200, accounting for some 30 percent of the area's population. The racial change took place at a varying rate, with an average of about five blocks a year being "broken." However, only one to three blocks a year were broken during 1947–1952, whereas there were ten in 1953, fourteen in 1954, and ten in 1955. At first the new Negro entrants were primarily veterans and buyers with large cash payments. They were succeeded by a new group of lower financial standing, which may have something to do with the lower standards of maintenance now observable. Some panic occurred at the time of first Negro entry. A number of community organizations worked to reduce the tensions of transition, but they have recently become discouraged because of the lower-class entrants now coming in and also because the proportion of Negroes now in the area is rapidly climbing to a level that will probably prevent stabilization on an interracial basis. No violence of any sort has occurred, however, and there is little outward evidence of bitterness.

The Control Area: Lehigh-Allegheny (C-1-P)

An area of about thirty-five blocks, two miles directly north of the Civic Center. Bounded by Allegheny Avenue, 5th Street, Lehigh Avenue, and 9th Street. Roughly rectangular in shape, this neighborhood is not distinguishable from the Strawberry Mansion test area, except that it has stayed all-white to the present time. General environment, neighborhood conditions, design, construction, and age of the dwellings are all closely comparable with the test area.

Price Analysis

Sales price information is available for the period 1943 to 1955, for a total of 49 quarters. This provides 16 quarters before nonwhite entry as a basis of comparison by which to judge price behavior after entry. Altogether there were 1,417 test sales recorded (average: 28.9 per quarter), and 768 control sales (average: 15.7 per quarter). Because the test and control areas are so very similar in all respects, direct comparison of selling prices is appropriate. Figure 32 depicts average sales prices over the entire period. Starting from almost the same average price of about $2,400, both areas moved together very closely throughout the period. Both showed a rising trend, but test area prices rose slightly faster, averaging $6,093 in the final quarter, compared with $5,337 for the control area. Percent increases over the period were:

Area	Average price before entry (16 quarters)	Average price after entry (last 4 quarters)	Increase	
			Amount	Percent
Strawberry Mansion (test).....	$2,846	$5,916	$3,070	107.9
Lehigh-Allegheny (control)....	2,786	5,011	2,225	79.9

Whereas control prices increased 80 percent over their own average level for the first 16 quarters, test prices climbed 108 percent. As a consequence, the margin of test prices over control prices grew considerably over the twelve-year period, as shown by the following table.

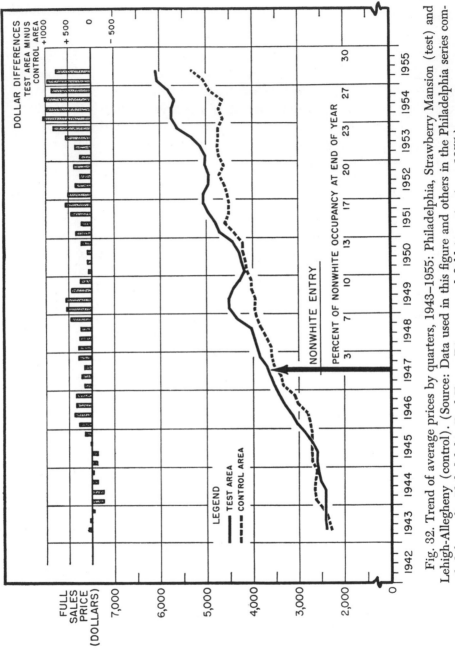

Fig. 32. Trend of average prices by quarters, 1943–1955: Philadelphia, Strawberry Mansion (test) and Lehigh-Allegheny (control). (Source: Data used in this figure and others in the Philadelphia series compiled from the Philadelphia Real Estate Directory and field investigations, 1955.)

STRAWBERRY MANSION AND LEHIGH-ALLEGHENY

Period	Average difference in dollars (test price minus control price)	Test price as percent of control price (averages)
Before entry Second quarter, 1943, to second quarter, 1947............	+60	101.8
After entry Year ending with second quarter of:		
1948...........................	+252	106.9
1949...........................	+441	111.2
1950...........................	+210	105.2
1951...........................	+213	104.9
1952...........................	+466	110.2
1953...........................	+311	106.6
1954...........................	+871	118.4
1955...........................	+905	118.2

In the continuing upward trend of test prices after nonwhite entry began, there were some rises and falls which were largely responsible for the variations in price differences. Nevertheless, it is clear that test prices were always higher than control prices, and by significant proportions, ranging from 5 to over 18 percent during the postentry period. This strong leadership over control prices took place while the test area was undergoing nonwhite entry that reached 30 percent by the end of 1955.

An informal polling of ten local real estate brokers revealed that eight believed values in the area had held up and had not been adversely affected by the racial change.[2]

HEAVY NONWHITE ENTRY:
TWO NEIGHBORHOODS

The Test Area: Cedar-Spruce (T-2-P)

Location.—In West Philadelphia, two miles directly west of the University of Pennsylvania, and one-third mile south of Market Street.

Boundaries, topography, and features.—A rectangular area of about thirty blocks, bounded by Pine Street, 55th Street, Cedar Avenue, and 59th Street. Topographically level and almost entirely residential, but with the normal amount of neighborhood stores and services. There are about 1,800 dwelling units in this neighborhood.

[2] Informal poll conducted by a volunteer staff member, July, 1956.

Structures.—The entire area is developed with two-story brick dwellings of the porch-front type; on many corner properties there are combination store-and-dwelling units. Houses are mostly built in rows, so that they touch each other, although there are about four blocks of twin units with each pair of units being detached. With few exceptions, all houses are single-family units and most have three bedrooms. Some located on the primary streets of the neighborhood have four bedrooms. These houses were built in the period 1905–1915; most of them are about 45 years old.

Condition (November, 1955): Good. Although fairly old, these homes are soundly built and have been well maintained.

Price range (November, 1955): Low to Medium, $6,000–$8,000 on secondary streets; $7,000–$10,000 on primary streets. Typical price: $7,000–$7,500. The price differences are almost entirely due to location by street, since the units are practically identical as to size and condition.

Socioeconomic characteristics.—West Philadelphia is considered one of the most desirable sections of the city in which nonwhites live, and it contains more Negro homeowners than any other Philadelphia area. Until after 1950, however, most Negroes lived north of Market Street, at least one-third mile north of the Cedar-Spruce neighborhood. The general area has served the housing needs of white working-class families, with large representations of Jewish and Catholic religious groupings. Owner-occupancy has typically been high, running to at least 90 percent.

Racial changes: Initial Negro entry took place in late May, 1952, and assumed large proportions very quickly because of the strong city-wide nonwhite demand for decent housing. About 100 Negro families moved into Cedar-Spruce each year after 1952, so that the total nonwhite population reached 320 families by the end of 1955. About ten blocks were "broken" each year. The entry of nonwhites appears to have come as a heavy shock to the white residents, and a severe panic existed through 1954. Considerable tension and high feelings are reported to have existed during this time, but no outbreaks or riots occurred. Reactions were more bitter than in Strawberry Mansion. An organized effort was begun to keep Negroes out, but failed. However, as fast as homes were put on the market by whites, it appears that nonwhite buyers were ready to take them. Judging by what has happened elsewhere in Philadelphia, nonwhite occupancy in Cedar-Spruce will continue to increase above its present 30 percent level, eventually becoming predominant.[3]

The Control Area: Elmwood (C-2-P)

A rectangular area of about twenty blocks in the Elmwood district, two and a half miles southwest of the University of Pennsylvania and a mile west of the Schuylkill River. Bounded by Elmwood Avenue, 65th Street, Guyer Avenue and Carroll Street. Closely comparable to the Cedar-Spruce test area but with no nonwhites living in it at the end of 1955.

Price Analysis

Price data for a total of 37 quarters have been analyzed, covering the period from the second quarter of 1946 to the second quarter of 1955. Twenty-five quarters are in the pre-entry period and provide a reference level against which to compare price behavior after nonwhite entry. Altogether, there were 620 sales recorded in the test area (average: 16.8 per quarter), and 475 control sales (average: 12.8 per quarter). Direct price comparisons are called for, since test and control areas are so similar except for the racial factor. Figure 33 presents prices averaged by quarters for each neighborhood.

From figure 33 it can be seen that the two areas showed closely parallel price behavior over the entire period. Both began at the low $4,000 level in 1946 and climbed to about $7,500 by mid-1955, with test prices slightly higher in most quarters. Evidently control prices rose a bit faster than did test prices, considering the pre-entry period as a basis for measurement:

Area	Average price before entry (25 quarters)	Average price after entry (last 4 quarters)	Increase	
			Amount	Percent
Cedar-Spruce (test)..........	$6,160	$7,369	$1,209	19.6
Elmwood (control)........	5,919	7,239	1,320	22.3

[3] This should not be taken as a generalization that this will inevitably happen in other white neighborhoods of Philadelphia. Assuming some relaxation in total nonwhite demand, coupled with nonwhite entry into higher economic-level neighborhoods, it is reasonable to expect that a few mixed neighborhoods may eventually stabilize on an interracial occupancy basis.

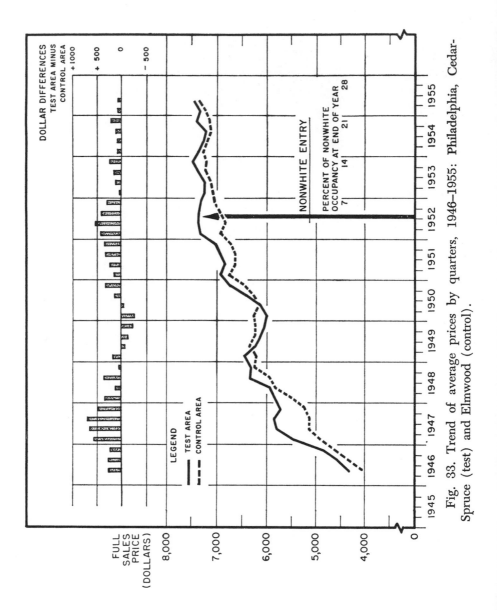

Fig. 33. Trend of average prices by quarters, 1946–1955: Philadelphia, Cedar-Spruce (test) and Elmwood (control).

Test prices dipped briefly below control prices during 1949–1950 (by 1 to 4 percent), but then resumed their superior position for the two years preceding nonwhite entry. The positive margin was maintained to the end of the observation period, although it became gradually smaller:

CEDAR-SPRUCE AND ELMWOOD

Period	Average difference in dollars (test price minus control price)	Test price as percent of control price (averages)
Before entry		
Second quarter, 1946, to second quarter, 1952.............	+240	104.3
After entry		
Year ending with second quarter of:		
1953.........................	+216	103.1
1954.........................	+155	102.1
1955.........................	+131	101.8

As nonwhite entry in Cedar-Spruce steadily climbed toward 30 percent, there was a very gradual reduction in test price margins over control prices. The change is so gradual, however, that it is hazardous to use it as a basis for generalization about a relative price decline in the test neighborhood. Continuing observation of these two areas is required to determine whether control prices will continue to move closer to test prices. It would seem safe to conclude, however, that nonwhite entry did not depress prices in Cedar-Spruce. In fact, on the basis of the price data available thus far, it is difficult to establish that nonwhite entry affected test area prices at all.

A comment by an experienced observer is worth noting:

The effect of this change [i.e., entry by nonwhites in 1952] was depressing values at first in the areas immediately adjoining. White buyers would not buy, owners were loathe to be the first to sell to Negroes. However, the pressure was so great due to the many properties placed on the market and the Negroes being desirous of moving into the area, that they paid premiums when making purchases. The Veterans Administration program of financing also made it possible for many of these people to acquire properties with little or no money. This movement has not affected the prices which can be obtained at the present time. The physical characteristics of the neighborhood seem to be maintained, as these newcomers are very desirous of keeping up the quality of their properties.[4]

Neither the price depression nor the premium prices mentioned by this observer appear to show up in the average price data. His general conclusions, however, confirm the statistical evidence that prices do not seem to have been affected by the changing racial picture.

The Test Area: Ogontz (T-3-P)

Location.—In northern Philadelphia, midway between the Germantown and Fern Rock districts, some six miles north of the Civic Center. The city limits lie about one and a half miles to the northeast.

Boundaries, topography, and features.—An irregularly shaped neighborhood of twelve blocks, containing about 850 homes. Bounded by Church Lane, Lambert Street, Sparks Street, Ogontz Avenue, Nedro Avenue, and Kemble Avenue. The area is gently sloped and is almost entirely residential in nature.

Structures.—Two-story brick or frame dwellings, the majority being of the porch-front type. Row construction for the most part, but some detached units. Almost exclusively single-family units, having three or four bedrooms, but with a sprinkling of two-family units. Average age is 30 to 35 years, most houses having been built during 1921–1925.

Condition (November, 1955): Good to excellent. Houses are well built and maintained.

Price range (November, 1955): Medium, $8,000–$10,000 (modal price about $9,200).

Socioeconomic characteristics.—This neighborhood has always been regarded as upper-middle class and superior to the two previously discussed Philadelphia areas (Strawberry Mansion and Cedar-Spruce). Until the recent racial changes began, the neighborhood was considered predominantly Jewish. Owner-occupancy has typically been about 90 percent. Some Negro occupancy existed west of the Ogontz neighborhood before January, 1952, when the test area first experienced nonwhite entry. Seven nearby blocks had from 10 to 50 percent Negro residence and three others each had a few Negro families.

[4] Letter from Samuel Sagan, Senior Member, Society of Residential Appraisers, Philadelphia, March 21, 1956.

Racial changes: The first Negro family bought and occupied a house in the Ogontz neighborhood on January 20, 1952. In the usual pattern, this family was the forerunner of other nonwhite purchasers who came in at a steady rate of about fifty families a year. Much fear and panic is reported to have arisen with the initial entry and persisted as each block was broken. Many homes were put on the market, with about twenty "For Sale" signs in evidence at all times over the period from 1952 to early 1955. Of late, the agitation has quieted somewhat, and the remaining whites do not appear emotionally disturbed to the point where they feel they must sell their homes immediately. No violence or widely organized opposition to the nonwhite entry arose at any time. By the end of 1955, Negro occupancy amounted to some 200 families, or 24 percent of all families in the neighborhood. There is reason to believe that nonwhite occupancy may not climb to the same proportion that it has in less expensive residential areas of Philadelphia, because of the relatively limited number of Negroes who can afford the higher financial commitments involved.

The Control Area: Olney (C-3-P)

An irregular rectangle of about twenty blocks, located a quarter mile east of the test area across Ogontz Avenue, a major dividing line. The area is bounded by Virginian Road, Grange Street, Nedro Avenue, 11th Street, Olney Avenue, and Chew Avenue. It is similar to the Ogontz area but contains some apartment buildings and income properties. These are indicative of the slightly higher price level as compared to Ogontz. Owner-occupancy units are alike in both areas, but those in the Olney area have generally brought about $1,000 more. Of significance is how nonwhite entry may affect this long-time differential. Only residential properties are represented in the price data. There were no nonwhite residents at the end of 1955.

Price Analysis

The observation period for this comparison extends over 41 quarters, from the second quarter of 1945 to the second quarter of 1955. The measurement base for price movements is the 27-

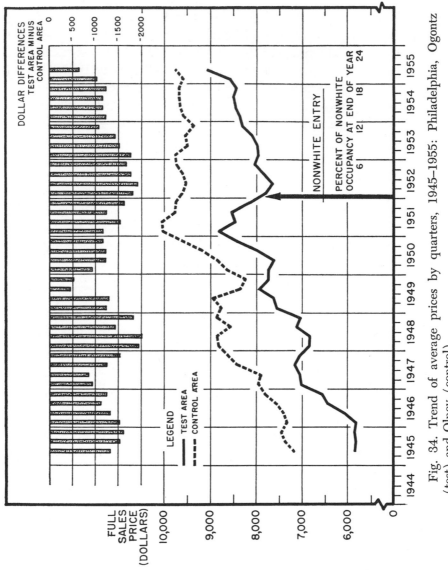

Fig. 34. Trend of average prices by quarters, 1945–1955: Philadelphia, Ogontz (test) and Olney (control).

quarter pre-entry period before the beginning of 1952. There was a total of 403 test sales (9.8 per quarter) and 278 control sales (6.8 per quarter). The analysis is conducted on the direct price comparison basis. Figure 34 shows prices averaged by quarters, for each neighborhood. By and large, test prices stayed parallel with control prices, drawing closer during 1947 and 1949 and farther away during 1952. Test prices started at just under $6,000 and rose steadily over the whole period except during 1951, the year prior to nonwhite entry. They ended at a little over $9,000. Control prices began slightly under $7,200 and finished at almost $9,800. Their rise was less regular than for test prices, however, since they showed dips during 1948–1949 and a long, almost unbroken decline from their 1951 high point of $10,000 to their concluding level. Test prices displayed a greater percent increase when measured against the average pre-entry level.

Area	Average price before entry (27 quarters)	Average price after entry (last 4 quarters)	Increase	
			Amount	Percent
Ogontz (test).............	$7,231	$8,652	$1,421	19.7
Olney (control)............	8,536	9,658	1,122	13.1

Test prices increased nearly 20 percent over the measurement base, as against a 13 percent gain for control prices. Consequently, the observation period closed with test prices closer to the control price level. This relatively faster increase for test prices occurred while nonwhite occupancy was moving toward a 24 percent level by late 1955. The gain on the part of test prices is clearly visible when yearly averages are considered.

OGONTZ AND OLNEY

Period	Average difference in dollars (test price minus control price)	Test price as percent of control price (averages)
Before entry Second quarter, 1945, to fourth quarter, 1951.............	−1,261	84.6
After entry Year ending with fourth quarter of:		
1952........................	−1,793	81.4
1953........................	−1,449	84.8
1954........................	−1,197	87.6
1955........................	−840	91.3

It appears that the increase in nonwhite occupancy in the Ogontz neighborhood was associated with a narrowing of the gap between test and control prices. Although the test price average dropped somewhat in the first year after entry, while nonwhite occupancy reached 6 percent, the next year saw a recovery to the pre-entry level. The last two years of the period, with 18 and 24 percent nonwhite occupancy, displayed a marked relative increase for test prices. For the last four quarters, test prices were 8.7 percent under control prices, whereas they had been 15.4 percent below during the pre-entry period.

While the sharp drop in test prices during 1951 suggests a market reaction to impending nonwhite entry, this theory is somewhat weakened by the occurrence of a similar—though not so sharp—drop in control prices for the same period. If the more severe character of the test price drop is alleged to have resulted from the threat of nonwhite entry, it must also be recognized that test prices quickly recovered to their old levels, and even higher, whereas control prices kept falling through 1953. Even after 1953, control prices rose slowly, while test prices were increasing very fast.

SUMMARY: PHILADELPHIA

Philadelphia's three test areas show the following comparisons with their control areas.

Test area and degree of nonwhite entry	Percent nonwhite occupancy in test area	Test price as a percent of control price (averages)		Percent change in test price/control price ratio
		For pre-entry period	For last 4 quarters	
Very heavy entry Strawberry Mansion........	30	101.8	118.2	+16.1
Heavy entry Cedar-Spruce..............	28	104.3	101.8	−2.4
Ogontz...................	24	84.6	91.3	+7.9

Two test areas show significantly large relative price increases over control areas; one shows a small relative decrease. The Philadelphia picture, then, indicates that nonwhite entry exercised a positive effect on selling prices.[5] The degree of nonwhite entry was about the same for all three areas, but the observed price behavior, relative to control prices, showed wide variation.

---

[5] This is supported by the evidence from another Philadelphia neighborhood in the Germantown area. All-white until late 1949, about half its homes were sold to Negroes over a four-year period. A careful review by the *Philadelphia Evening Bulletin* revealed that prices were not driven down by the racial changes; if anything, they were pushed upward. "Story of a 'Busted Block': Negro Sale Starts Rush But Nobody Loses Money," *Philadelphia Evening Bulletin,* January 24, 1954.

IX

Chicago and Kansas City

This chapter summarizes the results of studies by three other authors on real estate price changes associated with nonwhite entry into selected residence neighborhoods of Chicago and Kansas City.[1] The works of these writers are not strictly comparable with each other nor with the San Francisco-Oakland-Philadelphia studies described in preceding chapters because of differences in research procedures. However, the results of the several studies may be broadly compared.

CHICAGO'S SOUTH SIDE, 1920–1930

In 1930, Cressey gathered value data for comparable properties on Chicago's South Side, some in all-white areas and some in Negro areas. He reports that:

. . . In those blocks invaded by Negroes there was no actual decline in values and prices tended to remain approximately stationary, with possible slight increases four or five years after the general Negro occupancy of the blocks had occurred. But in comparable areas where there had been no Negro invasion, prices had constantly risen from year to year. . . . In other sections of the South Side a marked depreciation in values was noticeable before the entrance of Negroes into the area, and their appearance was only one contributing factor in

[1] Paul F. Cressey, "The Succession of Cultural Groups in the City of Chicago" (unpublished Ph.D. thesis, University of Chicago, 1930).

E. F. Schietinger, "Real Estate Transfers During Negro Invasion, A Case Study" (unpublished Master's thesis, Department of Sociology, University of Chicago, 1948); "Racial Succession and Changing Property Values in Residential Chicago" (unpublished Ph.D. thesis, Department of Sociology, University of Chicago, 1953); "Racial Succession and the Value of Small Residential Properties," *American Sociological Review*, XVI, no. 6 (December, 1951); "Race and Residential Market Values in Chicago," *Land Economics*, XXX, no. 4 (November, 1954).

Thomas L. Gillette, "Santa Fe: A Study of the Effects of Negro Invasion on Property Values" (unpublished Master's thesis, Department of Sociology, University of Kansas City, 1954).

the total situation. However, the entrance of Negroes seems not to have retarded the increasing value of at least some property on Michigan Avenue. The block between 42nd and 43rd Streets was entered by Negroes in 1924. In 1921 property here was worth $125 a front foot; in 1924 it was worth $140 and in 1928 it had increased to $200. This increase may in part be due, though, to the potential commercial value of Michigan Avenue. . . . An examination of the facts does not indicate anything of the magnitude of the depreciation on the sole responsibility of the Negroes for the losses in property values which it is often claimed is produced by Negro invasion into a white community.[2]

It should be noted that the character of racial change in Chicago during the 1920–1930 decade differed from more recent situations in at least two important respects: (1) it usually involved an *inundation* rather than a gradual settlement; (2) it involved nonwhites who were at a relatively low socioeconomic level and who were therefore renting or buying in less desirable neighborhoods. These differences imply other contrasts, such as white fear of being inundated; greater demand pressure by nonwhites, due to a more limited selection of residential locations; declining status of the neighborhood, making it more vulnerable to racial change; and "overloading" of dwelling units by more than one family, leading to even more rapid physical deterioration than before.

These conditions are substantially modified in the current scene. It cannot be stated with certainty, therefore, that Cressey's conclusions about the effects of nonwhite occupancy on property values are completely relevant to today's racial transition neighborhoods, particularly those with single-family dwelling units. In any event, his investigations throw some light on the race and property value question under conditions of a generation ago.

Cressey's findings should be further qualified in view of his primary value data source: Olcott's *Land Values Blue Book for Chicago*. The land values in this book are approximations, arrived at by deducting the *estimated* value of the structure from the *estimated* total value of the property. *They are not prices observed in the market.* Land usually represents only about 20 percent of total property value, which means that land value changes

---

[2] Cressey, "The Succession of Cultural Groups . . . ," pp. 245–246. Cited in Robert C. Weaver, *The Negro Ghetto* (New York: Harcourt, Brace and Company, 1948), pp. 287–288.

would be minimized—perhaps even indiscernible—in comparison with shifts in the total values themselves. Finally, the estimates are calculated by real estate appraisers, whose appraisals may be influenced adversely by their subjective views of the effect non-whites have on property values.

RECENT CHICAGO STUDIES

The principal recent work on race and property values in Chicago is that of E. F. Schietinger for the period 1940–1951. His data are observed sales prices of 880 individual properties in seven selected areas of Chicago's South Side, having medium to very heavy Negro entry over the period. The behavior of these prices is described in relation to assessed valuations in 1940 and subsequently to the grand average of prices within certain "stages of racial succession."

Racial succession stages are used to determine what price patterns emerge as Negro occupancy intensifies. Schietinger distinguishes five stages: "(a) pre-threat—absence of invasion or contiguity with an area of invasion; (b) threat—contiguity with a penetrated area; (c) penetration—presence of one or several invading residents in an area: (d) influx—rapid occupancy by invading residents subsequent to initial penetration; (e) saturation—complete or nearly complete occupancy by invading residents; (f) consolidation—occupancy subsequent to completion of the succession cycle." [3] His categories (c), (d), and (e) correspond approximately to the present study's terminology of light entry, medium and heavy entry, and very heavy entry.

It is important to observe that Schietinger was unable, for lack of resources, to carry out a central objective: the provision of all-white control areas to be used as yardsticks for the racially changing areas. Hence, the price movements within the individual areas are contrasted only with the average level when observation began, or with changing price levels in other transition areas. At no point are they compared against price levels in similar, all-white areas. Schietinger therefore leaves unanswered the basic question as to whether areas experiencing racial change show value behavior different from that in similar all-white areas.

Characteristics of Schietinger's seven observation areas are

---

[3] Schietinger, *Land Economics*, XXX, no. 4, 303, n. 7.

TABLE 4

CHARACTERISTICS OF SCHIETINGER STUDY AREAS

Area name	Census tract No.	Extent of Negro occupancy by 1948	Extent of Negro occupancy by 1951	Degree of entry in terms of present study	Ratio of No. of dwelling units to No. of structures	Comments
Woodlawn Area D	625	Nearly 100 percent; occurred during the 1920's	Same	Very heavy	2.4	"Long-established Negro residence." Single units outnumber duplexes.
Woodlawn Area C	623 624	"Saturated"; entered during 1940–1941	Same	Very heavy	3.9	A "recent settlement" area; resistance to entry, but tempered by white acceptance of "economic necessity" for Negro entry. Newer, better housing than in Woodlawn A, B, or D.
South Oakland	(A 6-block area)	About 50 percent; began in 1944	About 75 percent	Very heavy	5.8	"Moderately violent" reaction to entry. A high multiple occupancy area, but price data are for single units only.
Woodlawn Area B	627	About 20 percent; began in 1947	About 40 percent	Very heavy	4.3	"A transitional area—the core of the entire study." Near-blight condition. High multiple occupancy, with duplexes outnumbering singles. Strong opposition.
Greater Grand Crossing	885 888 889	About 10 percent; began in 1947	About 25 percent	Heavy	2.0	"More than usual hostility toward incoming Negroes." Better quality housing than Woodlawn areas.
Kenwood	(A 9-block area)	None; a "threatened area"	About 10 percent	Medium	1.0	Higher priced, single-family, older homes; "mansion-type."
Woodlawn Area A	629	None; a "threatened area"	About 10 percent	Medium	4.1	"Pronounced organizational resistance to entry." Better housing than in Woodlawn B or D; singles outnumber duplexes.

SOURCES: Data and descriptive material from S chietinger, "Racial Succession and Changing Property Values . . . ," and *Land Economics*, XXX, no. 4.

given in table 4. The next to the last column indicates the extent to which each area is characterized by multiple dwelling unit structures. The author finds some relationship between this variable and price behavior.

The price analysis begins with whatever stage of racial succession existed at the opening of the observation period and describes price movements from stage to stage. Price data were treated in the following manner.

Price estimates were summarized by size-of-structure and study area groups for time periods illustrating succession stages. Estimates of absolute price were converted into price relatives in order to achieve a modicum of standardization; this consisted of dividing each estimate by the assessed valuation which obtained for the structure in 1940. These price relatives were appropriately grouped and summarized as arithmetic means. To eliminate the influence of change in dollar values, prices for each area were reduced to an index based upon the grand mean [for all areas being compared] during that period.[4]

Price Behavior in Very Heavy Entry Areas

Over the six-year period, price relatives moved upward by from 43 to 75 percent for the very heavy entry areas. Woodlawn Area D, with long-established Negro residence, did not rise as fast as recently settled Woodlawn Area C, less heavily settled South Oakland, or Woodlawn B. Woodlawn Area D was also the area of lowest multiple-occupancy, while South Oakland and Woodlawn Area B were the highest.

MOVEMENT OF AVERAGE PRICE RELATIVES OF ONE- AND TWO-DWELLING
UNIT STRUCTURES, 1940–1951 (1940–1944 = 100)

Area	1945–1946	1947–1948	1948–1951
Woodlawn Area D	122	147	174
Woodlawn Area C	...	196	236
South Oakland	158	230	269
Woodlawn Area B			
White	200	263	309
Negro	150	239	263

SOURCE: Schietinger, "Racial Succession and Changing Property Values . . . ," table 14, p. 104. Placed on a 1940–1944 base by the present writer.

Apparently both South Oakland and Woodlawn Area B, which began to have Negro occupancy in 1944 and 1947 respectively,

---

[4] *Ibid.*, p. 304.

experienced larger relative price increases than the two areas with saturated occupancy going back to the beginning of the decade and before. Also, South Oakland and Woodlawn Area B had strong opposition to Negro entry, but this seemingly did not restrain the upward price surge. White-occupied homes in Area B showed larger relative price *gains* than did those with Negro occupants. However, in a detailed investigation of this area, Schietinger determined that Negroes *paid* "significantly more than did white purchasers for similar types of real estate in the same area during invasion," regardless of size of structure.

Price Behavior in a Heavy Entry Area

Greater Grand Crossing is Schietinger's only area classifiable as heavy entry. By 1951 it had a nonwhite occupancy of about 25 percent. It had better quality housing than the Woodlawn areas and also manifested more than the usual amount of hostility toward the incoming Negroes. Its relative price movements, separately recorded for one- and two-dwelling unit structures, were as follows (1940–1944 = 100):[5]

Type	1945–1946	1947–1948	1948–1951
One-dwelling unit structures........	119	155	169
Two-dwelling unit structures........	150	155	210

This area showed smaller relative price gains than any of the very heavy entry areas. The two-dwelling unit structures gained 110 percent over the 1940–1950 period, in contrast to a 69 percent gain for the single units.

Price Behavior in Medium Entry Areas

The price increases for the two medium entry areas are about the same as those for the heavy entry area. Woodlawn Area A— with higher multiple-occupancy structures—has the superior price performance. Both areas are characterized by higher priced housing, and Woodlawn Area A showed strong resistance to Negro entry (see tabulation, top of p. 200).

As a general summary of the price relative movements, it appears that the very heavy entry areas, as a group, showed the largest gains. All seven areas showed increases ranging

---

[5] Schietinger, "Racial Succession and Changing Property Values . . . ," table 14, p. 104. Placed on a 1940–1944 base by the present writer.

MOVEMENT OF AVERAGE PRICE RELATIVES OF ONE- AND TWO-DWELLING
UNIT STRUCTURES, 1940–1951 (1940–1944 = 100)

Area	1945–1946	1947–1948	1948–1951
Kenwood........................	125	148	168
Woodlawn Area A...............	125	197	216

SOURCE: Schietinger, "Racial Succession and Changing Property Values . . . ," table
14, p. 104. Placed on a 1940–1944 basis by the present writer.

from 68 to 209 percent. Areas with higher proportions of
multiple-occupancy structures showed larger relative price increases than one-dwelling unit areas with the same degree of
nonwhite occupancy.

Schietinger, as already mentioned, divided each price relative
by the grand mean for all price relatives in each time period,
thereby obtaining a price index reflecting the position of each
area relative to the average for all areas over the entire observation decade. The following table shows these price index figures
for the seven areas.

STUDY AREA PRICE INDEXES OF ONE- AND TWO-DWELLING UNIT STRUCTURES,
BY TIME PERIODS, 1940–1951

Study Area	1940–1944	1945–1946	1947–1948	1949–1951
Woodlawn Area D........	172	. . .	. . .	133
Woodlawn Area C........	99	118	103	104
South Oakland..........	99	109	121	119
Woodlawn Area B........	85	102	111	106
Greater Grand Crossing...	106	100	87	90
Kenwood................	70	61	55	53
Woodlawn Area A........	96	84	100	92

SOURCE: Schietinger, "Racial Succession and Changing Property Values . . . ," table
15, p. 106. These are not the same as the figures in the preceding tabulations, which
have been related to a base of 1940–1944 = 100 by the present writer.

Variation in relative price behavior is apparently not related
to the degree of nonwhite occupancy. However, there does seem
to be a positive relationship between rising prices and high
multiple-occupancy. The two relatively rising price areas and the
two relatively unchanging price areas are predominantly high
multiple-occupancy, ranging from 3.9 to 5.8 dwelling units average per structure. In contrast, the three areas with relatively
falling prices are predominantly low multiple-occupancy, rang-

ing from 1.0 to 2.4 dwelling units per structure. Schietinger observes:

> . . . *upward movement* took place . . . in high multiple-occupancy areas in the forefront of invasion [Woodlawn Area B and South Oakland]; *no movement* occurred in a multiple-occupancy area on the outer fringe of an invasion movement [Woodlawn Area B] and in an area saturated by Negro occupancy during the period of analysis [Woodlawn Area C]; *downward movement* occurred in an area of medium quality housing, low multiple-occupancy, and high resistance to invasion [Greater Grand Crossing]; in a "white elephant" mansion area in the forefront of invasion [Kenwood]; and in an area saturated by Negro occupancy some time before the period of analysis [Woodlawn Area D].[6]

As to the price movements over the racial succession cycle, Schietinger found no uniform effect of Negro occupancy on real estate prices in terms of time or area. The *threat of entry* did not produce price reductions in high multiple-occupancy areas and had no uniform effect on low multiple-occupancy areas. *Penetration* by Negroes was associated with price reductions in Woodlawn Area A for structures of one to four units, in Woodlawn Area B for structures of five to nine units, and in Kenwood for single units. In areas of high multiple-occupancy, *penetration* was apparently associated with either positive or negligible price changes.

Influx of Negroes was associated with the greatest general increase in price levels. Downward movements during this period were observed only for one- and four-unit structures in Greater Grand Crossing and in the Woodlawn Area B units occupied by Negroes as of 1948.

The periods of *saturation* and *climax* are represented by much less evidence, suggesting a mixed picture of both price stability and price reduction.

From the whole analysis of price trends, 1940–1951, in the seven Chicago areas with varying degrees of Negro occupancy, Schietinger lists the following conclusions:

1. The threat of Negro occupancy appears to have exerted a deteriorating effect upon property values only in areas of low multiple occupancy.

---

[6] *Ibid.*, p. 115. Italics supplied.

2. The typical effect of penetration by Negroes was improvement of the price level in the area affected, especially in areas of high multiple occupancy.

3. Influx of Negroes tended to be associated with maintenance of the price level reached during penetration.

4. The level of prices in an area of high multiple occupancy recently saturated by Negro residents compared favorably with the level maintained in other areas.

5. An area of low multiple occupancy long saturated by Negro residents evidenced a definite lag in the level of prices.

6. There is evidence that one- and two-family structures on the South Side did not keep abreast of price increases such as those recorded for North Side sales, except in areas of high multiple occupancy.

7. Variables associated with the prevailing price differences between areas suggest that the major price determinant of real estate is degree of use potential, in terms of either owner-occupancy or income.[7]

It is to be regretted that Schietinger's extensive research did not embrace an adequate system of all-white control areas. Nevertheless, his study demonstrates significant upward movement of prices over the observation decade in the seven areas studied. Prices did not fall with intensification of Negro occupancy. Against the background of much current theory on the subject, this is a significant conclusion.

A KANSAS CITY STUDY

In a 1954 master's thesis, Thomas Gillette carried out a well-documented comparison of real estate prices in two Kansas City neighborhoods—one a transitional area nearly 50 percent Negro-occupied, the other an all-white area.[8] His study design thus satisfies the basic condition that was absent from the Schietinger analysis.

In seeking his test area, Gillette had in mind one that had experienced relatively heavy Negro penetration since 1940, and, if possible, one that had been exposed to "invasion" long enough to get over any panic period that might have existed. He did not, however, want one in the final stages of influx.

He finally decided on Santa Fe, a fifteen-block area located in Census Tract 38, in the north-central part of Kansas City. The

---

[7] *Ibid.*, pp. 142–143.

[8] Gillette, "Santa Fe: A Study of the Effects of Negro Invasion on Property Values."

boundary streets are 27th Street on the north, Indiana Avenue on the east, 30th Street on the south, and Prospect Avenue on the west. This neighborhood is just southeast of one of the city's major Negro districts. Negroes began entering the neighborhood in January, 1949, and twenty-five Negro families were residing there by 1950. As of May, 1953, Negroes had acquired a total of 194, or 50 percent, of the 392 homes in the area. An average of about twenty-five Negro families entered the Santa Fe area during each six-month period from January, 1949, to June, 1953.

An all-white control neighborhood was selected, matching the Santa Fe area in respect to neighborhood age, size of dwelling units, type of construction, original sales prices, proximity to facilities and transportation, topography, land-use pattern, relation to central district, and neighborhood condition. The control area chosen was a twenty-four-block section, situated nine blocks southwest of Santa Fe, and bounded by 35th Street, Prospect Avenue, 38th Street, and Woodland Avenue.

Both areas are single-family dwelling neighborhoods, most of the homes being around 50 years old. Test area prices ranged from $6,000 to $15,500, while control prices were between $6,000 and $13,500.

Gillette compared the selling prices of fifty-two test area houses sold during 1949–1953 with the prices of fifty-two comparable houses in the all-white control area. Each pair of test–control houses was carefully matched with regard to age, type of construction, materials, number and size of rooms, date of sale, general condition, and other relevant factors.

Test area prices ranged from $4,000 above to $1,500 below the prices of matching control area units, with these *average* results:

1. In 35 of the 52 comparisons (67 percent), test-area prices exceeded control-area prices. The average excess was $1,135.

2. In 5 of the 52 comparisons (10 percent), test prices and control prices were equal.

3. In 12 of the 52 comparisons (23 percent), control prices exceeded test prices by an average of $702.

These comparisons of gross selling prices show a plus difference in favor of the mixed neighborhood price level. Approximately four out of five owners in the Santa Fe neighborhood received for their comparable properties as much as or more than did owners in the all-white control area; one out of five received less.

Gillette regards the higher prices paid by a majority of the Negro buyers in the test area as "a 'premium' which the Negro is forced to pay if he wishes to move into the area. These results indicate that prices in this particular neighborhood were enhanced rather than lowered through Negro entry. This evidence refutes the idea held by many people that Negro invasion must result in a drop in property values." [9]

The "premium" idea has been mentioned by many observers, and there is little doubt that sellers can frequently obtain more from a nonwhite buyer, who has fewer offerings to select from than a white. However, premiums would seem to be likely only for the first two or three sales to nonwhites in a neighborhood. After that, with most white buyers "scared off," an owner wishing to sell would have no choice but to offer his property to nonwhites. Raising his price to command a premium might mean another white owner would undersell him and his property would not be readily disposed of.

It may be more correct to consider the higher price level in the test area as a natural market effect brought about by strong demand for housing on the part of the pent-up nonwhite population. This views the higher price not as a penalty paid for being a nonwhite but as a competitive margin required to obtain the property in the face of spirited bidding by other home-seeking nonwhites. *Any* group entering a neighborhood under similar demand-supply conditions would, regardless of race, create the same price behavior. Of course, the higher price could still be considered an *indirect* penalty paid by nonwhites because of racial segregation, which limits their search for homes to only a few areas within local real estate markets.

Gillette's study includes an analysis of the occupations, educational attainment, and family incomes of whites and Negroes in both areas. Based on more than 200 interviews, he found the incoming Negro group superior to the white in all these respects indicative of socioeconomic status. A high proportion of the Negroes were professional people and civil servants, with most families reporting comparatively high incomes because both husband and wife were employed. These findings lead the author to

---

[9] *Ibid.*, pp. 60–61.

restrict the scope of his conclusion: "If the invading group had been on a significantly lower socio-economic plane, the level of prices might not have been elevated. This thesis does not contend that Negro invasion will inevitably result in a price increment, but does take the position that when the invading group is of a higher socio-economic composition than that of the group being invaded, the resulting trend in real estate values will be a positive upward trend, at least during the stages preceding succession." [10]

---

[10] *Ibid.*, p. 74.

X

Detroit and Portland

Two studies of Detroit transition areas exist. One deals with very heavy entry, the other with apparently heavy entry.

The first study is a master's thesis by Richard Wander,[1] completed in 1953. Wander observed real estate data covering three single-family areas over the 1940–1950 period. One area experienced Negro entry in 1948, with Negro occupancy reaching 30 percent by the end of 1950. The other two areas were chosen for their comparability with the test area, both remaining all-white throughout the period. All three areas are characterized as upper-middle class, the houses selling for $10,000 or more.

As a test area, Wander chose a neighborhood on Detroit's West Side, referred to as the Boston-Edison area. An older neighborhood of large, formerly expensive homes, 41 percent of its homes were built before 1920 and 53 percent from 1920 to 1929. Values in 1950 ranged from $10,000 up, and the typical resident was in the upper-middle income bracket.

The first Negro family moved in during 1948, and, by 1950, 55 of the 613 homes (8.7 percent) were occupied by Negroes. The incoming Negroes included doctors, lawyers, teachers, and businessmen.

Wander gives no direct description of white reactions to Negro entry but indirectly suggests that there was some panic during the initial stages in 1948–1949. Apparently, as entry continued after 1949, excitement tapered off and newcomers were absorbed without further excited departures by whites.

Two all-white neighborhoods known as the Golf Club area and Indian Village, were selected as bases for comparison. The Golf Club control area, also on the West Side, consists of nine blocks. Although its homes were valued at $10,000 or more in 1950, all but 17 percent were built during 1920–1939, and therefore did not have as high original construction costs as homes in the test

---

[1] Richard Stewart Wander, "The Influence of Negro Infiltration Upon Real Estate Values" (unpublished Master's thesis, Department of Sociology and Anthropology, Wayne State University, 1953).

area. Residents are described as having occupations similar to test area residents.

Indian Village consists of six blocks located on Detroit's South East Side. Wander states that age and architecture are similar to the test area, but that there are some signs of neglect.

Wander not only considered selling-price data, but looked at value figures, as declared by owners for the 1940 and 1950 Housing Censuses, and at assessed valuations for tax purposes. His analysis was twofold, comparing (1) value data for the test area as against the two all-white control areas, and (2) value data within the test area alone, as between homes in blocks containing nonwhites and homes in all-white blocks.

Summarizing the first branch of his analysis, he reports that "the Boston-Edison area still compares favorably in real estate values, and changes in them, with the other two areas." [2] The conclusion is necessarily rather indefinite, because the comparative value picture is a mixed one: the test area appears to have been slowly declining over the 1940–1950 decade in comparison with the two all-white control areas due to natural differences in neighborhood market desirability and life cycle.[3] But nonwhite entry in 1948, and the subsequent influx of more nonwhite families, seems to have checked, then reversed, the relative decline in the test area. Some details on this are illuminating. First, the census figures, which, of course, do not register the 1948 effects, are shown in the following table.

RATIO OF AREA AVERAGE DECLARED VALUE TO AVERAGE DECLARED
FOR ALL CITY PROPERTIES

Area	1940 (rental base)	1950 (market price base)[a]	Change 1940 to 1950	
			Amount	Percent
Boston-Edison (test).........	2.88	2.04	−0.84	−29.2
Golf Club (control)..........	3.09	2.50	−0.59	−19.1
Indian Village (control)......	3.40	2.01	−1.40	−41.2

SOURCE: Derived from data appearing at several places in Wander thesis.
[a] The change from a rental comparison to a market price comparison was necessary because the Housing Census for 1950 dropped the rental data.

[2] Ibid., p. 90.
[3] Factors other than race mentioned by Wander as possibly responsible for the test area's declining status are: (1) age of structures; (2) outmoded design; (3) large size; (4) expensive upkeep; (5) threat of encroachment by commercial enterprises. From this it would seem that test and control areas in this study were not closely matched with respect to factors influencing values.

Assessed valuations in the test area fell about 20 percent over the 1940–1950 period, rose 3.5 percent in the Golf Club area, and fell 13 percent in Indian Village. Thus, the test area did not keep up with either control area, when the entire ten-year span is considered. It is significant, however, that from 1948 to 1949— after nonwhite entry began—test-area valuations increased faster than those in the control areas. During 1949–1950, as Negro occupancy mounted, test-area valuations continued to increase at about the same rate as in the two all-white areas, but did not recover all the ground lost from 1940–1948.[4]

Both control areas showed greater price increases over the decade, yet test-area prices showed a strong recovery during 1949–1950, when Negro occupancy was approaching 30 percent. The comparative data are shown below.

COMPARATIVE SELLING PRICES

Area	Average ratio, 1950/1940 price	Average selling price percent change	
		1948–1949	1949–1950
Boston-Edison (test)..............	1.34	−7.8	+17.9
Golf Club (control)...............	2.13	+12.6	+31.7
Indian Village (control)..........	1.65	+29.1	−14.8

SOURCE: Derived from data appearing at several places in Wander thesis.

Over the 1940–1950 decade, test prices rose 34 percent, while control prices rose 113 percent and 65 percent, respectively, in the Golf Club and Indian Village areas. But after nonwhite entry had begun in 1948, test prices appeared to show up somewhat more favorably, particularly for the period 1949–1950. After a sharp drop (7.8 percent) in the first year of Negro entry, Boston-Edison prices came back with a strong 17.9 percent increase in 1949–1950.

Taken altogether, the data do not indicate that nonwhite entry in the Boston-Edison area harmed property values, relative to their level and direction before entry. Instead, there is some indication that nonwhite entry may have resulted in test area property values higher than they would have been had the area remained all-white. This conclusion can hardly be set down as a

---

[4] *Ibid.*, pp. 87–88.

long-term result, however, without more data for the years following 1950.

For the second part of Wander's analysis, the comparison of values in racially mixed as against all-white blocks within the Boston-Edison area, the same three value indices are employed.

With respect to values declared by owners for census purposes, the average value of homes in all test area blocks declined in comparison with Detroit city-wide values, but "the value attached to homes on mixed blocks decreased 11.4 percent less than that attached to those on homogeneous [all-white] blocks, from 1940 to 1950." [5]

Average assessed valuations, from 1940 to 1948, increased more for some blocks that became mixed in 1948, and decreased more for other mixed blocks, as compared with blocks that remained all-white. After 1948, while increases remained greater, decreases were smaller for the mixed blocks.

For selling prices—over the 1940–1950 period—the average on blocks that became mixed in 1948 increased 6.5 percent more than that for blocks which stayed all-white.

Thus there is a strong finding for this part of Wander's study that *within the test area* the prices for mixed blocks performed better than did those for all-white blocks.

An earlier study by the staff of the City of Detroit Mayor's Interracial Committee is reported to show generally favorable price findings for a racially mixed area of Detroit over the period 1946–1950.[6] Nonwhite entry is presumed to be heavy.

The selected test area was one with high Jewish occupancy, experiencing Negro entry during the four-year study period. A comparable all-white area was chosen as a control. The principal study findings are as follows:

1. The average price paid for two-family flats and single homes in the test area went up from its average level in 1946, and has come down only slightly.

2. Prices for these same types of property in the all-white area also went up but (a) in the case of two-family flats, came down to the

---

[5] *Ibid.*, p. 131.

[6] Richard Marks, "The Impact of Negro Population Movement on Property Values in a Selected Area in Detroit," City of Detroit, Mayor's Interracial Committee, January 16, 1950 (mimeo.). This is a summary of the complete study, which was not available for examination.

1946 level, and (b) dropped well below the 1946 average for single-family units.

3. Both areas showed considerable fluctuation in sales price/assessed valuation ratios over the four-year period, but the all-white area displayed the most marked fluctuation. Variation in the test area ratios did not appear to be associated with racial factors.

PORTLAND, OREGON

A survey by the Urban League of Portland is unique in focusing on comparative price behavior in five small neighborhood areas entered by only a single Negro family.[7] These are areas of predominantly single-family dwellings, selected according to the following criteria.

1. Representative residential districts, covering various price ranges.

2. Home purchased by nonwhite at least as new and attractive as the average white home in the area.

3. Test areas at least ten blocks distant from the Portland sections containing concentrations of nonwhites, and each in a different part of the city.

Each of the five test neighborhoods included all properties within 300 feet of the single nonwhite-occupied dwelling. This reflects a Portland zoning ordinance defining an "affected area" as all property within 300 feet of the property for which a zoning change is proposed.

A matching all-white control area was selected for each test area, closely similar in size, age and type of structures, value range, quality of streets and sidewalks, and general landscaping.

It is apparent, therefore, that the Portland Urban League study was focused on a particular type of problem: the influence of a single Negro-occupied dwelling upon the values of properties in the immediate vicinity. Moreover, by definition, buyers of such neighboring properties must all be whites; there is no question of replacing white by nonwhite demand as in many areas entered by nonwhites. Essentially, then, the study seeks to test the status of "affected" properties in the white market.

The survey compares selling prices in the five test areas with selling prices in the five matching control areas over the ten-year

---

[7] The Urban League of Portland, *Nonwhite Neighbors and Property Prices in Portland, Oregon* (1956).

period from 1944 to 1954. Sales data were gathered from county records. One of the test areas with high-value houses (average $40,000) did not yield enough sales to permit analysis. Comparative data for the remaining four pairs of test–control areas are summarized in table 5.

TABLE 5

Test Area–Control Area Comparisons: Portland, Oregon, 1944–1954

Item	Test 1	Control 1	Test 2	Control 2	Test 3	Control 3	Test 4	Control 4
Age of houses (years) ..	6 to 15	2 to 10	Wide range, few new	Same	Most 25 or more	Same	Most 25 or more	Same
Current value (1956, dollars)	6,500–12,750 av. 8,500	6,500–13,500 av. 10,000	5,500–14,000 av. 9,500	Same	Av. 14,000	Same	Av. 8,000	Same
Date of single Negro entry.............	1950	....	1951	....	1950	....	1940	....
Average selling prices (dollars)								
1944 or 1945........	6,287	6,300	6,000	4,300	7,690	8,260	4,400	4,100
1953 or 1954........	8,350	12,900	8,500	9,100	11,490	12,000	9,100	10,650
Percent increase in sales prices........	33	105	42	112	50	45	107	160
Number of sales after nonwhite entry....	5	3	6	5	7	11	9	12

Source: Compiled and adapted from Urban League of Portland, *Nonwhite Neighbors and Property Prices in Portland, Oregon* (1956).

Because of the small size of the test and control areas, the study is actually based on a very small number of sales. Selling price averages, therefore, are not highly stable and would be seriously affected by one or two transactions at an unusually high or unusually low price. There is also some reason to doubt that test and control areas were in fact properly matched with respect to all major factors affecting property values.[8] For these reasons, the results of the Portland survey do not warrant other than tentative conclusions.[9]

Subject to these reservations, the Portland study points to some significant facts. In the first place, in none of the five test areas was the entry of a Negro home buyer followed by a rush of sales. Real estate market activity appeared to be about the same

[8] The survey report asserts that house prices were apparently more influenced by factors such as the age, size, and type of house, and the attractiveness and desirability of the neighborhood than by the presence of a nonwhite. The former, however, are precisely the factors which the test area-control area procedure is designed to hold constant, allowing the effect of the racial factor to stand forth.

[9] It may be noted that the authors of the study appear to place more confidence in the results than does the present writer. Readers are referred to the Portland Urban League publication.

in both test and control areas, with a somewhat greater frequency of sales in two of the control neighborhoods.

In none of the four test areas shown in the table was the entry of a nonwhite family followed by a decline in the dollar value of properties. Instead, average selling prices moved upward with the general rise of real estate prices during the period considered. Relative to the control areas, however, the picture appears somewhat different. In two comparisons, the control areas show a wide margin of relative price superiority over the test areas; in another case, the advantage of the control area is less but still considerable; while one of the four comparisons finds test and control areas approximately on the same level with respect to price trends. Subject to the uncertain character of the data, therefore, it may be concluded that the entry of a single Negro family, not followed by others, did not absolutely depress but tended to retard the upward movement of house prices in the immediate vicinity, in three out of four cases studied.

XI

Financing of Transactions in Mixed Versus All-White Neighborhoods

The effects of financing upon price could be ignored in the present study if identical home financing opportunities were available to buyers regardless of race. Residential financing policies and practices could then be regarded as a general factor in each local real estate market. However, lending practices *do* vary with the race of the borrower.[1]

First, many *potential* sales to nonwhites fall through because institutional lenders will not make a loan. This is especially likely to happen when a nonwhite is trying to purchase a home in an all-white area. But since this study examines actual sales data, the fact that some potential sales failed to be consummated is not directly relevant.

Second, mortgage loans to nonwhites are frequently on less advantageous terms than to white borrowers because sources of credit tend to be different.[2] In analyzing sales that actually take place, most of which involve a loan or loans in addition to cash paid down, it is essential to ask whether whites and nonwhites receive comparable loans in comparable transactions. If they do, then lending practices are a general factor that can be ignored. If they do not, then the interpretation of sales price comparisons should take account of differentials in financing.

TERMS OF SALE AS AN INFLUENCE ON SELLING PRICE

Before presenting the analysis of financing for some of the areas covered by this report, it may be helpful to review the reasons

---

[1] A general analysis of mortgage financing in relation to minority groups is contained in Davis McEntire, *Residence and Race, Final and Comprehensive Report to the Commission on Race and Housing* (Berkeley: University of California Press, 1960), chapter xiii.

[2] *Ibid.*

why selling prices may be affected by differing financial arrangements.

In putting his house up for sale, every seller has some minimum price in mind. Naturally, he will try to get as much over
this price as he can, but he will not take less, unless he is under
strong pressure to sell. (If he does take less because of such
pressure, the resulting price is not regarded as one shaped by
normal market conditions, since it is not equally satisfactory to
seller and buyer.)

The seller's minimum price is set high enough so that, after all
selling commissions and other expenses are deducted and any
outstanding mortgage balances are paid off, he will receive a
net amount equal to his equity—as he defines it. In practice,
sellers differ considerably in the sophistication with which they
approach the calculation of their equities. While a few may try
to apply accounting and economic analysis to their home investment, most will take the real estate broker's advice as to what
they can expect to sell for. They may use the selling prices of
comparable homes in the area as a guide. Deducting selling
charges and outstanding loans yields their "equity" figure.[3]

For discussion purposes, assume the seller's house would bring
$8,000 in an all-cash sale, that he owes $5,000 on his old mortgage,
and that he would be satisfied with the $3,000 remaining to him
as his "equity." Selling expenses are not in point here and are
ignored.

There are several ways of financing the sale so that the seller
comes out with his full equity in cash. Obviously they all depend
on the buyer's ability to raise a total of $8,000. The buyer may
have $2,000 in cash and obtain a $6,000 first mortgage. He may
have $3,000 cash and assume the existing mortgage. He may have
no cash but be able to borrow the entire $8,000, perhaps resorting
to secondary financing or to a loan within the family.

---

[3] Of course, such an approach means that windfall gains or losses are lumped
into the "equity," depending on whether real estate prices have moved up or down
during the seller's period of ownership. The approach also ignores depreciation,
opportunity costs of alternative investments, imputed interest on actual investment, and imputed rental income; yet all have an important effect on a true equity
calculation. But the precise calculation of an owner's equity is not the issue here.
The important point is that the seller does have an "equity" figure in mind, and
this is what affects the eventual financing of the sale.

As long as the buyer shows up with $3,000 cash over and above the existing $5,000 mortgage, the seller's equity is fully realized. He need not trouble himself about how the buyer obtained the necessary financing. It is only when the buyer *cannot* get the $8,000 from "outside" sources that the seller's equity is affected, for the seller must then lend enough to the buyer to make up what he lacks (assuming that there is no better qualified buyer and that the seller decides to go through with the deal).

Thus, the seller's equity in cash is reduced by the amount of the loan he makes to the buyer, and he ends up with some amount of cash plus the seller's loan obligation for the equity balance. In most cases this loan obligation takes the form of a second mortgage on the property, since the buyer has already arranged for a first mortgage or assumed the existing one. The buyer is the mortgagor, the seller is the mortgagee, and the loan is made at an interest rate one to two points higher than the rates on first mortgages—around 6 or 7 percent at current levels.[4] Usually, the loan is payable in level monthly installments including a declining amount for interest, and has a payout period of from three to five years.

In theory, the higher interest rate on the second mortgage fully compensates the seller for the additional risks presumed to accompany a loan that takes "second place" to the first mortgage. In practice, it appears that, while the seller *might* be satisfied with the situation if he felt certain that he would hold the loan until it was fully paid up, he adjusts the sales transaction as though he definitely expected to sell the second mortgage to someone else *at a discount*. He performs this "adjustment" by making the total sales price high enough so that the necessarily larger second, when discounted, will bring in enough cash, when added to the cash down payment, to net him his $3,000 equity.

To know what his full sales price should be, the seller must assume some discount rate applicable to the expected future sale of the second mortgage. Currently, the second mortgage market is buying second mortgages for between 50 to 60 percent of the

---

[4] This is the *nominal* rate; the *effective* rate may be higher if the private lender charges a "premium." This can be done by having the borrower sign a note for more than is actually loaned him. The extent to which this happens is not known.

unpaid balance.[5] If the purchaser can get a $5,000 first mortgage and has $1,000 cash, he would be $2,000 short of the seller's "cash" price. Assuming a 50 percent discount on a second mortgage, the seller would now quote his minimum price at $10,000 rather than $8,000, offering to "take back" a second for $4,000. His arithmetic would look like this:

To be received from a buyer

Cash down payment..............................	$ 1,000
Proceeds of bank loan, secured by a first mortgage......	5,000
Promissory note for the balance, secured by a second mortgage held by the seller........................	4,000
	$10,000

The seller pays off the existing $5,000 mortgage, leaving $1,000 cash. Then he sells the second for $2,000 (discounts it 50 percent), thereby realizing his full $3,000 equity in cash. The buyer, of course, remains fully obligated for $4,000 and the house costs him a full $10,000 (plus loan interest and sales charges). As far as the seller is concerned, the "real" price is $8,000—he considers the discount involved in selling the second as just another selling expense.

Whoever buys the second stands to be repaid $4,000 (plus interest) on a $2,000 outlay—if nothing goes wrong. If the mortgagor defaults before the second is paid down to about $2,000, the mortgagee could lose some of his loan principal, because the selling price of the house would probably not cover the outstanding balance on both the first and second mortgages. The risk of loss would be even higher if real estate prices took a downturn. (Purchasers of second mortgages have fared very well indeed since 1940; defaults have been few and any that have occurred have probably been "covered" by a strongly rising real estate market.)

Of course, the seller may choose to hold the second mortgage rather than sell it on the discount market. In this case, he has really added an investment decision to his decisions bearing on the sale alone, and the eventual outcome of his investment as a lender should be thought of as an issue completely divorced from the sale. The reason for this is that he does have the opportunity

[5] In the San Francisco Bay Area, most buying of "seconds" is by individual investors; perhaps 10 percent is by small investment groups formed especially for this purpose. (Interviews with mortgage lenders and individual buyers of second mortgages, December, 1955.)

at the time of sale to receive his full equity in cash by selling the second, as already described. If he decides not to do this, then the consequences of that decision—whether good or bad—should not be treated as consequences of the sale itself.

In effect, the real meaning of his decision to hold the second mortgage is that he *has* received his full equity in cash ($3,000 in the example above) *and has then loaned $2,000 to the buyer,* secured by the second mortgage for $4,000. Whether he ever gets $4,000, plus interest, on his $2,000 investment, or later sells the second at a discount, is a separate issue entirely.

There is an additional refinement to this whole process as it occurs in "real life": sellers typically do not quote a minimum price and then raise it to buyers who have to ask for a seller-held second. Instead, their initial "asking price" is calculated on the assumption that any buyer will have to take a seller-held second for everything above the maximum loan commitment that can be obtained on the property.

In the example discussed above, if $5,000 is taken as the maximum loan obtainable and the discount on seconds is 50 percent, the asking price would be set at $11,000. A buyer with no cash of his own would have to pay this asking price, borrowing $6,000 on a seller-held second. This would net the seller $3,000 in the discount market, making up his required minimum price of $8,000.

The asking price could be proportionally reduced to correspond with the buyer's cash resources, if he uses the bargaining power available to him. Naturally, if the seller thinks he can net more than his $3,000 equity, he will try to do so. To a buyer with $1,000 to put down, the price could be $10,000; to one with $2,000, it could be $9,000; and for an all-cash buyer it could be $8,000. This is summarized in the following tabulation.

(1) Asking price (the "real" price from the buyer's point of view	$11,000	$10,000	$9,000	$8,000
(2) Cash down by buyer	0	1,000	2,000	3,000
(3) Maximum available first mortgage	5,000	5,000	5,000	5,000
(4) Second mortgage held by seller to cover the balance	6,000	4,000	2,000	0
(5) Net proceeds from sale of second mortgage (assuming a 50 per cent discount)	3,000	2,000	1,000	0
(6) Equity to seller (2) + (3) + (5) less $5,000 to pay off old mortgage	3,000	3,000	3,000	3,000
(7) Realized price (the "real" price from the seller's point of view (2) + (3) + (5)	8,000	8,000	8,000	8,000

The chief appraiser for a large savings and loan company sums it up this way: "When secondary financing is involved, the selling price is jacked up so that the seller will net roughly what he would on an all-cash-for-his-equity basis. Any price arrangements that yield him the same net that he would accept for an all-cash deal are equivalent to him—but obviously they aren't equivalent to the buyer." [6]

DISCOUNTED SECOND MORTGAGES AND "NET PRICE"

This lengthy commentary on the subject of second mortgage loans made by sellers is necessary in view of the heavy emphasis given it by the real estate business itself. Without exception, every broker, salesman, appraiser, and lender interviewed for the present study discussed it as an important feature of home resales, especially if nonwhite buyers are involved.

Most of those interviewed take the position that observed market prices for transactions involving the discounting of seller-held mortgages should be adjusted to reflect the sellers' realized price—that is, net of discount. In saying this, they are not suggesting that the "adjusted" prices would necessarily come out at a level below normal for the area concerned. They are following the exposition developed above: that sellers have set their asking prices high enough to allow for second mortgage discounts.

This is a reasonable position. But downward adjustment to observed market prices—so far as the objectives of the present study are concerned—would seem necessary only if sales in areas undergoing racial change involve a significantly higher proportion of seller-held financing than do sales in areas remaining all white.

The facts uncovered in studying the financing of sales in some of the areas discussed in this study show that all-white areas have the same proportion of seller-firsts and seller-seconds, and a 50 percent *higher* proportion of seller-thirds and above. Table 6 summarizes the financing information that was available for 1,413 sales in the San Francisco areas. While similar information for the other areas studied was not available, there is little reason to

---

[6] Interview, Oakland, California, September 7, 1955.

TABLE 6

MORTGAGES CLASSIFIED BY TYPE, FOR TRANSACTIONS
IN SAN FRANCISCO AREAS, 1949–1955

San Francisco areas compared	Number of transactions analyzed	Percent	Percent of transactions involving					
			First mortgage		Second mortgage		Third mortgage or higher	
			Seller mortgagee	Other than seller mortgagee	Seller mortgagee	Other than seller mortgagee	Seller mortgagee	Other than seller mortgagee
Summary comparison								
6 Test areas[a]......	665	100.0	1.9	63.5	16.8	14.8	0.8	2.2
8 Control areas....	748	100.0	1.2	68.9	16.4	11.1	1.2	1.2
Individual comparisons between comparable test and control areas:								
Test: Lakeview....	178	100.0	2.3	61.8	18.2	13.6	0.9	3.2
Control: Sunnyside	108	100.0	1.6	65.8	16.3	11.4	0.8	4.1
Test: Oceanview...	57	100.0	...	67.7	9.7	19.4	3.2	...
Control: Sunnyside	108	100.0	1.6	65.8	16.3	11.4	0.8	4.1
Control: Glen Park	112	100.0	...	63.5	17.6	14.9	2.7	1.3
Test: Silver Terrace A.........	124	100.0	1.3	70.8	16.5	10.1	...	1.3
Control: Geneva ..	26	100.0	...	80.0	15.0	5.0	...	...
Control: Silver-Alemany.......	102	100.0	0.8	69.4	16.1	12.9	0.8	...
Test: Silver Terrace B.........	98	100.0	0.9	69.2	14.0	15.0	...	0.9
Control: Visitacion Valley..........	87	100.0	...	73.0	8.1	16.2	...	2.7
Control: Mission-Geneva Terrace	112	100.0	...	75.0	19.2	5.8	...	...
Control: Silver-Alemany.......	102	100.0	0.8	69.4	16.1	12.9	0.8	...
Test: North of Ridge Lane.....	97	100.0	3.1	61.4	16.2	15.4	0 8	3.1
Control: Sunnyside	108	100.0	1.6	65.8	16.3	11.4	0 8	4.1
Test: South of Ridge Lane.....	111	100.0	...	60.0	30.0	10.0	...	...
Control: Glen Park	112	100.0	...	63.5	17.6	14.9	2.7	1.3

SOURCE: Files of Multiple Listing Service, San Francisco.

[a] Financial arrangements for sales in the other two test areas (Sunset and Ingleside Heights) are analyzed separately elsewhere in this chapter (p. 230).

suppose that financing differed significantly from that in the San Francisco areas.

From table 6 it can be seen that, of all seller-held financing in all areas, only second mortgages account for a large enough share of the total mortgage picture (about one-sixth) to constitute a possible reason for making downward adjustments in observed market prices. The categories of seller-held firsts and seller-held thirds and above account for only 2 to 3 percent of all mortgages, and their possible influence can be disregarded.

Of the 665 transactions occurring in the six test areas, only one in six (16.8 percent) involved a seller-held second. The proportion is almost exactly the same for the 748 control-area transactions (16.4 percent). With the same proportion of seller-held seconds in both types of areas, the only other possible variable would be in the average ratio of second mortgage to selling price.[7]

For all test area sales involving seller-held seconds, the second mortgage averaged 26 percent of the total purchase price. The corresponding control-area figure is 21.3 percent.[8] Translated into actual loan figures, this means that a $10,000 house selling in a test area would carry an average seller-held second loan of $2,600, as against one for $2,130 if it sold in a control area. The difference of $470 does not appear to be very significant, in view of these two points:

1. If the seller *did* sell the second,[9] and assuming a 50 percent discount is applicable, the average amount discounted would be $235, or 2.3 percent of the average selling price. This is a minor variation as compared with observed fluctuations in neighborhood prices.

2. Not only is the discount a small proportion of the sale price, but, as already observed, seller-held second mortgages, on the average, were involved in but one sale out of every six. This held for test areas as well as control areas. Any adjustment for these sales, therefore, would not affect the total picture appreciably.

With respect to individual areas studied, table 6 shows some variation in the test–control comparisons of seller-held seconds. Control areas have a larger proportion of mortgages in this category in five comparisons, while the test areas exceed in the remaining ones. No matter which areas have larger proportions of seller-held seconds, the differences are relatively small in most cases. If the test-area excesses alone are considered—and this would give all possible leeway to the view that areas of racial change have numerous seller-held seconds and their market prices

---

[7] It is important to keep in mind that these statistics refer only to the second mortgages that are held by sellers. When *all* second mortgages are considered, irrespective of holders, the evidence indicates greater dependence on this type of financing by nonwhite than by white buyers.

[8] These figures are very close to those for *all* second mortgages as a proportion of purchase price: 25.3 percent in the test areas and 21.7 percent in the control areas. (See table 10, p. 229.)

[9] No statistics are available to show the proportion of sellers who hold, rather than sell, the secondary financing for which they are the mortgagees. Interviews with mortgage lenders and private buyers of mortgages yielded the estimate that three-fourths of all sellers hold such financing to maturity because of "good investment" and "small risk."

should therefore be scaled down—there is but one that is significantly large: South of Ridge Lane (30.0 percent) vs. Glen Park (17.6 percent). Some readers may wish to consider this in reviewing the relative behavior of market prices in those areas. Adjusting for differences in seller-held seconds would make a net average reduction of $272 in test prices relative to control prices. This is not enough, however, to alter the findings for that pair of areas.

To summarize, then, the similarity between test and control areas in regard to seller-held seconds results in market prices in both types of areas being affected in about the same way. Thus the whole subject can be disregarded in connection with the present examination of comparative market price behavior.

VA LOANS: A SPECIAL CASE

Some comment is called for concerning the price effects of discounting practices frequently arising in connection with Veterans Administration-guaranteed loans. As in the case of secondary financing that may be subject to eventual discount, transactions involving a discounted VA loan may be closed at a price higher than that which would result from an all-cash or non-VA transaction. It is argued by some that observations of market prices should allow for the boosting effect produced by any discounted VA loans.

VA-guaranteed loans were a significant financing element for only a few of the specific neighborhoods studied for this report. Most VA loans are made on new or fairly new homes, usually in tract developments. The only study areas having characteristics that made them eligible for significant numbers of these loans were:

Test Areas	Control Areas
Brookfield Village (Oakland)	San Lorenzo (San Lorenzo Village)
Columbia Gardens (Oakland)	North of Davis (San Leandro)
Silver Terrace A (San Francisco)	South of Davis (San Leandro)
Silver Terrace B (San Francisco)	Sobrante Park (Oakland)
Sunset (San Francisco)	Silver-Alemany (San Francisco)
	Geneva (San Francisco)
	Visitacion Valley (San Francisco)

Brookfield Village and *Columbia Gardens* were the two test areas most affected by VA financing during the period of observation. But it should be kept in mind that their comparable control areas (the first four listed) experienced about the same amount of such financing, so that the price-boosting effects that probably occurred were common to test and control areas alike. For all areas where the point discount system was standard procedure, white buyers were subject to the same "loan brokerage fee" as non-whites. The only differential factor that was linked to race in the whole situation was that areas undergoing racial change carried about one additional discount point in comparison with all-white areas.[10] This is such an insignificant differential that it may be disregarded.

OTHER ASPECTS OF FINANCING
IN SAN FRANCISCO AREAS

All but a minor percentage of sales in the test areas—after the all-white pattern was broken—were to nonwhites. The financial details for these sales therefore provide an opportunity to check certain aspects of financing in the test areas against the same aspects in the white control areas.[11] In this way, some light can be shed on a number of significant questions relating to the financing of nonwhite home purchases.

Cash, primary, and secondary financing.—The general pattern of financing showed appreciable differences as between white and nonwhite purchases. It may be seen from table 7 that about one white buyer in eight (12.8 percent) paid all cash, whereas only one nonwhite buyer in twenty (5.7 percent) did so. Each test area shows a lower proportion of all-cash sales than does the matching control area—the single exception being Silver Terrace B, where all-cash sales were more frequent than in two of its three control areas.

Cash plus a first mortgage accounted for a more nearly similar proportion of sales: 53.6 percent in the control areas, compared with 48.4 percent in the test areas.

Secondary financing appears to have been necessary to a greater extent in the test areas: second mortgages were resorted to in

---

[10] Based on interviews with institutional lenders, loan brokers, and real estate firms, July to September, 1951; August to September, 1953; September to November, 1955.

[11] Financing details were not available for all sales in the areas studied. The discussion that follows is based on financial data for 665 test sales and 748 control sales in San Francisco.

TABLE 7

NUMBER AND PROPORTION OF TEST AND CONTROL AREA TRANSACTIONS INVOLVING CASH ONLY, FIRST MORTGAGE, AND ADDITIONAL MORTGAGES, SAN FRANCISCO, 1949–1955

San Francisco areas	All transactions		Transactions involving										
			All cash[a]			First mortgage only[b]			First and second mortgage[c]			Three or more mortgages[d]		
	No.	Total dollar amount (000)	No.	Percent	Dollar amount (000)	No.	Percent	Dollar amount (000)	No.	Percent	Dollar amount (000)	No.	Percent	Dollar amount (000)
All Test Areas[e]	665	7,340	38	5.7	386	322	48.4	3,574	279	42.0	3,093	26	3.9	287
T-1 South of Ridge Lane (C-1)	111	1,088	6	=5.4	46	30	27.0	285	75	67.6	757	..	..	..
T-2 Silver Terrace A (C-2, C-3)	124	1,446	4	3.2	36	70	56.5	822	46	37.1	542	4	3.2	46
T-3 North of Ridge Lane (C-4)	97	1,054	3	3.1	26	51	52.6	553	38	39.2	421	5	−5.1	54
T-4 Silver Terrace B (C-2, C-5, C-6)	98	1,281	8	+8.2	125	56	57.1	726	30	−30.6	381	4	4.1	49
T-5 Lakeview (C-4)	178	1,882	15	8.4	133	81	45.5	834	71	39.9	794	11	−6.2	120
T-7 Oceanview (C-1, C-4)	57	589	2	3.5	20	34	+59.7	354	19	−33.3	198	2	−3.5	18
All Control Areas	748	9,034	96	12.8	1,254	401	53.6	4,919	228	30.5	2,601	23	3.1	260
C-1 Glen Park	112	1,145	6	5.4	51	50	44.6	530	48	42.9	491	8	7.1	73
C-2 Silver-Alemany	102	1,083	4	3.9	37	59	57.8	620	37	36.3	400	2	2.0	26
C-3 Geneva	26	379	2	5.3	20	12	63.1	244	12	31.6	115	..	..	..
C-4 Sunnyside	108	1,126	12	11.1	108	62	57.4	654	27	25.0	281	7	6.5	83
C-5 Mission–Geneva Terrace	112	1,474	18	16.1	259	68	60.7	852	26	23.2	363	..	..	..
C-6 Visitacion Valley	87	1,016	3	3.4	45	54	62.1	653	27	31.1	284	3	3.4	34
C-7 Lincoln–Judah	201	2,811	51	25.7	734	96	48.2	1,366	51	25.7	667	3	0.5	44

SOURCE: Files of Multiple Listing Service, San Francisco.

a Test areas generally show smaller proportion of sales for all cash. Exceptions are marked + (greater) or = (equal).

b Test areas generally show smaller proportion of sales for cash plus first mortgage. Exceptions are marked + (greater).

c Test areas generally show higher proportion of sales with a second mortgage. Exceptions are marked − (smaller).

d Test areas generally show higher proportion of sales with three or more mortgages. Exceptions are marked − (smaller).

e Six test areas are shown. Matching control areas are shown in parentheses. Financial arrangements for sales in the other two test areas (Sunset and Ingleside Heights) are analyzed separately elsewhere in this chapter.

42 percent of all sales, as compared with 30.5 percent for the control areas.[12] Sales with three or more mortgages accounted for 3.9 percent of test sales and 3.1 percent of control sales.

It seems reasonable to infer from the data in table 7 that non-whites were relatively less able to purchase homes for all cash or with cash plus a first mortgage. Thus, they had to employ secondary financing in over two out of five sales (46 percent), while white buyers needed to do so in only two sales out of six (34 percent).

Down payments.—The determination of final selling price for a home is partially a function of the size of down payment. Presumably, a seller faced with two offers to buy, one involving $1,000 cash down, and the other $2,000 cash down, would be willing to quote a price to the larger cash buyer which was lower by an amount equal to (or less than) the difference between $1,000 and the value of a $1,000 note discounted to the present at some expected rate of interest. This assumes, of course, that the seller would have to carry the extra $1,000 himself if he sold to the lower cash bidder. If outside financing were available for the full amount of the balance involved in either offer, there would be no reason for the seller not to quote the same price to both buyers.

Thus, the down payment is significant insofar as its size may or may not involve the seller in some seller-held financing. The relevance of this factor for the present study is obvious: other things being equal, a price comparison between two identical houses sold to buyers with differing amounts of cash down might lead an observer erroneously to infer the existence of a difference in "value," traceable to some distinct features of the properties themselves. It must be determined, then, whether amounts paid down by nonwhites differed enough, on the average, from those paid down by whites to cause what might be considered serious price reactions under conditions of nonwhite purchase.

Judging from the financial data available for the San Francisco areas, there is some evidence that nonwhites are not able to put as

---

[12] As already noted, when *all* second mortgages are examined, rather than just those held by sellers, it is evident that nonwhites depend on them more heavily than whites.

much cash down as are white buyers. Table 8 shows that non-white buyers averaged cash down payments of from one-fifth to one-eighth of purchase price. As might be expected, plural mortgages were accompanied by relatively smaller cash down payments.

TABLE 8

PERCENT OF PURCHASE PRICE PAID IN CASH, BY TYPE OF FINANCING,
SAN FRANCISCO TEST AND CONTROL AREAS, 1949–1955

San Francisco areas	Cash down payment as a percent of purchase price, for sales involving		
	First mortgage only	First and second mortgage	Three or more mortgages
Test areas and matching control areas			
T-1 South of Ridge Lane (C-1)...........	17.9	12.8	...
T-2 Silver Terrace A (C-2, C-3)...........	17.3	16.7	15.3
T-3 North of Ridge Lane (C-4)...........	25.1	16.0	10.9
T-4 Silver Terrace B (C-2, C-5, C-6)......	19.2	14.3	⎰ 8.2
T-5 Lakeview (C-4).....................	21.6	13.3	12.5
T-6 Oceanview (C-1, C-4)...............	24.1	15.4	14.0
Weighted[a] average, test areas..........	20.7	14.3	12.1
Control areas			
C-1 Glen Park.........................	31.0	15.4	17.1
C-2 Silver-Alemany.....................	23.4	16.3	1.9
C-3 Geneva............................	17.8	14.3	...
C-4 Sunnyside.........................	26.1	17.6	10.4
C-5 Mission-Geneva Terrace.............	32.3	16.7	...
C-6 Visitacion Valley...................	26.0	19.7	25.1
C-7 Lincoln-Judah.....................	31.0	20.1	13.8
Weighted[a] average, control areas.......	28.3	17.5	14.4

SOURCE: Files of Multiple Listing Service, San Francisco.
[a] Weighted by number of transactions.

The proportion of purchase price paid in cash by white buyers ranged from over a fourth to one-seventh, again varying according to the type of financing structure adopted. By comparison, then, cash down payments by nonwhite buyers averaged from 16 to 25 percent less than those by white buyers using comparable financing. Individual test-control comparisons in table 8 show the same general pattern, although there is some variation from the average for the test–control comparisons as a whole.

The finding that nonwhites, on the average, make smaller down payments than do whites is not an unexpected one. It is a direct reflection of their weaker earnings—and assets. More notable is the high percent of purchase price paid in cash by whites and nonwhites alike during a period characterized by large-scale reliance on VA-guaranteed and FHA-insured mortgages with high loan-appraisal ratios. Of course, one would not expect to find small cash down payments of 10 percent or less, as is so often observable in sales of new tract homes. By far the majority of all sales, in both test and control areas, involved used homes, and— in the case of FHA applications, at least—these could not qualify for as large appraisals or loans as could new properties. Nevertheless, the down payments—particularly where first mortgages only are involved—are quite substantial.

Size of loan.—It is frequently alleged that racial discrimination may affect lending policies so that nonwhites—if they receive loans at all—do so on terms less favorable than those which would be available to white borrowers on the same properties. That lenders are acutely aware of changing racial patterns, and that their awareness may lead them to formulate lending policies accordingly, is quite clear from their own statements.[13] However, it is equally clear that most lenders are referring to one of two situations when they speak of limiting or denying loans to nonwhite applicants. The first situation is that of property in a long-established "mixed" area of varied older structures, many of which have been converted to multiple-unit rentals—an area generally considered to be deteriorating and therefore associated with a high risk factor. The second situation involves property in an all-white neighborhood.

In the first situation it is likely that *any* borrower, regardless of race, will be denied a loan (or will get one with a smaller loan/appraisal ratio), simply because the general neighborhood is going through the downward swing of its "life cycle" and is considered less desirable than other areas of the city. By contrast, the second situation may frequently lead a lender to refuse a loan to a nonwhite because of personal prejudice, lending policy, or apprehension concerning unfavorable neighborhood reaction.

Neither situation is relevant to a loan application by a nonwhite seeking to buy in an already mixed neighborhood of comparable

---

[13] See chapter ii above. See also McEntire, *Residence and Race* . . . , chapter xiii.

homes in good physical condition. Judging by the statements of some lenders, they would evaluate such a loan application just as though it were made by a white.[14] The San Francisco test areas, for which financing information is available, involved many such loan applications and therefore provide an opportunity to check loan terms against those extended to white borrowers in the all-white control areas.

It cannot be determined how many nonwhite loan applications covering test area properties were denied outright—if any were. But those that did arise out of favorable lender decisions may be set alongside loans extended to whites on comparable control-area homes.

In table 9 the weighted average loan observed for six test areas and seven control areas is listed by type of mortgage, type of mortgagee, and interest rate. The proportion of loans in various interest rate categories is also shown, as is the proportion of loans in the several mortgage-type classifications.

Two main conclusions emerge from these data: (a) With respect to average loan size, the significant classification is first mortgages, because the size of secondary mortgages is directly affected by the size of the average down payment. It has already been shown that nonwhites have smaller down payments and therefore somewhat larger second and third mortgages. For all first mortgage categories the weighted average test-area loan exceeded the weighted average control-area loan in five cases and fell short in three. This implies that nonwhites were generally loaned as high a proportion of the purchase price as were whites, when they were able to obtain a first mortgage. It should be recalled that these loans were made on comparable properties in comparable neighborhoods so that the parallel performance of white–nonwhite loans is highly significant. (b) With respect to interest rates, all mortgage categories may be considered. Again, it appears that nonwhites obtained about the same proportion of loans at each rate of interest as did whites, implying equal treatment by lenders. Nonwhite borrowers actually fared better than whites for seller-held firsts and other than seller-held third and higher mortgages in that they had larger proportions of loans at

---

[14] Interviews with officials of lending institutions, August to November, 1951.

TABLE 9

AVERAGE DOLLAR SIZE AND RELATIVE SIGNIFICANCE OF LOANS, BY TYPE OF MORTGAGE,
TYPE OF MORTGAGEE, AND INTEREST RATE, SAN FRANCISCO AREAS, 1949–1955

Classification of mortgage, mortgagee, and interest rate	Weighted average loan (dollars)		Percent of each classification		Percent of all mortgages	
	Test areas[a]	Control areas	Test areas[a]	Control areas	Test areas[a]	Control areas
All mortgages...............	....	....	....	....	100.0	100.0
First mortgages.............					65.4	70.0
With seller mortgagee......			100.0	100.0	(1.2)	(1.4)
5 percent	10,033	8,750	42.9	28.6		
5½ percent	6,000	....	14.2	....		
6 percent	9,633	8,290	42.9	71.4		
With other than seller mortgagee...........			100.0	100.0	(64.2)	(68.6)
3 percent	....	8,500	....	0.2		
4 percent	8,074	7,477	31.5	27.1		
4½ percent	9,537	9,156	28.1	28.5		
4¾ percent	7,300	10,000	0.5	0.5		
5 percent	7,333	7,890	5.8	11.5		
5½ percent	8,790	8,197	2.6	5.9		
6 percent	6,217	6,650	31.2	26.3		
7 percent	11,500	....	0.3	....		
Second mortgages..........					31.6	27.5
With seller mortgagee......			100.0	100.0	(16.8)	(16.4)
5 percent	725	3,262	2.0	5.2		
5½ percent	2,825	....	1.0	....		
6 percent	3,041	2,530	94.0	94.8		
7 percent	2,772	....	3.0	....		
With other than seller mortgagee...........			100.0	100.0	(14.8)	(11.1)
4 percent	1,684	1,204	3.4	7.4		
4½ percent	....	....	....	....		
5 percent	1,990	1,387	1.1	5.6		
6 percent	2,754	2,397	81.0	87.0		
7 percent	3,460	....	3.4	....		
Third and higher mortgages...					3.0	2.4
With seller mortgagee......			100.0	100.0	(0.8)	(1.2)
6 percent	1,074	1,596	100.0	100.0		
With other than seller mortgagee...........			100.0	100.0	(2.2)	(1.2)
5 percent	550	....	6.7	....		
6 percent	1,947	1,064	92.3	85.7		
7 percent	....	2,750	....	14.3		

SOURCE: Files of Multiple Listing Service, San Francisco.
[a] Data for test areas are for period *after* nonwhite entry only.

the lower interest ranges. They fared worse than whites in the case of all second mortgages, but only to a minor degree.[15]

Loan as a percent of purchase price.—The financial data for the San Francisco areas provide an additional piece of evidence that strengthens the suggestion that nonwhites who obtained loans in those areas were treated in the same way as white borrowers. This evidence is found by examining the loan as a percent of purchase price. Discriminatory lending policy would show up in the form of lower loan/price percents for nonwhite borrowers. Table 10 presents loan/price percents for all categories of mortgages and various rates of interest.

TABLE 10

AVERAGE LOAN/PRICE PERCENTAGES, BY TYPE OF MORTGAGE AND BY RATE
OF INTEREST, SAN FRANCISCO AREAS, 1949–1955

Mortgage category and areas	Rate of interest (percent)						All rates combined (weighted)
	4	4½	5	5½	6	7	
First mortgages							
Test areas..........	71.5	82.2	66.1	62.2	61.7	...	69.3
Control areas........	70.7	76.7	64.2	61.6	63.7	...	68.6
Second mortgages							
Test areas..........	16.2	...	14.5	21.5	26.4	29.1	25.3
Control areas........	29.6	15.0	23.7	13.8	21.9	21.8	21.7
Third and higher mortgages							
Test areas..........	...	...	3.6	...	15.5	...	14.9
Control areas........	...	...	...	...	11.8	24.0	12.3

SOURCE: Files of Multiple Listing Service, San Francisco.

[15] Discussion of interest rates must remain incomplete, however, in the absence of any data on the *effective* rates of interest charged by private lenders. For example, the records may show a $2,000 seller-held second with a stipulated 6 percent interest rate. But the borrower may have received only $1,800 as proceeds of the loan. Assuming a five-year payout period, the extra $200 premium raises the *effective* interest rate to around 10 percent.

Many private lenders undoubtedly make such "premium" loans, but since no records of such transactions exist, the extent of this practice is unknown. White and nonwhite buyers alike would presumably be subject to such premium payments, but some lenders might charge higher premiums to nonwhites. If they do, this becomes a hidden extra cost of shelter for nonwhite purchasers, charged them either because the lender really believes a higher loan risk is involved or because he wants to give expression to his prejudice.

It should be noted that comparisons of interest rates paid before 1940 showed nonwhites paying noticeably higher rates. This was primarily due to the poorer quality of the housing they were purchasing during that time. Since 1940, they have been able to buy property generally comparable to that purchased by whites.

First mortgages are, again, the significant subject for analysis, for the reason already discussed above. It is apparent that non-whites received the same loan/price percent, on the average, as did whites. The combined loan/price percents, weighted by number of loans at each interest rate, are remarkably close: test areas —69.3; control areas—68.6. At individual rates of interest, the loan/price percent is noticeably higher in the test areas, except at the 6 percent rate.

For secondary loans, the average percent of loan to purchase price is higher in the test areas, confirming the already established fact that nonwhites resort to larger second and third mortgages.

TEST AREAS WITH LIGHT ENTRY
OR UNDER "THREAT" OF ENTRY

Two test areas—Sunset and Ingleside Heights—have been omitted from the preceding analysis of financing in the San Francisco neighborhoods studied. They are singled out for special attention in order to see whether any abnormal financing patterns for *white* borrowers developed under the conditions of very light nonwhite entry (Sunset) or during a period of anticipated heavy nonwhite entry (Ingleside Heights).

The Sunset area, it will be recalled, had between twenty-five to thirty nonwhite families moving in, beginning in 1952, with the nonwhite proportion reaching a little over 3 percent by late 1955 (see chap. vi, p. 114). Eight or ten of these families were of Chinese or Japanese stock.

Ingleside Heights, a heavy entry area, was in the path of a westward nonwhite settlement pattern, and its white occupants had clear notice that nonwhites would eventually be buying in their neighborhood. Contiguous areas just to the east had non-white occupancy of from 8 to 12 percent for one or two years before the first Negro family moved into Ingleside Heights.

Financing patterns in the Sunset area *during* light nonwhite entry and in the Ingleside Heights area *before* heavy nonwhite entry were contrasted with those for both the individual and grouped white control areas. The results show no significant differences in any of the financing aspects, including structure of financing, cash down, average loan size, range of interest rates, and percent of loan to purchase price. White borrowers in these two test areas, although exposed to the racial influences just described, obtained loans with characteristics similar to those made to borrowers in the all-white control areas.

XII

Standards of Property Maintenance
by Nonwhite Owners

Although very little reference to standards of property maintenance by nonwhite homeowners is found in the real estate literature, many white property owners, judging from their frequent mention of the subject, appear to believe that nonwhites do not keep up the property they occupy.[1] If this were so, it would naturally have a deteriorative effect on neighborhood appearance and a decrease in values would probably follow.

It is not this chapter's purpose to explore the subject exhaustively—that would constitute a major project in itself. However, the condition of property is intimately bound up with the price-formation process, and it is therefore appropriate to present some evidence on the comparative maintenance performed by nonwhite and white homeowners.

Writing for the *Insured Mortgage Portfolio* in 1949, Margaret Kane reported on the answers of FHA field directors in a survey of their experience with Negroes as credit risks and property owners. The following, she says, is a typical statement: "In summary, on the basis of contacts with lending institutions, builders, and investors who have had experience with Negroes in home financing on sound economic principles, a uniformly excellent record with Negroes as credit risks has been established. In addition to favorable credit experience, *these groups are enthusiastic about the way Negroes maintain and improve their properties.*"[2]

In 1944, the National Association of Real Estate Boards surveyed local boards in eighteen important American cities to determine

---

[1] Based on statements gathered in interviews with white homeowners in transition areas, August to December, 1951; September to November, 1955.

[2] Margaret Kane, "A Wider Field for Mortgage Lending," *Insured Mortgage Portfolio* (Washington, D. C.: Federal Housing Administration), Fourth Quarter, 1949, pp. 15–18. Italics supplied.

local experience with Negroes as credit risks and property maintainers. The press release of the survey stated that "thirteen out of 18 answered yes to the question, 'Does the Negro take care of his property if it is in good repair when he obtained it?' Eleven out of 18 answered yes to the question 'Does the Negro take as good care of property as other tenants of comparable status?' " [3]

A recent study by the Legislative Information Committee of the National Community Relations Advisory Council reports that "statistics accumulated by the United States Housing Authority and the Federal Housing Authority show that Negroes and whites of comparable incomes have practically identical records of property maintenance and payment, regardless of whether they live in mixed or segregated neighborhoods. In fact, these statistics show that Negroes have a slightly better record in this respect than whites." [4]

Perhaps the most thorough analysis yet made of property maintenance in a local neighborhood is the one described in Gillette's property value study, already discussed in chapter ix.[5] Santa Fe, the Kansas City neighborhood he analyzed, had 392 homes, of which 194 were Negro-owned and -occupied in May, 1953, when he made his observations. He interviewed a majority of these Negro homeowners and personally inspected their homes, as well as those of whites, both in that neighborhood and in an all-white control neighborhood. On the basis of 202 interviews and inspections, Gillette reported that a higher percentage of Negro homeowners had made and were making repairs and improvements than were white homeowners of comparable properties. He concludes that the nonwhite homeowners were raising the general physical condition of the Santa Fe neighborhood.

Gillette gives two possible reasons for the greater home maintenance and repair activities on the part of the nonwhites: (a) The test area may have needed more repairs because whites foresaw the invasion and let their properties go relatively untended.

---

[3] National Association of Real Estate Boards, *Press Release No. 78* (November 15, 1944). Cited in Robert C. Weaver, *The Negro Ghetto* (New York: Harcourt, Brace and Company, 1948), p. 292.

[4] *Equality of Opportunity in Housing, A Handbook of Facts* (New York: National Community Relations Advisory Council, June, 1952).

[5] Thomas L. Gillette, "Santa Fe: A Study of the Effects of Negro Invasion on Property Values" (unpublished Master's thesis, Department of Sociology, University of Kansas City, 1954).

(No evidence one way or the other is presented on this point; even if it were true, the fact that the Negroes made the needed repairs is a positive piece of evidence.) (*b*) The incoming Negro group was of a higher socioeconomic level and therefore had a greater drive to raise neighborhood property maintenance standards and improve homes. (Gillette found a marked superiority in educational background, occupational level, and income for the incoming Negro families as compared with whites in either the transition or all-white areas.) An additional possible explanation is that the Negroes were new homeowners, behaving toward their properties in the way that new owners frequently do, whereas most whites in the control area had been in possession of their properties for considerable periods of time.

In the scores of interviews held with real estate brokers familiar with the neighborhoods studied for the present report, a virtual unanimity of opinion prevailed as to the nonwhite homeowner's good record in property upkeep. A sampling of typical statements follows:

Colored owners maintain properties better than whites do in this neighborhood. About 70 percent of the colored make repairs and paint up their property.

The average colored owner takes pride in his property and keeps it up well. Some of the newer owners may neglect homes because they have never owned property before. VA financing has enabled them to buy, but they have only a small equity in their property, and treat it almost like rental. But this is also true of whites in the same situation.

There has been a decided improvement in property maintenance since the Negroes started moving in. They're doing a better job than the original white owners.

Inside and out, the colored homes look as good as or better than they did when their white owners occupied them.

The neighborhood condition is good. Maintenance by the Negroes is up to average standard, or better.

Whites staying in the neighborhood say that the colored upkeep is up to or better than what the previous owners did.

Confirmation of the brokers' opinions was provided through the writer's personal inspections, on a repeated and intensive basis, of all the areas studied. Judging by the physical appearance alone of the neighborhoods and individual dwelling units, it was impossible to distinguish which ones had nonwhite occupants. These observations were not limited to house exteriors only; over 100 interviews with white and nonwhite homeowners permitted a close view of interior maintenance, furnishings, and standards of cleanliness. On all counts, the nonwhites as a group at least matched the whites, according to the writer's observations. In the absence of any systematic measurement of maintenance conditions these observations were necessarily subjective; yet the general maintenance comparability of two properties is not a complex thing to judge.

On one occasion, in 1953, the writer set aside a weekend for the specific purpose of checking the number of properties in all the San Francisco areas that were being painted or otherwise treated by the owners for exterior maintenance. A street-by-street coverage of every one of the fifteen test and control areas produced a total tally of 83 major projects, such as exterior painting, reroofing, and extensive landscaping. Out of these, 55 were for homes with nonwhite occupants. As houses in all the areas studied are predominantly owner-occupied, it may be presumed that the nonwhite occupants of these 55 homes owned them.

In addition to the normal motivations of homeowners to property maintenance, many of the nonwhite owners interviewed by the present writer indicated incentives of "race pride" and feelings of being on trial. Following are two characteristic statements:

We certainly intend to have our property look at least as good as the rest of the homes in this neighborhood. Some white people in this block are hurting neighborhood appearances by not keeping their lawns and houses up very well. Why are they concerned with possible value effects [from new nonwhite neighbors] when they are responsible for definite value effects?

We feel that anyone who behaves objectionably should be called down for it, regardless of race. We are trying hard to improve the appearance of the place in every way, and I've talked with Mrs. J—— [a Negro neighbor] to try to do more with the garden in front. Good maintenance helps Negroes in general to find better housing.

The fragmentary and unsystematic evidence presented on the subject of nonwhite property maintenance cannot be taken as conclusive. But the evidence that is available strongly suggests that nonwhites who are buying homes in formerly white neighborhoods are "keeping up with the Joneses" in taking care of their property. It is quite probable that much of the white-held belief about substandard maintenance by nonwhites stems from observation of overcrowded slum areas, where nonwhites are predominantly tenants and where most landlords spend little, if anything, to maintain the appearance of property in which their only interest is the derivation of income.

Appendices

Research Method

Supplementing the discussion of research methods in chapter iii, further information is presented below concerning the selection of test and control neighborhoods and sources of price data.

SELECTING THE TEST NEIGHBORHOODS

For reasons already given in chapter iii, this study focused on formerly all-white residential neighborhoods outside the central city area which had experienced various amounts of nonwhite entry during the study period. These were identified through official city records and real estate offices.

The redevelopment agencies, in most cities where they exist, are accumulating as much information as they can concerning the residential location of nonwhites, since this has an important bearing on their relocation policies. The three cities studied—San Francisco, Oakland, and Philadelphia—had enough official data to permit a broad identification of neighborhoods undergoing recent racial change. To check on whether any neighborhoods might have been overlooked, the mailing lists of several local Negro, Chinese, and Japanese publications were analyzed and officials of the principal nonwhite organizations interviewed.

The next step was to become familiar with each of these neighborhoods through close inspection, conversations with residents, and interviews with real estate brokers actively selling in them. In this way, the details on the dates and extent of nonwhite entry were obtained, and each neighborhood was classified according to price range, type and age of structures, and access to services.

Every one of these neighborhoods in San Francisco and Oakland—eight and nine, respectively—were used as test areas for the study. In Philadelphia, however, because of time and budget limitations, three of the most typical neighborhoods were selected out of a total of some eighteen. These three were chosen in accordance with the considered judgment of four of the city's leading appraisers, men who knew the city so well that they could readily evaluate neighborhood-by-neighborhood comparisons. The selection was made so as to yield a range of selling prices and a variation in the degree and speed of nonwhite entry.

NEIGHBORHOOD BOUNDARIES

A broad neighborhood selection of the kind just described was not enough. Specific boundaries had to be defined for each test area—and for each control area as well—so that selling price data could be gathered according to street and block.

The neighborhood boundaries of significance for this study are those surrounding groups of residences the prices of which react more or less together in response to the play of market factors. Such uniformity of price behavior comes about when topography or street pattern or likeness of structure—separately or together —link a number of residences into an economic unit. If, for example, several owners neglect their properties, the selling price of every house in that neighborhood will probably be lowered because the general desirability of the area will have fallen.

When this kind of price interdependence is present, one is clearly dealing with a neighborhood which constitutes a local market area. Its boundaries are usually quite distinct, being partially formed by some natural feature such as a ravine or ridge, or by a man-made barrier like a freeway, primary street, or park. Because of the way in which most neighborhoods are built up, one almost always finds that the architectural and structural features of homes change when such neighborhood boundaries are crossed, and this is usually accompanied by differences in original costs. Naturally, this reinforces the tendency of such areas to behave as local market units.

The neighborhood concept involved in the property value question would logically seem to be the one empirically developed by those most familiar with neighborhoods as *market areas:* the real estate brokers and salesmen. These businessmen generally subdivide their areas of operation into fairly small neighborhoods, averaging about ten to fifteen blocks each. These are usually well defined by physical boundaries, often carry widely recognized names, and possess some degree of community consciousness. It is these types of areas that real estate practitioners and writers have in mind when they refer to neighborhoods affected by nonwhite entry. Direct interviewing repeatedly revealed that brokers and salesmen look upon these areas as economic units, each responding fairly cohesively to all the factors that affect value trends in a particular locality. Since each neighborhood has a predominant—often uniform—type of residential structure, selling prices move up and down in a reasonably compact cluster.

By working closely with real estate brokers, salesmen, and appraisers who were intimately familiar with the test areas already broadly determined, it was possible to identify the precise market-area boundaries for each one. The basic consideration governing these boundary determinations was that there be a clear distinction between the average price level and general price behavior on one side of the boundary as compared with the other. It would seem that there could be no better authorities for such a determination than those who daily handle transactions on both sides of those boundaries.

Using this method, the twenty test neighborhoods were bounded as shown by maps 2, 4, and 6.

Simultaneously, the boundaries of nineteen control neighborhoods were established by the same general methods, again guided by the real estate authorities familiar with the areas concerned. As outlined in the text, the criteria for selecting the control neighborhoods were such as to make them similar to the test areas in every regard but one—they experienced no nonwhite entry or threat of entry during the period covered by the study.

One further comment concerning neighborhood boundaries: obviously the behavior of average prices would have been distorted if the boundaries had erroneously been set too widely, exceeding the natural market area and embracing portions of adjoining market areas. The distortion would have been up or down, depending on the relative price levels in these neighborhoods. To avoid this, in the few instances where no distinct physical feature was present to form a boundary and there was some difference of opinion among the experts as to just where the boundary should be set, the problem was resolved by moving the boundary toward the center of the neighborhood until all the real estate consultants agreed that it clearly did not include any part of an adjoining neighborhood. While this procedure reduced the size of several neighborhoods somewhat under what their natural market area might have been, it ensured that all sales occurring within the boundaries as established were influenced by the same set of market factors.

THE COLLECTION OF PRICE DATA

As described in the text, about 85 percent of the selling price data for the thirty-three San Francisco and Oakland test and control neighborhoods was obtained from the central files of the multiple listing offices operating in and near those cities. The remaining 15 percent was furnished by coöperative real estate offices contacted during the neighborhood selection process. For Philadelphia, which has no multiple listing office, all prices were obtained from published real estate directories.

These sources of price data were not ideal, but they appeared to be the only practicable ones for a large-scale study of this kind. To collect enough reliable price data to reveal average price movements in each of the selected neighborhoods during 1943–1955 required access to uniform, continuous, and accurate records. Theoretically, there were three other sources that might have been used: title insurance company files, public records of deeds of trust, or the individual records kept by real estate offices. In practice, each of these has one or more drawbacks so serious as to eliminate it from consideration.

Title insurance company files.—Title companies, as they are called, insure a property owner's title against legal defects that may arise out of previous transfers of ownership. They necessarily keep comprehensive and accurate records of every sale within a broad area of operation. However, since these records are regarded as confidential, no one can consult them who is not a title company employee. While some companies are willing to coöperate by having one or two of their employees tabulate sales data for indicated neighborhoods on a spare-time basis, this is far too slow a procedure to be acceptable. Several trials indicated that the rate at which this method would yield data would have meant waiting more than a year to cover all the neighborhoods studied.

Public records of deeds of trust.—When real estate changes hands, the new deed of trust is made a matter of public record in the county recording office. Although the actual selling price does not appear, the deed facsimile shows the federal documentary tax stamps which are required to be affixed to the deed in the amount of $0.55 for each $500 or portion thereof of consideration received in cash by the seller. It would seem that the actual sales price could be fairly accurately calculated from the face value of the tax stamps.

This would be so except for two serious defects in the process. First, the tax stamps reveal only the *cash* consideration; if the new owner assumes the existing loan or loans on the property, this fact is not directly recorded. Actually, well over half of all the transactions studied involved the assumption of an existing loan. If the assumed loan is fairly large, the price calculated from tax stamps would be obviously lower than normal, but since the amount of the loan is not recorded, no adjustment can be made to arrive at the full price.

Second, it is a common practice for the purchaser to affix more stamps to the deed than the law requires. This is done to give some future buyer the impression that the property sold for a higher price than was actually the case. To test the frequency of this device, two checks were made, each involving some 100 transactions. Actual selling prices were obtained from coöperating real estate offices. These were compared with the selling prices for the same properties as estimated from the tax stamps. It was found that the calculated prices averaged about 5 percent higher than actual prices, with the distortion reaching 10 percent and over in several instances. Such variations could easily produce arbitrary deviations of $500 and more in the test area–control area comparisons, concealing or exaggerating the differences in average prices.

In addition to these objections, recorded deeds do not reveal the terms of sale. Since this study had the secondary objective of not only analyzing the effects of financing on selling prices but determining how financing terms are affected by the buyer's race, the lack of information regarding terms of sale was a conclusive reason for rejecting this possible data source.

Individual records kept by real estate offices.—This would have been an ideal source—if available. Unfortunately, very few offices were willing to open their files to yield the data needed for this study.

Having discarded these three data sources, the necessary information was obtained from the only other possibilities: The San Francisco, Oakland, and Southern Alameda County Multiple Listing Offices and the Philadelphia Real Estate Directory.

The multiple listing offices had significant advantages as a data source: (*a*) their records were coöperatively made available; (*b*) information covering all the San Francisco Bay neighborhoods was centralized in just four record locations; (*c*) actual selling prices and terms of sale were fully, accurately, and consistently recorded; and (*d*) physical details of each property were completely listed, permitting a secondary check on any "abnormal" features of particular houses.

On the other hand, there was one major disadvantage: only a portion of all sales in the areas studied was handled through multiple listing channels. For the years involved, the proportion averaged about 40 percent, ranging from 30 percent in the earlier years to 50 percent and above in a later period. As discussed in chapter iii (Sources of Price Information), this may mean that the average price levels computed for each neighborhood were somewhat lower than those that might have been derived from complete sales records. This downward bias, however, if present, operated equally on test and control areas alike.

A few real estate offices in San Francisco and Oakland were willing to make their sales records available. Approximately 15 percent of the total price data for all the San Francisco Bay Area neighborhoods came from such files. These data were complete and highly accurate and brought the average sales coverage to about 45 percent of all transactions.

For Philadelphia, in the absence of any multiple listing office, the Real Estate Directory constituted the only practicable data source. Although the Directory contained no information on financing arrangements, its great advantage consisted in the completeness and accuracy of its records on selling prices.

Individuals and Organizations Who Assisted This Study

The "Acknowledgments" to this study have already mentioned a number of people and organizations to whom an especially large debt of gratitude is due. Those listed below have also contributed greatly. Not only have they furnished market data and information on neighborhood conditions, but their familiarity with the neighborhoods studied and their interest in the question being explored resulted in many valuable insights and suggestions.

All have earned the thanks of the author and the Commission on Race and Housing.

SAN FRANCISCO

Real Estate Brokers and Appraisers

San Francisco Real Estate Board, Aladdin Realty Company, Anchor Realty Company, Anthony E. Maggio, Barney Ritter, Blade Realty Company, Blanchard Realty Company, DeBiew Realty Company, Donner Realty Company, Earle Realty Company, Frank Fahs Realty Company, George T. Alvers, George M. Del Seccho, Golden Bear Realty Company, H. S. Adams Realty Company, J. C. Alaimo Realty Company, Jules Saxe, Louis A. Gatti, Maxwell Realty Company, O'Connor and Savasta, Pacific Brokerage Company, Sala and Sala Realty Company, Sanford Pearl, Transbay Cities Realty Company, True and Jensen, Valencia Realty Company, Vargas Realty Company, Walter Renner, West States Realty Company, Williams and Son Real Estate.

Financial Institutions

Baldwin and Howell, correspondents for New York Life Insurance Company; Bank of America N. T. & S. A.; Bayview Federal Savings and Loan Association; California Savings and Loan Association; Crocker First National Bank; Franklin Savings and Loan Association; Golden Gate Federal Savings and Loan Association; Marble Mortgage Company, agents for Penn Mutual Insurance Company, Mutual Life Insurance Company of New York, and Provident Mutual Life Insurance Company of Philadelphia; Prudential Life Insurance Company; Transbay Savings and Loan Association.

Other Sources

Robert Eisner, Supervising Appraiser, Assessor's Office, City and County of San Francisco; Benjamin Henley, President, California-Pacific Title Insurance Company; James Howard, Land Appraiser, Assessor's Office, City and County of San Francisco.

OAKLAND AND VICINITY

Real Estate Brokers and Appraisers

A. B. Stevenson, Realtors; Dean Allen, Fidelis Real Estate Company, Jim Woodard and Company, Martha Scott Adams Realtors, Tim Meldrum and Company.

Financial Institutions

Don Mitchell, Executive Vice-President, Berkeley Savings and Loan Association; Joseph Spicer, Spicer Insurance Service; Royce Slewing, Chief Appraiser, First Savings and Loan Company.

Other Sources

William Brothers, Appraiser, Assessor's Office, Alameda County; E. Horwinski, Executive Director, Oakland Housing Authority; Mortimer Smith, President, Oakland Title and Guarantee Company.

PHILADELPHIA

Real Estate Sources

Ambrose Winder, Appraiser and Consultant; Edward Worthington, Appraiser; Isadore Martin Real Estate Company; John T. Dolde, Appraiser; Samuel Sagan, Realtor.

Other Sources

Philadelphia Commission on Human Relations; Institute for Urban Studies, University of Pennsylvania; Philadelphia Housing Association; William Erwin, Jr., Assistant Vice-President, Commonwealth Title Company of Philadelphia.

Bibliography

BOOKS

Abrams, Charles. *Forbidden Neighbors*. New York: Harper and Brothers, 1955.

Babcock, Frederick M. *Valuation of Real Estate*. New York: McGraw-Hill Book Company, Inc., 1932.

Fisher, Ernest M. *Principles of Real Estate Practice*. New York: The Macmillan Company, 1923.

Gist, Noel P., and Halbert, L. A. *Urban Society*. 3d ed., New York: Thomas Y. Crowell Company, 1950.

Hoagland, Henry E. *Real Estate Finance*, Chapter VI. Homewood, Illinois: Richard D. Irwin, Inc., 1954.

Hoyt, Homer. *One Hundred Years of Land Values in Chicago*. Chicago: University of Chicago Press, 1933.

Johnson, Charles S. *Negro Housing*. Report of the Committee on Negro Housing for the President's Conference on Home Building and Home Ownership. Washington, D. C.: The Conference, Vol. VI, 1932.

———. *Patterns of Negro Segregation*. New York: Harper and Brothers, 1943.

May, Arthur A. *The Valuation of Residential Real Estate*. New York: Prentice-Hall, Inc., 1942.

McMichael, Stanley L. *How to Finance Real Estate*. New York: Prentice-Hall, Inc., 1949.

———. *McMichael's Appraising Manual*. 4th ed., New York: Prentice-Hall, Inc., 1951.

———. *Real Estate Subdivisions*. New York: Prentice-Hall, Inc., 1949.

———, and Bingham, Robert F. *City Growth and Values*. Cleveland: The Stanley McMichael Publishing Organization, 1923.

Myrdal, Gunnar. *An American Dilemma*. New York: Harper and Brothers, 1944.

Schmutz, George L. *The Appraisal Process*. North Hollywood, California: George L. Schmutz, Publisher, 1951.

Schneider, George A. *California Real Estate Principles and Practices*. New York: Prentice-Hall, Inc., 1927.

Weaver, Robert C. *The Negro Ghetto*. New York: Harcourt, Brace and Company, 1948.

Weimer, Arthur M., and Hoyt, Homer. *Principles of Real Estate*. 3d ed., New York: The Ronald Press, 1954.

ARTICLES AND PAMPHLETS

Abrams, Charles. "Race Bias in Housing," statement sponsored jointly by the American Civil Liberties Union, National Association for the Advancement of Colored People, and American Council on Race Relations (July, 1947), pp. 24–28.

Anliot, Richard B. "The Effect of Negro Occupancy in a Public Housing Project or Private Housing on the Value of Neighboring Residences." Youngstown, Ohio: Fair Employment Practice Committee, November, 1953.

American Institute of Real Estate Appraisers. *Appraisal Terminology and Handbook*. Chicago: The Institute, 1950.

Bay Area Real Estate Report, Fourth Quarter, 1954.

Beehler, Jr., George W. "Colored Occupancy Raises Values," *The Review of the Society of Residential Appraisers*, XI, No. 9 (September, 1945).

"How One Negro Found a Home for His Family." *San Francisco Chronicle*, July 22, 1951.

University of Pennsylvania, Institute for Urban Studies. "Program for Eastwick Housing Market Development Analysis." Philadelphia: University of Pennsylvania, Institute for Urban Studies, December, 1954 (Mimeo.).

Laurenti, Luigi M. "Effects of Nonwhite Purchases on Market Prices of Residences," *The Appraisal Journal*, XX, No. 3 (July, 1952).

———. "Real Estate Price Behavior in Neighborhoods Entered by Nonwhites," *Bay Area Real Estate Report*, Fourth Quarter, 1954.

Marks, Richard. "The Impact of Negro Population Movement on Property Values in a Selected Area in Detroit." Detroit: Mayor's Interracial Committee, January 16, 1950 (2 page summary, Mimeo.).

McDonald, A. M. "Appraising Residential Property," *The Appraisal Journal*, XXI, No. 2 (April, 1953).

McEntire, Davis. "A Study of Racial Attitudes in Neighborhoods Infiltrated by Nonwhites," *Bay Area Real Estate Report*, Second Quarter, 1955.

Merton, Robert K. "The Self-fulfilling Prophecy," *The Antioch Review*. VIII, No. 2 (Summer, 1948).

Minnesota, The Governor's Interracial Commission. "The Negro and His Home in Minnesota." Minneapolis: The Commission, June, 1947.

Morgan, Belden. "Values in Transition Areas: Some New Concepts," *The Review of the Society of Residential Appraisers*, XVIII, No. 3 (March, 1952).

National Association of Real Estate Boards. *Code of Ethics.* June, 1924 (Revised November 17, 1950).

National Community Relations Advisory Council. *Equality of Opportunity in Housing: A Handbook of Facts.* New York: The Council, June, 1952.

"The Negro in San Francisco." *San Francisco Chronicle,* November 6, 1950.

Neiswanger, David. "Appraising the Small Home," *The Appraisal Journal,* V, No. 2 (April, 1937).

Parker, Elsie Smith. "Both Sides of the Color Line," *The Appraisal Journal,* XI, No. 3 (July, 1943).

Philadelphia, Commission on Human Relations. "Philadelphia's Negro Population—Facts on Housing." Philadelphia: The Commission, October, 1953.

Phillips, George A. "Racial Infiltration," *The Review of the Society of Residential Appraisers,* XVI, No. 2 (February, 1950).

Ross, Thurston H. "Market Significance of Declining Neighborhoods," *The Appraisal Journal,* XXIII, No. 2 (April, 1955).

Schietinger, E. F. "Race and Residential Market Values in Chicago," *Land Economics,* XXX, No. 4 (November, 1954).

————. "Racial Succession and the Value of Small Residential Properties," *American Sociological Review,* XVI, No. 6 (December, 1951).

Schmutz, George L. "The Hazards of Residential Locations," *Review of the Society of Residential Appraisers,* XVIII, No. 5 (May, 1952).

Stern, Oscar I. "Long Range Effect of Colored Occupancy," *The Review of the Society of Residential Appraisers,* XII, No. 1 (January, 1946).

————. "The End of the Restrictive Covenant," *The Appraisal Journal,* XVI, No. 4 (October, 1948).

U. S. *News and World Report.* A special report, November 16, 1951.

GOVERNMENT PUBLICATIONS

Coe, Paul F. "Nonwhite Population Changes," *Insured Mortgage Portfolio,* Vol. 16, No. 4 (Second Quarter, 1952). Washington, D. C.: Federal Housing Administration.

Hoyt, Homer. *The Structure and Growth of Residential Neighborhoods in American Cities.* Washington, D. C.: Federal Housing Administration, 1939.

Kadow, Stanley. "Observations on the Minority-Group Market." Reprinted from *Insured Mortgage Portfolio* (Summer, 1954). Washington, D. C.: Federal Housing Administration.

United States Census of Housing: 1950. Vol. I, *General Characteristics,*
Chap. 1, "U. S. Summary." Washington, D. C.: U. S. Government
Printing Office, 1953.

United States Census of Housing: 1950. Vol. IV, *Residential Financing,*
Part I, "United States." Washington, D. C.: U. S. Government Printing Office, 1952.

U. S. Supreme Court. *Buchanan* v. *Warley,* 245 U. S. 60.

"A Wider Field for Mortgage Lending," *Insured Mortgage Portfolio*
(Fourth Quarter, 1949). Washington, D. C.: Federal Housing Administration.

UNPUBLISHED STUDIES

Cressey, Paul F. "The Succession of Cultural Groups in the City of
Chicago." Unpublished Ph.D thesis, University of Chicago, 1930.

Gillette, Thomas L. "Santa Fe: A Study of the Effects of Negro Invasion on Property Values." Unpublished Master's thesis, Department
of Sociology and Anthropology, University of Kansas, Lawrence,
Kansas, 1954.

Jensen, Constance C., Lindberg, John, and Smith, George L. "The
Minority Group Housing Market in San Francisco, with Special
Reference to Real Estate Broker and Mortgage Financing Practices." Unpublished Master's research project, School of Social Welfare, University of California, Berkeley, 1955.

Schietinger, E. F. "Racial Succession and Changing Property Values
in Residential Chicago." Unpublished Ph.D. thesis, Department of
Sociology, University of Chicago, 1953.

———. "Real Estate Transfers During Negro Invasion, A Case Study."
Unpublished Master's thesis, Department of Sociology, University
of Chicago, 1948.

Star, Shirley. "Interracial Tension in Two Areas of Chicago: An Ex-
ploratory Approach to the Measurement of Interracial Tension."
Unpublished Ph.D. thesis, University of Chicago, December, 1950.

Wander, Richard. "The Influence of Negro Infiltration upon Real
Estate Values." Unpublished Master's thesis, Department of Sociology and Anthropology, Wayne State University, Detroit, Michigan,
1953.

Index

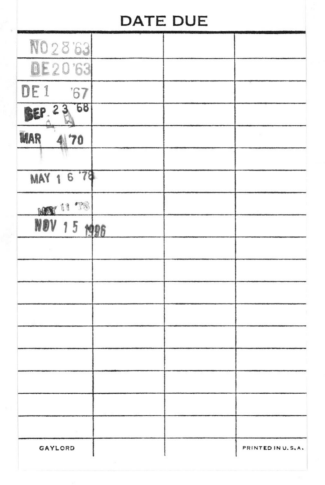

DATE DUE

NO 28 '63			
DE 20 '63			
DE 1 '67			
SEP. 23 '68			
MAR 4 '70			
MAY 1 6 '78			
MAY 11 '78			
NOV 1 5 1996			
GAYLORD			PRINTED IN U.S.A.